NOTES FROM THE SICK ROOM

NOTES FROM THE SICK ROOM

Steve Finbow

Published by Repeater Books
An imprint of Watkins Media Ltd

19-21 Cecil Court
London
WC2N 4EZ
UK
www.repeaterbooks.com
A Repeater Books paperback original 2017
1

Distributed in the United States by Random House, Inc., New York.

Cover design: Johnny Bull
Typography and typesetting: JCS Publishing Service Ltd
Typefaces: Minion Pro and Gill Sans

ISBN: 978-1-910924-97-6
Ebook ISBN: 978-1-910924-43-3

To Marie… Love and Scars…

Contents

Sickness was what restored me to reason.

Friedrich Nietzsche – *Ecce Homo*

CHAPTER I

Moments of Being

Induction as Introduction

The doctor will see you now. If you follow me, we can commence the tour of the hospital, but first a short induction. The title — *Notes from the Sick Room* — stems from three sources: *Life in the Sick-Room: Essays by an Invalid* (1844), by the social theorist Harriet Martineau, a treatise and memoir on chronic suffering; *Notes from Sick Rooms* (1883), a healthcare manual written by Julia Princep Stephen, Virginia Woolf's mother; and *Death in the Sick Room* (1885), a painting by Edvard Munch, now in the Munch Museum, Oslo. Artists, writers and theorists are the source of this investigation — how they deal with illness and injury and how they work through and within their affliction or, indeed, cease to create because of the physical and psychological trauma.

The evaluation will be of physical complaints: broken bones, cancer, tuberculosis, HIV/AIDS and any attendant problems; it will not cover mental illnesses apart from when these are secondary symptoms of the main condition. There are excellent studies on creativity and mental illness (or the "Sylvia Plath effect", as it has become known), but not many on physical illness and the problems of creating while living with disability. Of course, a change in the physical wellbeing of an artist may induce forms of mental illness, but the primary goal of this examination is the effects of trauma on an artist and the subsequent effects on their work and life.

On our journey through the hospital — and the sanatorium that stands within its gardens — we will meet some of the patients: Christopher Hitchens and Kathy Acker in the cancer ward; Frida Kahlo and Denton Welch in the orthopaedic department; Bruce Chatwin and Michel Foucault in the HIV/AIDS unit; and, John Keats, the Brontës, Robert Louis Stevenson, Katherine Mansfield and D.H. Lawrence *et alia*, when we take a tour of the tuberculosis sanatorium. Along the way, we will also encounter Bob Dylan, Roland Barthes, Andy Warhol, Joris-Karl Huysmans, Roberto Bolaño, Fritz Zorn, Frigyes Karinthy and many others in a time-travelling compound from which we will distil their thoughts and creations within and through their disorders.

Helping us with our ward rounds will be specialists, resident theorists who will either concur with our diagnosis or provide a second opinion. These consultants include: Roland Barthes (when he's not in a hospital bed), Michel Foucault (likewise), Anton Chekhov (doctor, patient, writer), J.G. Ballard, Georges Bataille, E.M. Cioran, Jean-Luc Nancy, Gilles Deleuze, Félix Guattari, Oliver Sacks and a host of other interns, medical officers, registrars and heads of department. Susan Sontag, who is on sabbatical, will join us for the conclusion of the disquisition. The overriding theory derives from our chief physician, Dr Friedrich Nietzsche, whose health and illness informed his life and work and whose *The Gay Science* (1882) (more recently translated as *The Joyous Wisdom*) is the manual we will be turning to as a guide to our probings and proddings.

And here is Dr Nietzsche's abstract for the book from his own "Preface to the second edition" (1886) of *The Gay Science*: "A psychologist knows few questions as attractive as that concerning the relation between health and philosophy; and should he himself become ill, he will bring all of his scientific curiosity into the illness. For assuming that one is a person, one necessarily also has the philosophy of that person; but here there is a considerable difference. In some, it is their weaknesses that philosophize; in others, their riches and strengths. The former *need* their philosophy, be it as a prop, a sedative, medicine, redemption, elevation, or self-alienation; for the latter, it is only a beautiful luxury, in the best case the voluptuousness of a triumphant gratitude that eventually has to inscribe itself in cosmic capital letters on the heaven of concepts. In the former, more common case, however, when it is distress that philosophizes, as in all sick thinkers — and perhaps sick thinkers are in the majority in the history of philosophy — what will become of the thought that is itself subjected to the *pressure* of illness?"

We will examine the patients' case notes, their medical history and lifestyles, question them on symptoms and pain management, and hope to form a diagnosis of the correlation, or otherwise, between illness and creativity. The primary source material will be their letters, journals, memoirs and the biographical data written about them. We will also study the fiction and non-fiction produced by writers, songs and pieces written by musicians and artworks created by artists.

There will be a brief introductory chapter on the hospital and its creation and the emergence of medicine as a separate science through the works of Hippocrates, Empedocles and other Classical scholars, plus a study of Asclepius, the Greek god of medicine, plus other non-Western founders of medicine and its studies. Throughout the text, so as not to appear aloof and indifferent, we will also scrutinize my own medical history and how it relates (or otherwise) to the bed-ridden writers and artists within the hospital. The germ of this study began when I was recuperating in Chitose City Hospital, Hokkaido, Japan, after complications from a norovirus illness, and had lapsed into a coma over the 2006 Christmas period (of which more later). On regaining consciousness, I realized that I had nearly missed the deadline to enter the Willesden Short Story Competition. I asked my partner to print out and bring in the short story, it still needed editing and I had one day to get it finished. It was six-thousand words long and I wanted to get it down to under four-thousand. My throat was full of exudative pharyngitis, white clumps of bacteria or fungus surrounded my pharynx, probably caused by the doctors who saved my life. My taste buds were shot — tea tasted like Bovril, the mackerel in tomato sauce the nurses brought me for breakfast suggested Battenberg cake, the miso soup accompanying it was more like Lucozade. I was on an intravenous drip for my electrolytes and an insulin pump because of my type-one diabetes (the cause of my coma). I took the pages of "Mrs. Nakamoto Takes a Vacation" and went at the text with a red pen, an inky scalpel with which I excised the tumorous material and resected the mass. Because of the deadline, I worked quickly, but this was also because of my fatigue and my focus. If I had been healthy and at home, I would have dithered, read a book, gone for a walk, played on the Wii, maybe even added five hundred words to the story, thought it was good enough. But in the hospital room I looked at the words and saw the text needed excoriating, the skin needed to be taken off so all that was left was its muscle and bone structure. The first paragraph eventually read: "She fixes herself a bowl of miso soup, steamed rice, and pickled plums and takes them on a tray into the living room to eat while watching the weather report on television. The day is going to be warm — a thin layer of cloud burning off by midday. Mrs. Nakamoto nods, finishes the last drops of her soup, fills a bottle with water and leaves the house. The journey to the station takes fifteen minutes and she walks in her usual manner — small steps, head slightly bowed, turning her neck left and right and dipping her forehead as a greeting to people she knows, people she sees most mornings. The people do the same. Nothing is said, just the incline of the head and the muffled grunt of acknowledgement. But she doesn't recognize anyone this morning. Where is the man with the excitable dogs? Where are the schoolchildren eating persimmons? Where is the old man with the red umbrella?" For me that is concise, and it is so because of the concentration of thought(s) while recovering from a diabetic coma in the strange environment of a Japanese hospital.

An earlier serious illness in 2003 had honed my reading habits and helped me realise the correlation between knowledge and self-examination, a pursuit of escape while trapped in a diseased body, an understanding of how the body functions and not just as a vehicle for the mind. On 4 October, 2012, just as I was preparing the book proposal for *Notes from the Sick Room*, I collapsed in my house and was taken to Whipps Cross Hospital with a burst appendix. Here are the details of admission: "Mr Finbow was admitted on the 4/10/12 with DKA (diabetic ketoacidosis) and a painful plus tender abdomen. After appropriate resuscitation, he was found to have a very tender and peritonitic abdomen. A CT scan was performed which showed some fluid in the pelvis and some small locules of gas. In view of his known diverticulosis" — not known to me at the time — "a perforated sigmoid diverticulum was suspected. His observations started to improve, but he remained very tender in all 4 quadrants. It was decided to take him to theatre to perform a laparoscopy +/- proceed. At this time, large amounts of pus were found in the abdomen and it was decided to convert to a full laparotomy. A perforated appendix was found with an adherent loop of sigmoid attached to it. Apart from the appendix, the rest of the bowel was healthy and intact." Before surgery, the stoma nurse had visited me, regarding the possible necessity of a colostomy bag:

"The appendix was resected and the abdomen was washed out thoroughly. Mr Finbow was treated with antibiotics post op and made a good recovery. He did however complain of an episode of coffee ground vomit during his admission. An OGD (oesophago-gastro-duodenoscopy) was therefore performed, and this was normal." The OGD was thoroughly uncomfortable, it reminded me of the scene in *The Matrix* where Neo wakes up in the human-harvesting farm. "He will be discharged today. We will arrange district nursing to remove the remainder of his wound clips next week." Along with the above, I had intestinal colic and peritonitis. While recovering at home, my wound became inflamed and was "oozing yellow exudate," so iodine was applied and antibiotics prescribed, it then developed granulomas, which had to be cauterized with silver nitrate.

I now have a scar that runs from my xiphoid process to my pubic bone, cutting through my six-pack (I wish). I have a longer scar than Carson, the appendicitis patient in John Updike's "The City" (1987): "His scar was not the little lateral slit his classmates had shown him but a rather gory central incision from navel down; he had been opened up wide, it was explained to him, on the premise that at his age his malady might have been anything from ulcers to cancer. The depth of the gulf that he had, unconscious, floated above thrilled him. There had been, too, a certain unthinkable intimacy. His bowels had been 'handled,' the surgeon gently reminded him, in explaining a phase of his recuperation. Carson tried to picture the handling: clamps and white rubber gloves and something glistening and heavy and purplish that was his. His appendix had indeed been retrocecal — one of a mere ten percent so located. It had even begun, microscopic investigation revealed, to rupture." I felt the same way. During my rehabilitation, I focused on what was and what was not going to be included in the book, what references to use, and I was determined to make it theoretical yet readable, in which I hope I have succeeded.

Now it's time for the induction, and I will hand you over to one of our resident specialists, Mrs Virginia Woolf, who will provide some guidance on being ill and its effects on the creative mind. In this case, I will provide the second opinions as they refer to the study to come. Mrs Woolf? "Considering how common illness is, how tremendous the spiritual change that it brings, how astonishing, when the lights of health go down, the undiscovered countries that are then disclosed, what wastes and deserts of the soul a slight attack of influenza brings to view, what precipices and lawns sprinkled with bright flowers a little rise of temperature reveals, what ancient and obdurate oaks are uprooted in us by the act of sickness, how we go down into the pit of death and feel the waters of annihilation close."

Illness is universal, everything is ill or becomes ill at some stage. Some were born ill, we will all most surely die ill. Illness is the internal shadow of our being. I'm not sure about spiritual change, psychological no doubt, psychosomatical, even hypochondriacal and I suppose some patients get a kind of religious enlightenment through near-death events — certainly not Nietzsche or Hitchens. Does spirituality disappear in the onslaught of the corporeal? But I agree with Mrs Woolf's undiscovered countries — Progeria, Pemphigus, Sciatica and Neutropenia among them. The wastes and deserts are more of the mind, which, while ill or convalescing, seems to expand to featureless horizons only distantly glimpsed while healthy. Her "bright flowers" are the signs of our keener awareness of life and so, even more so, death and flowers were a motif for cancer in the works of Danilo Kiš. Our ideas about our bodies, our selves, are the "obdurate oaks" that are uprooted when we consider our illness and our survival, as we swim frantically against the "waters of annihilation."

Please continue, Mrs Woolf. "Don't you agree," she says, "it becomes strange indeed that illness has not taken its place with love and battle and jealousy among the prime themes of literature?" I do, but I hope to redress this in this study. But you are forgetting that illness is a theme in many works: Daniel Defoe's *A Journal of the Plague Year* (1722); Alphonse Daudet's *Land of Pain* (1930) (syphilis); Thomas Mann's *The Magic Mountain* (1924) (tuberculosis), his *Death in Venice* (1912) (the plague) and *Doctor Faustus* (1947) (syphilis); Aleksandr Solzhenitsyn's *Cancer Ward* (1968); Albert Camus' *The Plague* (1947); John Berger's *A Fortunate Man* (1967); Pierre Guyotat's *Coma* (2006) and Philip Roth's *Nemesis* (2010) (polio), to name just a few that I haven't already mentioned.

Mrs Woolf frowns and lifts that haughty nose, "Literature does its best to maintain that its concern is with the mind; that the body is a sheet of plain glass through which the soul looks straight and clear, and, save for one or two passions such as desire and greed, is null, and negligible and non-existent." I agree to a certain extent, but looks at the works, letters and journals of Franz Kafka, Anton Chekhov, Katherine Mansfield and J.G. Ballard to understand how these writers investigated illness and injury, how disease and deformation of the body informs the mind. In a short story "You and Me and the Continuum" (1966), Ballard writes: "'Kodachrome. Captain Kirby, MI5, studied the prints. They showed: (1) a thick-set man in an Air Force jacket, unshaven face half-hidden by the dented hat-peak; (2) a transverse section through the spinal level T-12; (3) a crayon self-portrait by David Feary, 7-year-old schizophrenic at the Belmont Asylum, Sutton; (4) radio-spectra from the quasar CTA 102; (5) an antero-posterior radiograph of a skull, estimated capacity 1500 cc.; (6) spectroheliogram of the sun taken with the K line of calcium; (7) left and right handprints showing massive scarring between second and third metacarpal bones.' To Dr Nathan he said: 'And all these make up one picture?'" And as he explained later in an interview, "Exactly. They make up a composite portrait of this man's identity." Rather than a sheet of plain glass, the body is a technology through which we experience the world.

Mrs Woolf sniffs. "But," she rejoins, "all day, all night the body intervenes; blunts or sharpens, colours or discolours, turns to wax in the warmth of June, hardens to tallow in the murk of February. The creature within can only gaze through the pane — smudged or rosy; it cannot separate off from the body like the sheath of a knife or the pod of a pea for a single instant; it must go through the whole unending procession of changes, heat and cold, comfort and discomfort, hunger and satisfaction, health and illness, until there comes the inevitable catastrophe; the body smashes itself to smithereens, and the soul (it is said) escapes." I concur with most of this, but the easy dichotomy of comfort and discomfort, health and illness becomes blurred when illness or injury strike. The body, rather than being smashed to smithereens (an exceptional case would be Frida Kahlo), experiences a metamorphosis (particularly within cancer and HIV/AIDS patients) and the soul (whether it ever existed) rather than escaping is obliterated.

Mrs Woolf places the long fingers of her right hand on my shoulder, "To look these things squarely in the face would need the courage of a lion tamer; a robust philosophy; a reason rooted in the bowels of the earth." I gesture over my shoulder at the large marble bust of Friedrich Nietzsche that occupies an alcove in reception. "Yes, yes," she says becoming a little miffed, "but the public would say that a novel devoted to influenza lacked plot." I disagree, the stages of influenza are the plot: the infiltration by the virus, it replicates, becomes contagious, symptoms present themselves — aches, fevers, sneezing, coughing, sore throat — and then the immune system begins its battle against the invader, fatigue sets in, then the virus is gone, you are healthy once more — until the sequel, that is.

Mrs Woolf smiles, and I agree with her when she observes, "Yet it is not only a new language that we need, more primitive, more sensual, more obscene, but a new hierarchy of the passions; love must be deposed in favour of a temperature of 104; jealousy give place to the pangs of sciatica." I sit forward and rub the ache in my lower back, the fireworks of pain behind my knee and down into my calf muscle. She continues, "There is, let us confess it (and illness is the great confessional), a childish outspokenness in illness; things are said, truths blurted out, which the cautious respectability of health conceals." I agree, just look at the letters of Chekhov and Lawrence, the stories of Kafka and Mansfield, the paintings of Munch and Modigliani, the essays of Hitchens and Chatwin.

"One more thing before you go on your rounds," she says, "In illness words seem to possess a mystic quality. We grasp what is beyond their surface meaning, gather instinctively this, that, and the other — a sound, a colour, here a stress, there a pause — which the poet, knowing words to be meagre in comparison with ideas, has strewn about his page to evoke, when collected, a state of mind which neither words can express nor the reason explain." Interesting. I'm not sure about "mystic," words that are occult or ethereal. You implied earlier that the language we needed should be "more primitive, more sensual, more obscene," now that sounds like Mr David Herbert Lawrence to me. But I do agree that illness causes a certain synaesthesia, a heightening of the senses that reason cannot explain. But back to Mr Lawrence…

Mrs Woolf interjects, raises an eyebrow, and I know what's coming, "I read Lawrence with the usual sense of frustration:

and (know) that he and I have too much in common — the same pressure to be ourselves: so that I don't escape when I read him: am suspended: what I want is to be made free of another world. This Proust does. To me Lawrence is airless, confined: I don't want this, I go on saying. And the repetition of one idea. I don't want that either. I don't want 'a philosophy' in the least: I don't believe in other people's reading of riddles. What I enjoy (in the Letters) is the sudden visualization: the great ghost springing over the wave (of the spray in Cornwall) but I get no satisfaction from his explanations of what he sees. And then it's harrowing: this panting effort after something: and 'I have £6.10 left' and then Government hoofing him out, like a toad: and banning his book: the brutality of civilized society to this panting agonized man: and how futile it was. All this makes a sort of gasping in his letters. And none of it seems essential. So he pants and jerks. Then too I don't like strumming with two fingers — and the arrogance. After all, English has one million words: why confine yourself to 6? and praise yourself for so doing."

Phew! Well, we will meet the airless, panting, gasping, jerking Lawrence on our tour and he can give us his own "philosophy" and advice on life, writing and illness. I thank Mrs Woolf and she walks through reception to the on-call rooms to have a lie down. I will page someone and ask them to pop in while she's asleep and remove those stones from her white coat.

So let us start our tour of the hospital. On our way we will encounter some scenes that will be upsetting, some that will be uplifting and some that will be remarkable in their concision and clarity. What they will mostly be is humbling. I will leave the last thoughts to Marcus Aurelius who, putting it bluntly, wrote: "Hippocrates cured many diseases then died of disease himself. The Chaldean astrologers foretold the deaths of many people, then their own fated day claimed them. Alexander,

Pompey, Julius Caesar annihilated whole cities time after time, and slaughtered tens of thousands of horse and foot in the field of battle, and yet the moment came for them too to depart this life. Heraclitus speculated long on the conflagration of the universe, but the water of dropsy filled his guts and he died caked in a poultice of cow-dung."

I apologize for the waiting time. The doctor *will* see you now.

CHAPTER 2

Depth Advertised

Gastroenterology as Gestation

I had had no signs, or so I thought. No symptoms. Well, apart from the constant pain in my chest, the redness of my face, the discolouration of my urine, the occasional bloody stool. But these could have been symptoms of many things and were not, as I discovered much later, indications of the major problem, just indications that I was not living healthily, that I was drinking too much, eating the wrong food, being stressed, not sleeping enough; basically, that I was a forty-something man living in London at the beginning of the twenty-first century. Didn't we all suffer from similar prodromes? What was there to worry about? Apart from these minor manifestations — and the fact that I was hypertensive and asthmatic and had had operations on my left knee — I was healthy. I still managed the odd game of football — the cause of my anterior cruciate ligament surgery and six-inch scar — most days I walked from Primrose Hill to Soho and back. At the weekends, I walked miles, mostly around London and, sometimes, the countryside. Apart from the knee surgery in 1994, I hadn't been hospitalized since I was a young boy. What was there to worry about?

The day before, 12 February, 2003, I had had the day off and accompanied K to Slade School of Fine Art where she had an interview to study for an MA. That was mid-afternoon, the interview had gone well and we had walked back to Primrose Hill and stopped for drinks in our local, The Prince Albert.

After a few pints, no more than usual, we went home to the flat and K cooked a chicken stew while I read. During the rest of the evening, I probably had a couple of vodka tonics and went to bed as usual, reading before I fell asleep.

I woke early as usual the next morning, readied to leave for work, drank tea — I never ate breakfast — and, feeling somewhat tired, decided for a change to take the tube from Chalk Farm to Tottenham Court Road, a journey of about fifteen minutes that, it being around 6am, wouldn't be too intolerable. I might even find a space to read, either W.G. Sebald's *After Nature* (1988) or David Peace's *Nineteen Seventy Seven* (2000) — I always read two books, one fiction, one non-fiction — a habit I no longer maintain. In the past three or four years, my taste has moved towards non-fiction, and I'm sure it has something to do with what happened on that day, Thursday, 13 February, 2003.

I walked to the station, took the spiral staircase down to the platform and waited for a Charing Cross-bound train. The sign read "1 MORDEN via CHARING CROSS 4 mins", which meant 6 mins in the convoluted time-space discontinuum of the Northern Line. The train arrived and I got on and stood by the back door of the carriage as I usually did, took out the Sebald and read the lines about a delirious crew suffering from some unknown disease, for some reason their gums are swollen, their limbs stiff with blood and their internal organs swollen.

Only a few people were on the train commuting into the centre of London from the likes of Edgware, Hendon, Golders Green and Hampstead, reading newspapers and books, the smartphone's mass usage being a few years in the future. At Camden Town some passengers got on and off and a middle-aged man sat alone on the bank of seats to my left. I continued reading and Sebald was going on about the Hippocratic oath and surgery and incapable physicians.

I do not remember feeling ill before the next event; I may have been perspiring a little, I always did on the tube. I may have felt nauseous from the beer and the stew and the vodka tonics, maybe tired from the five hours' sleep, but I don't think so. The man to my left began picking his nose, vigorously, deeply, more an excavation than a pick, like the Channel Tunnel drills, like the prisoners in *The Great Escape*. I looked away, tried to concentrate on my reading — Sebald was now banging on about enduring suffering.

Before we reached Euston, the man's fingers were excavating the interior of his nostrils like naked mole-rats in the darkness. After burrowing and digging for minutes, he extracted his finger, inspected the treasures that were once within and then popped his finger in his mouth, licked and swallowed, and began the tunnelling again. By the time the train reached Warren Street, I was feeling sick. I put my book into my bag and jumped off at Goodge Street and got on the carriage behind, now sweating heavily from the effort to keep from vomiting. I gulped and gasped and opened the carriage window to let in some fresh air.

Tottenham Court Road. I got off, took the stairs and escalators to the surface and walked to the office in Manor House, Soho Square. I was usually the first one to arrive and I made a cup of tea and, surprisingly for me, drank a glass of water. Feeling better, I sat at my desk and read my emails. The day ahead would be the usual mixture of deadlines and deliveries, meetings and budgets, staff problems and disagreements, stress and boredom, or would it?

By 10am, most people had arrived and were discussing the previous evening's television shows, what they had eaten, the usual stuff. I walked down the main corridor to the room where two of my assistants did what they did. Only F was in and she asked me something or other about something. I felt sick and excused myself. In the toilet, I looked in the mirror. I was very pale, very unlike me. I took some deep breaths, put my head perfunctorily over the toilet bowl, gagged a bit, coughed, but nothing came up. I splashed my face with cold water and returned to F to find out what that something or other about something was.

As I entered the main office, I felt a ball of pain in the centre of my chest behind the xiphoid process — I knew it was called this because I fractured it, along with several ribs, falling off a slide while on holiday in Whitburn with my family when I was about nine or ten years of age; my brother hit his head, we were fighting walking up the slide. The process has, since then, been a place that I don't like touching or letting others touch. The chest pain felt like heartburn and I thought maybe I was feeling ill because of the beers and the chicken stew and the vodka tonics and decided to call K to see if she was feeling the same and, if she was, I could blame it on her cooking.

I felt faint and nauseous but returned to my assistants' room and asked F to explain to me the something about something. She looked up and said, "Are you all right?" The pain intensified and, for some reason, I lifted my arms in the air to alleviate the burning sensation. I couldn't breathe properly. "I'll get some water," I said, and stepped into the corridor and toppled to the floor. People rushed out of the reception. I vomited copiously, a substance that looked but didn't taste like coffee grounds. G, the office manager and one of the assigned first-aid people, asked what I thought was wrong. I said I didn't know, all I said was, "Call an ambulance." Something inside me (and out) knew that those coffee grounds were not from Nescafé.

Apparently, I then passed out until the ambulance arrived and I was taken down on a stretcher, vertically at times, in the lift, Schindler's lift, to the waiting ambulance. A friend of mine, B, accompanied me and, while the paramedic was checking my vitals and giving me some serious painkillers, he told them I was asthmatic, hypertensive and had had amoebic dysentery the previous year after a trip to Morocco with K. He also asked whether it was a heart attack and they said no, they didn't think so, the coffee-ground vomit indicated the liver, pancreas, or stomach, it could be ulcers. Later, I discovered that haematemesis (coffee-ground emesis) is also a sign of yellow fever, haemophilia B and the Ebola virus. Luckily, I had been reading W.G. Sebald and not Peace, "The viscera are in various parts viz: The uterus and kidneys with one breast under the bed, the other breast by the right foot, the liver between the feet, the intestines by the right side, and the spleen by the left side of the body. The flaps removed from the abdomen and thighs are on the table." I passed out again from either the pain, which was intense, or the drugs. I was on my way, unconscious, to University College Hospital.

Above the entrance to *our* imaginary hospital, cast in bronze, stands a statue of the Greek god of doctors, medicine and healing. His head is handsome, he has Zeus-like hair and a beard that seems to have been hewn from the clouds surrounding Olympus. He wears a chlamys and we see a muscled chest and ripped abdomen, suggesting vigorous health and strength. In his right hand, he holds a staff that reaches down to the base of the sculpture, a snake wraps itself around this rod, its tongue flickering up towards the healer's hand. This is Asclepius, son of the Thessalian princess Koronis and Apollo, the god of the arts. According to Samuel Butler's translation of Homer's *The Iliad* (1898), snatched from his mother's burning womb — the cuckolded Apollo had killed both Koronis and her lover and set her on a pyre but saved his unborn son — he was sent to the god-Centaur Chiron to be trained to hunt and to heal: "They passed through the spreading host of the Achaeans and went on till they came to the place where Menelaus had been wounded and was lying with the chieftains gathered in a circle round him. Machaon passed into the middle of the ring and at once drew the arrow from the belt, bending its barbs back through the force with which he pulled it out. He undid the burnished belt, and beneath this the cuirass and the belt of mail which the bronzesmiths had made; then, when he had seen the wound, he wiped away the blood and applied some soothing drugs which Chiron had given to Aesculapius (Asclepius) out of the good will he bore him."

Homer mentions Asclepius several times in *The Iliad*, mostly in reference to being the father of Machaon, "Nestor knight of Gerene did as Idomeneus had counselled; he at once mounted his chariot, and Machaon son of the famed physician Aesculapius, went with him," and "these were commanded by the two sons of Aesculapius, skilled in the art of healing, Podalirius and Machaon. And with them there came thirty ships." He not only sired Machaon and Podalirius, both surgeons and proto-pharmacists, but five daughters: Aceso – goddess of healing, Iaso – goddess of recuperation, Aglaea – goddess of good health, Panacea – the goddess of remedies and cures, and Hygieia – the goddess of good health and cleanliness. The mother to Asclepius' children was Epione – the goddess of soothing pain. There was another son, a strange dwarf who always wore a cowl and travelled with his father, Telesphoros — "bringer of fulfilment" — god of convalescence, recuperation and regeneration — of transfiguration. There is also a small statue of Telesphoros in the intensive-care unit of our hospital, it is marble not bronze and the figure wears a heavy Thracian cloak concealing his stunted body, his face is simultaneously youthful and wise and the sculpture has a soothing effect on patients.

There were many hymns to these gods and goddesses of health and medicine, and these were used in ritual healings throughout Ancient Greece and its Archaic Empire. Most of the hymns to Asclepius invoke his father, Apollo, the god of medicine and healing, of plague and illness, and the god of literature and music, of art and philosophy. Hermes, Apollo's half-brother, also carries a rod — a caduceus — with wings and two snakes entwined along its length; some health organizations use it as their symbol, but it is more related to commerce. Even Thomas Mann, in his novel set in a TB sanatorium — *The Magic Mountain* — confuses the two, "It was a fancy flag, green and white, with the caduceus, the emblem of healing, in the centre." If Apollo is the god of health and medicine, Hermes is the god of the zone of transit, an intermediary between two worlds, life and death. But it is Apollo who interests us here, father of Asclepius, grandfather of that god-family of doctors, carers and proto-pharmacists — the first clinicians at the birth of the hospital.

The bronze figure of Asclepius that stands above the entrance to the hospital was probably sculpted by pupils of the Athenian artist Myron (active 480–440 BC), whose works comprised, among others, statues of athletes, animals and gods, including Apollo. Visiting Athens from his native Kos sometime during this period, the father of clinical medicine, Hippocrates himself, may have seen the figures of Asclepius and Apollo and they, in turn, could have inspired the opening lines of his oath: "I swear by Apollo the healer, by Aesculapius, by Health and all the powers of healing, and call to witness all the gods and goddesses that I may keep this Oath and Promise to the best of my ability and judgement."

Another contemporary of Myron's may also have seen the sculptures. Empedocles lived from 492 BC to 432 BC — a great rival of Hippocrates, also a great healer and surgeon, he placed philosophy at the centre of medical studies rather than the practical application of care. He may have been one of the first physician-writers, for Empedocles dabbled in poetry, philosophy and science. His best-known work — *On Nature* — heralds his profession as both poet and healer.

Empedocles travelled the Ancient Greek lands, dispensing poetry along with medicine, wisdom infused with diagnoses. Empedocles believed himself to be a banished god, he had thousands of followers and was a prototype "wise old man," an archetype, a forerunner of Nietzsche's Zarathustra, wandering the countryside. He echoed Zarathustra's transformation through illness and convalescence, that echo evident in Kahlo's paintings, Welch's writings and Dylan's post-accident songs. "What happened, my brothers? I, the sufferer, overcame myself, I carried my own ashes to the mountains, I made for myself a brighter flame. And behold! the phantom *fled* from me! / Now to me, the convalescent, it would be suffering and torment to believe in such phantoms: it would be suffering to me now and humiliation," as Nietzsche has it.

The phantom is the self before illness, before the transmigration through convalescence to awareness. Empedocles wished to replace the Olympian gods with the four elements — earth, sea, air, and fire; Nietzsche wanted to replace God with the new man stripped of any disabling morality. Empedocles saw the universe as a battle between love and strife, and here we return to Apollo because Empedocles' philosophical system centres on a dynamic dualism, which overlaps with Nietzsche's theory of the Apollonian and Dionysian, an important symptom of the illness — the creativity prognosis.

"Over in the corner stands a large and heavy trunk, his only asset, containing two clean shirts and a fresh suit. Aside from these, only books and manuscripts. On a shelf, innumerable bottles, flasks and tinctures: for headaches, which regularly occupy so many wasted hours, for stomach cramps, spasmodic vomiting, intestinal weakness, and above all, those terrible medicaments to control insomnia — chloral and veronal. A horrifying arsenal of poisons and narcotics." This is not exactly a vision of the *Übermensch* — the superman, the destroyer of God, but it was the day-to-day reality for Nietzsche as described by Stefan Zweig. Whether because of brain cancer or the long-term aftereffects of syphilis, Nietzsche lived the life of a sickly man. Zweig again: "Sometimes he spends the whole day confined to bed. Vomiting and cramps until he loses consciousness, searing pain in the temples, sent almost blind." In his illness, Nietzsche existed within the worlds of strife, a Dionysian hell of pain.

In the moments between these bouts, Nietzsche wrote in an Apollonian zone of order, structure and individuation, but Apollonian through intoxication, through pain and narcotics, a Dionysian chaos: "My written productions (I would prefer not to say 'books' and also not 'pamphlets') I have virtually tricked out of myself during rare vacations and times of sickness; I even had to dictate the Straussiad, because at that time I could neither read nor write," he confesses in a letter to Hans von Bülow on 2 January, 1875.

Zweig quotes Nietzsche as claiming that, "at all stages of life, the surplus of pain has in my case been immense." Nietzsche attempted to write and think his way out of the illnesses, only to be trapped in an eternal recurrence of disease until a drug put him to sleep. Yet Nietzsche — despite his letters of complaint — in *Ecce Homo* (1888), saw himself as healthy: "The concepts 'soul', 'spirit', ultimately even 'immortal soul' invented so as to despise the body, to make it sick — 'holy' — so as to approach with terrible negligence all the things in life that deserve to be taken seriously, questions of food, accommodation, spiritual diet, the treatment of the sick, cleanliness, weather! Instead of health the 'salvation of the soul' — in other words *folie circulaire* between penitential cramps and redemption hysteria!"

Nietzsche was both patient and doctor: he explored the symptoms and administered the medication, he used his analysis of illness to create a symptomatological philosophy, a pathology of humanity. Without his various maladies there would have been no incisive books — his thinking was surgical and his books were examples of auto-vivisection. Zweig argues that "suddenly he draws from himself the very malady that saps his soul and presses it hard against his heart. Then comes the truly mysterious moment (whose date we cannot pinpoint precisely), one of those dazzling inspirations at the heart of his work, where Nietzsche 'discovers' his own sickness."

Nietzsche perceived illness as transformative, as life-affirming, he saw the world as unhealthy and himself as the diagnostician of its maladies — indeed, without sickness, there would be no world, there would be no writing. On 2 January, 1875, he wrote in a letter to Hans von Bülow: "But since I am now in a good physical state, with no prospect of sickness, and my daily cold baths offer no likelihood of my ever being sick again, my future as a writer is almost hopeless." By 8 December of the same year, he was spending thirty-six hours in bed every two or three weeks "in real torment," and complained in a letter to Erwin Rohde that "there is no pleasure left in life," and that he really is "surprised how difficult living is. It does not seem to be worth it, all this torment."

During this time, he was working on *Untimely Meditations* (1876), his study of European culture in which "the unhistorical and the historical are equally necessary to the good health of a man, a people, and a culture." Nietzsche questioned the historical determinations of health and sickness, saw them as both trans-formative and individuating — the history of an illness became the unhistorical and imaginative projection of a healthy future. Ten years later, in writing taken from *Late Notebooks*, he asserts: "Health and sickliness: be careful! The yardstick remains the body's efflorescence, the mind's elasticity, courage and cheerfulness — but also, of course, how much sickliness it can take upon itself and overcome — can make healthy. What would destroy more tender men is one of the stimulants of great health."

This was a personal summation not only of his own body but that of contemporary Europe and of Ancient Greece, a precarious balance between Apollo and Dionysus, history and unhistory, of health and sickness. He wrote in a letter to Franz Overbeck in September 1882: "…on the whole I have a right to talk of recovery, even if I am often reminded of the precarious balance of my health."

Illness animated Nietzsche, in essence, it was a will to life, a will to power, a recovery from life into life, an affliction become philosophical reflection, a theory of convalescence and what he called "the intoxication of recovery," the use of the Dionysian to attain the Apollonian, the movement through strife to discover love. This is how Nietzsche interpreted the world, how he examined himself. He wrote to his mother and sister on 27 December, 1871: "This Apollonian effect is through my Dionysian one […] and after that, through the Apollonian-Dionysian double effect of my book." The book was *Die Geburt der Tragödie aus dem Geiste der Musik* (*The Birth of Tragedy*) (1872), in which Nietzsche sets out his "double effect." It is interesting to note that around the time of the publication of *The Birth of Tragedy*, Nietzsche wrote several drafts for a play about Empedocles, which had the same working title as Hölderlin's *The Death of Empedocles* (circa 1800). We can take a closer look at the double effects of therapy and convalescence, of illness and recovery, from within the Apollonian-Dionysian prognosis and its antecedent, Empedocles' dynamic dualism — love and strife.

For Empedocles, love, when mixed with the four elements of earth, water, fire and air, forms the primal sphere, it is the uniting bond, a proto-singularity. When this sphere is invaded by strife or hate (from within — as a kind of genetic abnormality or cancer), or from without (bacteria or virus), then the singularity inflates and explodes, creating everything we now know but in a chaotic sense expanding and proliferating until another collapse is imminent. It is only with love's power that the world we know can be bound together in an ordered and harmonious whole.

The body, likewise, is a balance of the four elements, made healthy with love. It is only when invaded by dis-ease (strife) that it becomes unstable and reins in chaos until love (care, convalescence) regains power and creates equilibrium. In his play *The Death of Empedocles* (1797–1800), Hölderlin has the philosopher proclaim, "poison heals the sick / And one sin punishes the others."

"Poison heals the sick," reverberates in Nietzsche's proclamation that that which didn't kill him made him stronger, and both can allude to the process of immunization. Strife is the antigen used to stimulate love's response. Strife and chaos are poisons that heal by a restoration of love's (care's) binding power. Nietzsche believed that bouts of sickness — dis-ease, strife — led to his strength, to his creative powers, and that only by overcoming strife, through experiencing it, can we move forward as individuals, as a society, even as a species. Empedocles' theory of love becomes Nietzsche's Apollonian order and structure, while strife (hate) becomes Dionysian chaos and intoxication. In health terms and in the process of creativity, these duelling and dualistic "twofold truths" (Empedocles) or "double effects" (Nietzsche) concern individuation and sociality.

The artist and the patient are in a constant process, an eternal recurrence, of individuation. In writing and painting, in illness and convalescence, there is a process of becoming and becoming again; if individuation is an ongoing event, a constant search for an "I", then this impossibility of a perfect sphere of being, this constant "imitating" of the self, and art, writing, music, becoming well again after illness, are means of, or attempts to, reveal or regain what Nietzsche called "unity with the innermost core of the world" through order and structure, but also through artistic and narcotic intoxication. In *Acting Out* (2009), Bernard Stiegler claims, "I never cease to find myself *other than myself*, I never cease to find myself *divided*, while at the same time the group *alters* and *divides itself* — and it does this because a process of individuation is structurally incapable of completion."

Diversity unifies, strife is legitimized by love, there is Apollonian and Dionysian equilibrium, but all of this is an ongoing process and, I would argue, that the essence of creativity — the spark of inspiration — and the singularity of illness — the point at which the "I" teeters on divisibility (its own big bang) — is symptomatological as well as asymptotical. It is the moment we get closest to the "I," the diagnosis of the symptoms that make up individuation and the point at which there is a need to share that with others, the group, the "we" through art and through convalescence.

Thomas Bernhard investigates this link in *Correction* (1975): "I've lived half my life not in nature but in my books as a nature-substitute, and the one half was made possible only by the other half. Or else we exist in both simultaneously, in nature and in reading-as-nature, in this extreme nervous tension which as a form of consciousness is endurable only for the shortest possible time."

Jean-Luc Nancy writes in *Corpus* (2003): "Why indices? Because there's no totality to the body, no synthetic unity. There are pieces, zones, fragments. There's one bit after another, a stomach, an eyelash, a thumb-nail, a shoulder, a breast, a nose, an upper intestine, a choledoch, a pancreas: anatomy is endless, until eventually running into an exhaustive enumeration of cells. But this doesn't yield a totality. On the contrary, we must immediately run through the whole nomenclature all over again, so as to find, if possible, a trace of the soul imprinted on every piece. But the pieces, the cells, change as the calculation enumerates in vain." That's what I've always felt about my body, that it's a sum of its parts and since I no longer have some of these parts, it has become more fragmented, shifting, not really *Middlemarch* but more William S. Burroughs' *The Soft Machine* (1961): "Metamorphosis of the Rewrite Department coughing and spitting in fractured air — flapping genitals of carrion — Our drained countess passed on a hideous leather body — We are digested and become nothing here."

From the age of three or four, I felt that my body had been rewritten, that it metamorphosed before I started school, at about the time I learned to read. Some of my earliest memories, friable and fractured, are of being in hospital. I remember my parents visiting me when I was in an isolation ward, they wore surgical masks and brought me books. Maybe Thomas Bernhard was correct when he declared that "books were meant for grown-ups, they'd go to your head like a disease, mother always used to say." And they did. I remember reading the *Janet and John* series, "This is Janet. This is John," with their colourful covers and prim and proper nuclear families. I also read the *Peter and Jane* books published by Ladybird. I also read Ladybird's "Adventures from History" series and distinctly recall *Captain Scott*, *Stone Age Man in Britain* and *Julius Caesar and Roman Britain*. But I may not have read them, I may have just looked at the pictures or read them when I was older but, in my mind, they sit on the bedside table in the hospital along with a bottle of Tree Top orange squash and a bar of Caramac.

However friable my memories of the past, I have always associated illness with reading; the smell of camphor becomes the odour of books, foxing is the eczema on my chest. Patterns of disease become narratives, human life a fabulation of linearity, a medical metafiction. Maybe that is why I flinch when I see people break a book's spine or cruelly dog-ear the pages. Towards the end of writing this book, I decided to obtain my medical records to shore up the facade of some of my shakier memories and those more so of my mother and father. So please note that throughout the book there will be brief passages from my medical autobiography (autopathography) with notes from others that I hope will give relief and offer guidance to this solipsistic time-travelling. As Mark Leyner writes, "memory (and, in a sense, autobiography) is like a rash that blossoms and fades," and I am itching to get on with it.

There are roughly 250 pages of records (the length of the average-sized contemporary novel) dating from 12 October, 1965 moving through the 70s, 80s, 90s and into the twenty-first century to January 2016. There are a few gaps in the chronology due to the times I have lived abroad — New York in the late 80s, Thailand and Japan from 2006 until 2011 and South Africa intermittently.

The first photocopied record from the earliest notes resembles the black page from Laurence Sterne's *The Life and Opinions of Tristram Shandy, Gentleman* (1759), that metafictional novel which fragments and rewrites itself, breaks all the rules of linear narrative and highlights the artificiality of fiction as well as of human life. Sterne died of pulmonary tuberculosis at the age of fifty-four, the age I was when I started to write this book. So the missing records also resemble the missing chapters in *Tristram Shandy*, the black page signifying Yorick's death, whilst the near-black page of the records indicate the birth of my medical history.

The first note, written in the clichéd doctor's illegible handwriting, is near impossible to decipher, the darkness of the photocopy hindering my efforts further, but I can make out the dates: 12/10/65 (I was four and three-quarters) to ?/?/67. On the right side of the page, I can read a few words. "12/10/65 — tonsillitis." Beneath that what looks like "Nembutal," could that be right? Nembutal was something William Burroughs used as an antidote to the toxic effects of yagé while exploring the Amazon in 1953. "23/12/65 — gargled" something. "02/02/66 — Tonsillitis with running, itching nose. ENT URT infection." Then a list of drugs, eleven of them. "22/03/67 — recurrence of asthma. Grass or flower allergy." I have never suffered from these allergies, I have never had hayfever (allergic rhinitis).

There is a clearer page dated 07/09/65 and an end date of 13/09/65, so a month before these dark pages begin. It is an admission/discharge form from West Middlesex Hospital. The chief of department is one M. Dynski-Klein. A little research uncovers a Martha Dynski-Klein who authored a book called *A Colour Atlas of Paediatrics* and is also quoted in *Pediatric Allergy, Asthma and Immunology* by Arnaldo Cantani. The diagnosis is bronchial asthma. It reads, "present attack began at 11pm last night and he was taken to doctor but with temporary relief only and was sent for admission at 9pm" [sic]. I must have been time-travelling again. "Attack began with breathlessness and coughing; later he vomited. At 11am, he became white and limp, eyes turned up, but no convulsions, or tongue biting, or incontinence." This made me think of Louis-Ferdinand Céline's *Guignol's Band* (1944), "Like a crisis in his illness, his asthma. When that got him! what a panic! [...] Should've seen his eyes then! [...] the horror that seized him!" There are many pages in the doctor-writer's works that detail suffering and illness, and we will encounter him regularly throughout the book. Céline died on 1 July, 1961, five months after I was born, from a subarachnoid haemorrhage, otherwise I would have transplanted him to Isleworth to be my physician.

The record continues, "First started having attacks of asthma at age of three months. He was well from 7 months until 2 ½ years and started again after moving. No other illnesses. Immunizations — triple, polio, smallpox." Thanks to whoever immunized me against polio because, as Philip Roth wrote in his novel *Nemesis* about a polio epidemic in New Jersey in the summer of 1944, "polio is a disease that we have to live with every summer. It's a serious disease that's been around all my life. The best way to deal with the threat of polio is to stay healthy and strong." I had no chance of that, just a memory of being constantly in bed, the white cotton, the camphor, milk that I came to detest, my body becoming an object to be probed and prodded and subject to medical commentary — the critical and the clinical.

On examination — "Wheezing, skinny child in mild respiratory distress. No cyanosis. Subcostal recession. Audible wheeze. Sibilant rhonchi all over chest. Bilateral rales." I rattled when I breathed, the breath crackled out of me. Breath was a hidden language, a substance, a reluctant material trapped within a small skinny body, my lungs became my internal enemy. I remember staring in the mirror disassociating parts of my body with their functions, a skinny body without organs, *a la* Deleuze and Guattari from *A Thousand Plateaus* (1980): "In doses. As a rule immanent to experimentation: injections of caution. Many have been defeated in this battle. Is it really so sad and dangerous to be fed up with seeing with your eyes, breathing with your lungs, swallowing with your mouth, talking with your tongue, thinking with your brain, having an anus and larynx, head and legs?" I did not breathe with my lungs, I couldn't swallow with my mouth, talking with my tongue was difficult, thinking about breathing is not breathing. It was around this time that I began to have a problem with people's heads, I will explain further when I reach my teenage years.

I would like to return to the imaginary hospital now and, after a quick tour, apply this prognosis to certain case studies of artists who have suffered from illnesses and disabilities and used these (or denied the effects of them) in their work. So pick up your clipboards and notebooks and follow me on a time-travelling ward round. Ready? Do follow me, if you please.

On meeting Hans Castorp at the Berghof sanatorium high in the Swiss Alps, Dr Krokowski responds to Hans' assertion that he is perfectly healthy by proclaiming, "Then you are a phenomenon worthy of study. I, for one, have never in my life come across a perfectly healthy human being." Eight years after the publication of *The Magic Mountain*, our good doctor Louis-Ferdinand Céline stated in *Journey to the End of Night* (1932), "He's written, says he's sick […] Big deal! Sick! I'm sick too! What does he mean sick? We're all sick. You'll be sick yourself before you know it! That's no excuse! What do we care if he's sick!" We are all sick and most of us are in denial about our sickness. How do we come to terms with this denial? In a Nietzschean way? Using our illness as a means of attaining insights into our future evolution? As a way of testing the limits of our morality and the ethics of society in the form of doctors, nurses, caregivers?

On entering hospital, whether conscious or unconscious, we give ourselves over to the institution, to society in microcosm, but one that is more concerned with the body and its functions and malfunctions, with its maintenance and the threats of disability, decay and death. There may be chapels and prayer rooms in hospital but they are usually out of the way, almost furtively situated. The hospital is the space of sickness, blood and death, it is the space of health, care and convalescence, a space where the body undergoes extreme violence as a means of sustaining life. It is a place in Foucault's *The Birth of the Clinic* (1963), where "doctor and patient are caught up in an ever-greater proximity, bound together, the doctor by an ever-more attentive, more insistent, more penetrating gaze, the patient by all the silent, irreplaceable qualities that, in him, betray — that is, reveal and conceal — the clearly ordered forms of the disease. Between the nosological characters and terminal features to be read on the patient's face, the qualities have roamed freely over the body. The medical gaze need hardly dwell on this body for long, at least in its densities and functioning."

I would like to take that clinical gaze and those nosological characters and turn them critical and biographical in this study of certain artists, writers and musicians and their relationship to their disease, debilitation and/or disability. I agree with Foucault that, "like civilization, the hospital is an artificial locus in which the transplanted disease runs the risk of losing its essential identity." I hope we do not contract some type of nosocomial infection such as MRSA or tuberculosis, for "we must place ourselves, and remain once and for all, at the level of the fundamental *spatialization* and *verbalization* of the pathological, where the loquacious gaze with which the doctor observes the poisonous heart of things is born and communes with itself." We will observe and discuss these medical cases and attempt to diagnose the patients' forms of creativity as related to illness — a symptomatological study of inspiration and artistic practice.

As we walk beneath the statue of Asclepius, the serpent posed in an eternal marmoreal flicking of its tongue, the automatic sliding doors to reception open in an asthmatic wheeze and we are in the coolness and antiseptic glow of the hospital. We can hear the faint Doppler effect of ambulance sirens, ferrying the sick and the injured to our multidimensional and time-travelling hospital. One may be carrying Roland Barthes, an oxygen mask over his bloodied face, his chest crushed by the impact of a laundry van as he was crossing the Rue des Écoles. He wrote, "Life can only imitate the book, and the book itself is only a tissue of signs, a lost, infinitely remote imitation." Barthes will imitate life for another month before succumbing to his injuries. He had become passionless and humourless after the death of his mother; he had written in *Camera Lucida* (1980): "I who had not procreated, (I) had, in her very illness, engendered my mother. Once she was dead I no longer had any reason to attune myself to the progress of the superior Life Force (the race, the species). My particularity could never again universalize itself (unless utopically, by writing, whose project henceforth would become the unique goal of my life). From now on I could do no more than await my total, undialectical death."

His total, undialectical death; all the more poignant and ironical as he had endured tuberculosis from the age of nineteen, like Hans Castorp, spending years in various sanatoria. Whereas Nietzsche's illness had spurred him on to biologically and morally improve the race, the species, through a superior Life Force, the *Übermensch* and the *Wille zur Macht* (will to power), Barthes' injuries debilitated his sense of self to such an extent that he craved death, he preferred a depersonalized silence. It is as if observing Barthes' crushed body, we are creating in our clinical gaze his own theory of photography, "The presence of the thing (at a certain past moment) is never metaphoric; and in the case of animated beings, their life as well, except in the case of photographing corpses; and even so: if the photograph then becomes horrible, it is because it certifies, so to speak, that the *corpse* is alive, as corpse: it is the living image of a dead thing."

For a month after his accident, Barthes was a living corpse. The "real" to him, his mother, had died, he had nursed the death of the "real" and he wanted to believe that she would live but now his whole life was one of "this-has-been," there is no Nietzschean overcoming, there is no consolation in convalescence, he gave up the body's formality to become a corpse.

In the hospital reception area, the foyer and the open-plan waiting section, the walls are decorated with paintings and banners depicting brightly coloured, even Day-Glo, flowers — I believe they are hibiscuses. They were donated to the hospital by one of our regular patients, an artist of sensitive, one could even say exaggerated, thoughts about his own health, or lack thereof. Like Nietzsche, he was a sickly child, he suffered from bouts of St Vitus Dance, contracted scarlet fever, broke his arm, had his tonsils out, came down with rheumatic fever that left him with facial tics, low muscle mass, and reddish-brown blotches all over his body. Brian Dillon wrote in *Tormented Hope: Nine Hypochondriac Lives* (2010) that "until his death in 1987, he remained genuinely preoccupied with the problem of his body, with the problem of having a body and what (or what not) to do with it, and with whom. He was tormented by beauty, but also by the threat of illness and its remembered reality. Warhol was a hypochondriac for whom health and aesthetics were inextricably linked, an artist who confronted the truth of the body as fearlessly as he did its fantasies, and yet remained quite unable, in private, to accommodate himself to the reality of his own physical decline and the illnesses (and deaths) of those closest to him. In his pathological investment in the ideas of beauty and ugliness, health and disease, and in his inability to tell those two continuums apart, he is our contemporary. Warhol's fears are our own and we have to choose between the conflicting means he found to express and assuage them."

Unlike Barthes, but in a similar fashion to Nietzsche, Warhol explored how the body and mind reacted to illness, how sickness manifested itself in personal philosophy and how disease made us human, all too human. Between 1962 and 1967, Warhol worked on a series of silkscreen canvases with the group title "Death and Disaster," originally titled "Death in America." He used images and headlines from the front pages of contemporary newspapers and created works such as, *Deaths on Red, Red Disaster, Gangster Funeral, Silver Car Crash (Double Disaster), Race Riot, Green Disaster #2* and *Ambulance Disaster*. At the time, Warhol was obsessed with death, particularly the death of celebrities, and had been working on a series of silkscreens of Marilyn Monroe who had died on 5 August, 1962, just two months before Warhol began the "Death and Disaster" pictures with *129 Die in Jet*, the newspaper dated 4 June, 1962. It was to further extend this series that Warhol founded the first Factory at 231 East 47th Street, New York City.

Warhol used the repetition of disaster, death, riot and executions to anaesthetize the horror, to immunize the viewer against a mediatized terror. If something is repeated enough, it either becomes absurd or becomes nothing. These violent images are washed in blues, pinks, greens, oranges and sliver as if they were created as decoration, as greeting cards for some gruesome new celebration. These are still lives, *nature morte*, concerning contemporary modes of death, they are examinations of how the human body interacts with modern technology — jet planes, cars, ambulances, electric chairs, and of how the flesh is weak when impacted with the violence of speed and steel. They are rainbow-hued meditations on the temporal disease of the self and snapshots of the very moment that existence terminates. Alongside the works on Marilyn Monroe and Elizabeth Taylor (Warhol began his silkscreens of Taylor when she contracted pneumonia and had a subsequent tracheotomy during the filming of *Cleopatra*), these visions of violence and death and sex and celebrity would inspire the writing of J.G. Ballard — in particular *The Atrocity Exhibition* (1970) and *Crash* (1973). Both men had a cold, almost depersonalized gaze, a surgeon's unflinching eye: "At the same time it seemed to me that Vaughan was selecting certain sexual acts and positions in his mind for future use, the maximum sex act within the automobile. The clear equation he had made between sex and the kinaesthetics of the highway was in some way related to his obsessions with Elizabeth Taylor."

Ambulance Accident (1964), one of Warhol's "Death and Disaster" canvases, shows the double image of a crashed ambulance, a body of a young man thrown out of the window, arched like a diver, arms thrown out, face covered in blood, the ambulance number visible on the crumpled bodywork, the crash almost ironical. Was the ambulance on the way to the hospital when it crashed? It is as if the automobile and the human body have become one in the instant of the photograph, as if the silkscreen version, bleached clinical white, is the reification of Warhol's statement in an interview in *Art News* in 1963 that, "I want to be a machine," and in *POPism: The Warhol Sixties* that, "What I liked was chunks of time all together, every real moment." The double image provides us with a mirror that reflects nothing, an almost Pierre Menard-like contemplation on authenticity, representation, reproduction and simulacra. What is real? What is image? In the opening pages of *The Philosophy of Andy Warhol* (1975), Warhol and his interlocutor "B" discuss mirrors and their representation of the self: "Some critic called me the Nothingness Himself and that didn't help my sense of existence any. Then I realized that existence itself is nothing and I felt better. But I'm still obsessed with the idea of looking into the mirror and seeing no one, nothing."

The mirror reflects the death of the self, it makes trauma a surface negation, but the image forces us to stare, to confront that crisis of existence. The silkscreen exemplifies Barthes' theory in *Camera Lucida* of the punctum as "also: sting, speck, cut, little hole — and also a cast of the dice. A photograph's punctum is that accident which pricks me (but also bruises me, is poignant to me)." By repeating the image, mirroring it, colouring it — almost like iodine over a wound — Warhol invests the image with punctum, "News photographs are very often unary (the unary photograph is not necessarily tranquil). In these images, no *punctum*: a certain shock — the literal can traumatize — but no disturbance; the photograph can 'shout', not wound." These pictures of death and disaster are blue bruises, pink scars, red wounds, yellow fever dreams of the body's vulnerability and the constant presence of a perfunctory death. Just a year after concluding the series, Warhol experienced his own moment of death and disaster.

From *Camera Lucida* again: "I now know that there exists another *punctum* (another 'stigmatum') than the 'detail'. This new punctum, which is no longer of form but of intensity, is Time, the lacerating emphasis of the *noeme* ('*that-has-been*'), its pure representation." After 3 June, 1968, Warhol would carry his own stigmata, his own punctum, as a reminder of time, of the pure representation of his body and "what-has-been" through his roadmap of scars. "'What about your scars?' B said. 'I'll tell you about your scars. I think you produced *Frankenstein* just so you could put your scars in the ad. You put your scars to work for you. I mean, why not? They're the best things you have because they're proof of something. I always think it's nice to have the proof.'"

Warhol created his flower paintings between 1964 and 1965, using variations on an original photograph by Patricia Caulfield. In a similar manner to the "Death and Disaster" silkscreens, Warhol experimented with colour and repetition. Not as shocking as the images of suicide, riots and car accidents, the flower paintings that adorn the walls of the hospital reception, although they brighten up the institutional-taupe of the walls, still remind us of impermanence, of the fading of beauty and of life. They are psychedelic versions of still lives, *memento mori*; hibiscus flowers represent delicate beauty and purity but also immortality, and are forerunners of Warhol's skull paintings of the mid-1970s. Several of the paintings show red or pink flowers on a darker background and these resemble the entry and exit wounds of bullets, the petals peeled open flesh, the disk of the flower the dark entry to the body.

All of the paintings Warhol executed during the mid-1960s are concerned with the fragility of the body as it encounters technology (car crashes) and/or time (Marilyn Monroe and flowers). These remind us of death, yet Warhol denied death its place in human existence and focused on the transitory nature of life, on its diseases and its decay. "I don't believe in it, because you're not around to know that it's happened. I can't say anything about it because I'm not prepared for it," he wrote in *The Philosophy of Andy Warhol*. Warhol's paintings and films highlight our temporal existence, they confront us with our mortality, they are projections of our "being-towards-death," their inauthenticity highlights our everyday existence and they fuse the morbid (car crashes, skulls) with the beautiful (Monroe, hibiscuses).

Warhol reinterprets death in his work, a continual repetition of dying but not the impossible experience of death. Who would have thought that Warhol was a Heidegger and *Being and Time* fan? "*The closest closeness which one may have in being towards death as a possibility, is as far as possible from anything actual.* The more unveiledly this possibility gets understood, the more purely does the understanding penetrate into it *as the possibility of the impossibility of any existence at all.* Death, as possibility, gives Dasein nothing to be 'actualized', nothing which Dasein, as actual, could itself *be.* It is the possibility of the impossibility of every way of comporting oneself towards anything, of every way of existing."

Warhol reaffirmed the nothing of being towards death in his paintings of surface, his projection of the possibility of the impossibility of permanent time, he states, in *The Philosophy of Andy Warhol,* that "the thing is to think of nothing, B. Look, nothing is exciting, nothing is sexy, nothing is not embarrassing. The only time I ever want to be something is outside a party so I can get in." Warhol is a blank, a nothing, a possibility.

Before we look more closely at the event of 3 June, 1968 and its aftermath, let us go back to Warhol's sickly childhood and a crucial point in his becoming an artist. In *An Afghan Picture Show* (1992), the author William T. Vollmann has written an account of how illness and reading inspired him to become a writer, how being off school sick led to his mother reading to him and this kindled his feverish imagination to invent worlds of his own: "The idea of a world beyond the window, which was now a translucent slab of light, or for that matter of any other possibility than that of lying in my bed immobile, became as dry and strange as some ontological argument of the Middle Ages, and by degrees ever less likely, until when at mid-morning, my mother came in to bring me a cup of tea or some soup, I refused politely, in the same way that I would have done if she'd come to ask whether I would be willing to study law at the university. This inability to grasp my own state of existence of the day before would have possessed me so much that by mid-afternoon, when my mother came in to read to me, I no longer shifted my position beneath the blankets at all, but lay absolutely still in the hot faintness of my malady as though I were one of those people one reads about in old books who are always getting becalmed in the tropics."

Warhol recounts a similar experience: "I had had three nervous breakdowns when I was a child, spaced a year apart. One when I was eight, one at nine, and one at ten. The attacks — St Vitus Dance — always started on the first day of summer vacation. I don't know what this meant. I would spend all summer listening to the radio and lying in bed with my Charlie McCarthy doll and my un-cut-out cut-out paper dolls all over the spread and under the pillow. My father was away a lot on business trips to the coal mines, so I never saw him very much. My mother would read to me in her thick Czechoslovakian accent as best she could and I would always say "Thanks, Mom," after she finished with Dick Tracy, even if I hadn't understood a word. She'd give me a Hershey Bar every time I finished a page in my coloring book."

Vollmann and Warhol's childhood illnesses resulted in periods of leisure during which they spent mostly solitary hours "playing" with their imagination, using material — words for Vollmann, paper dolls and colouring books for Warhol — which introduced them to the possibility of creativity. This transforming power, away from the anxieties of peer pressure — both were made fun of at school and bullied because of their appearance — emerged from the binary factors of a fevered mind and the imaginative need to escape boredom and solitude, the impulse to create, the drive to invent a world that one feels safe within and that one can control.

From childhood onward, both Warhol and Vollmann created works that impel the viewer/reader to acknowledge an ephemeral reality, one that constantly reminds us of encroaching death. From *An Afghan Picture Show*: "And when I lay in bed all day, the eerie luminescence of my sickness in me and all about me, my inability to recall my healthy state in any real sense made the wrinkles of my own 'Land of Counterpane' seem a menacing *memento mori*." Warhol is obsessed with illness, with brands, with media, with attempting to re-establish the period in which his mother gave him a chocolate bar for finishing his artwork, a time in which he ventriloquized his silence and internalized the art of the cartoon. Vollmann created miniature landscapes of war (counterpain) from which he would go on to explore in his writing the history of violence and colonialization. Both used illness as a means of imagination and both carried this through their later work in ever-evolving yet self-referential processes — Warhol's repetitive images and Vollmann's re-writing of American history.

On the afternoon of 3 June, 1968, outside the Decker Building at 33 Union Square West and East 16th Street, Andy Warhol and his boyfriend Jed Johnson invited the writer Valerie Solanas to join them in the new Factory space. Previously Andy had lost one of her scripts and Valerie had been hassling him to pay compensation. Valerie thought Andy was giving her the runaround and was not being honest with her, she thought his staff were making excuses to her and lying about where Andy was when she called on the phone or in person. Andy was wearing makeup and pimple cream to hide his blotchy skin and spots. Some of the usual crew were in the Factory — Fred Hughes, Andy's business manager, the film director Paul Morrissey, and the superstar actress Viva was calling from a hair salon. Mario Amaya, the art critic, was also there to discuss a project.

Viva was talking to Morrissey and then Andy and, as Andy passed the phone to Hughes, Valerie Solanas took a

.32 automatic pistol from a paper bag she was carrying and fired a shot. The bullet missed, Andy cried out for her to stop and threw himself to the floor, Valerie Solanas fired again and missed again. Andy had by now crawled under a table for protection. Valerie Solanas stepped forward and fired a third shot, this time the bullet penetrated Andy's right side, travelled through his body and exited through Andy's back on the left side. Believing she had murdered Andy, she fired two more shots at Mario Amaya, one of which entered just above his hip and exited clean, leaving no critical damage. She now turned to Fred Hughes, who begged her not to shoot. She seemed to have slaked her blood thirst and moved toward the elevator doors and pushed the call button, but before the elevator arrived she returned to Hughes and held the gun to his head, pulled the trigger, the mechanism jammed. Valerie Solanas took another gun, this time a .22, from the paper bag, but the elevator doors opened, she stepped in and the doors closed.

Fred Hughes called the emergency services and I am sure he had in his mind Andy's silkscreens, particularly *Ambulance Disaster* and *Double Elvis*. The photographer/poet Gerard Malanga and the musician Angus Maclise appeared to find Billy Name crouching over Andy's body. After ten minutes or so, the ambulance team put Andy into a wheelchair and took him to Columbus Hospital, three blocks away on 19th Street. Surgeons found that the bullet had ricocheted in Andy's body, around his abdomen and up into his chest; on its trajectory it penetrated his spleen, gall bladder, liver, oesophagus and both lungs before exiting. At one point, the doctors pronounced Andy clinically dead and used internal cardiac massage to resuscitate him. The action took ninety seconds before Andy was revived. They operated on him for nearly six hours, removing his spleen in the process. Snap.

Andy Warhol spent nearly four weeks in hospital recovering from the shootings, he hated every minute of his stay, as his interlocutor "B" in *The Philosophy of Andy Warhol* reminds him, "Remember how embarrassed you were in the hospital when the nuns saw you without your wings? (sic) And you started to collect things again. The nuns got you interested in collecting stamps, like you did when you were a kid or something. They got you interested in coins again too." Warhol returned to his childhood hobbies of philately and numismatics, the serried ranks of stamps prefiguring his repetitive silkscreens, the coins as forerunners of his multiple dollar-bill prints he created before beginning the "Death and Disaster" series. Warhol disliked the bureaucracy of the hospital and saw it as mercenary, "B: Hospitals are unbelievable. A: When I was dying I had to write my name on a check." He spent his time recording telephone conversations he had with friends, family and associates, these were disembodied voices reminding him that he was back from the dead and Andy realized that the traumatic shooting — the near-death experience, a confrontation with his own mortality — was a transforming event: "Before I was shot, I always thought that I was more half-there than all-there — I always suspected that I was watching TV instead of living life. People sometimes say that the way things happen in movies is unreal, but actually it's the way things happen in life that's unreal. The movies make emotions look so strong and real, whereas when things really do happen to you, it's like watching television — you don't feel anything. Right when I was being shot and ever since, I knew that I was watching television. The channels switch, but it's all television."

Warhol would never recover fully from his injuries, he would have to wear a surgical corset, had trouble with his lungs and suffered from gallstones, which would eventually lead to his death on 22 February, 1987 from cardiac arrhythmia following a gallbladder operation.

In 1960, before he began to work mainly with silkscreens, Warhol painted *Where is Your Rupture?* It is based on a newspaper advertisement for the Brooks Appliance Company who made trusses and corsets. Between 1965 and 1967, the years she attempted to ingratiate herself into Warhol's circle, the would-be assassin, Valerie Solanas, wrote *SCUM Manifesto* (1967) while living at the Chelsea Hotel. The radical tract opens with the rallying cry: "'Life' in this 'society' being, at best, an utter bore and no aspect of 'society' being at all relevant to women, there remains to civic-minded, responsible, thrill-seeking females only to overthrow the government, eliminate the money system, institute complete automation and eliminate the male sex." An analysis of the work alongside Warhol's pre and post-trauma artwork may provide an insight into the transformative nature of his shooting and its aftermath, the bullet as caregiver, the scars as convalescent stigma.

In *SCUM Manifesto* (SCUM may be an acronym for the Society for Cutting Up Men), Solanas wrote, "To call a man an animal is to flatter him; he's a machine, a walking dildo. It's often said that men use women. Use them for what? Surely not pleasure." The machine could have been anything. Warhol wanted to be a machine, free from pain, from imperfections, but the machine could also be his process of creation, the Factory itself, a machine of human parts. In *Where Is Your Rupture?*, the body is desexualized, a torso, an anatomical toy, a dildo replacing the penis that it is missing, the vagina it may or may not have. The whole Solanas/Warhol saga could be subtitled "Gender Trouble," and Warhol's art could be as a prompt to Judith Butler's book of the same name: "I continue to hope for a coalition of sexual minorities that will transcend the simple categories of identity, that will refuse the erasure of bisexuality, that will counter and dissipate the violence imposed by restrictive bodily norms."

Warhol's paintings, his use of transsexuals and transvestites in his films, the blurred oscillation of his own sexuality — heterosexual, homosexual, bisexual, asexual — made him a surprising target for Solanas. But *Where Is Your Rupture?* acted *as* a target for Solanas; it showed her the way into the body, *Double Elvis* provides her with the method, the Marilyn Monroe and Elizabeth Taylor portraits with the motive, and the "Death and Disaster" silkscreens with the projected denouement. Although it was Solanas who carried two guns to the Factory that day, she states in the manifesto, "Hatred and Violence: The male is eaten up with tension, with frustration at not being female, at not being capable of ever achieving satisfaction or pleasure of any kind; eaten up with hate — not rational hate that is directed at those who abuse or insult you — but irrational, indiscriminate hate... hatred, at bottom, of his own worthless self." Yet Warhol counters in *The Philosophy* that "some people think violence is sexy, but I could never see that." After he recovered from the shootings and the operations, Warhol began to corporatize his life and work, his silkscreens of skulls and guns resembling harmless decorations, impotent signs of violence and death, as if, from the brink of non-existence, Warhol returned with a new view of the world. "Some people, even intelligent people, say that violence can be beautiful. I can't understand that, because beautiful is some moments, and for me those moments are never violent. A new idea. A new look. A new sex."

Warhol's post-shooting activities proliferated, he became involved in magazines, television, films, music and fashion, as if the shot Andy had multiplied, as if he had become one of his own repetitious paintings. In order that a singular Andy could never go through the trauma and pain again, he multiplied his self and the events he was involved in, all the while maintaining a detached aura, a distant personality although in the midst of celebrity and the media. Solanas states: "'Great Art' and 'Culture': The male 'artist' attempts to solve his dilemma of not being able to live, of not being female, by constructing a highly artificial world in which the male is heroized, that is, displays female traits, and the female is reduced to highly limited, insipid subordinate roles, that is, to being male. The male 'artistic' aim being, not to communicate (having nothing inside him he has nothing to say), but to disguise his animalism, he resorts to symbolism and obscurity ('deep' stuff). The vast majority of people, particularly the 'educated' ones, lacking faith in their own judgment, humble, respectful of authority ('Daddy knows best'), are easily conned into believing that obscurity, evasiveness, incomprehensibility, indirectness, ambiguity and boredom are marks of depth and brilliance."

In *Where Is Your Rupture?* there are no depths, the numbered black arrows point to places on the desexualized surface indicating possible locations of rupture, whether of the body's surface or the invisible organs within, they also become the future trajectory of bullets fired at Warhol or the points at which the bullet bounced and deflected through tissue, bone and organ within his body. They could also be the preliminary sketches of the scars on Warhol's body, the surface reflection of the trauma. This is what Warhol, "the great artist," communicated after the traumatic event, that this surface, this television screen, is what you see and what you get, there is no "symbolism and obscurity," no "ambiguity." All Warhol's post-traumatic work returns his own affectless gaze; the self-portraits in particular are non-evasive, the skulls that appear with Andy mean exactly what we think they mean — death — and death is not heroized. Solanas, however, does want to become immortal, she has not been near to death and believes that "all diseases are curable, and the aging process and death are due to disease; it is possible, therefore, never to age and to live forever. In fact the problems of aging and death could be solved within a few years, if an all-out, massive scientific assault were made upon the problem." But this won't happen because men are in charge and men know nothing about death and disease. Even though Warhol wanted to become a machine, to be a part in the process of a machine, Solanas goes on: "Lack of automation. There now exists a wealth of data which, if sorted out and correlated, would reveal the cure for cancer and several other diseases and possibly the key to life itself. But the data is so massive it requires high-speed computers to correlate it all. The institution of computers will be delayed interminably under the male control system, since the male has a horror of being replaced by machines."

The male horror at being replaced by machines echoes in Warhol's repetitive artwork, in the desexualized bodies, in the Factory itself, but, rather than fearing this, Warhol embraces it, captures the affectless gaze of the automaton, and Warhol may have had the last word on the subject in an interview years earlier in *Art News*: "Someone said Brecht wanted everybody to think alike. I want everybody to think alike [...] Everybody looks alike and acts alike, and we're getting more and more that way. I think everybody should be a machine [...] because you do the same thing every time. You do it again and again." This is a depersonalization brought about through trauma, a multiplying of the self because of the loss of the self in the near-death experience, a flattening out of the self, a means of avoiding penetration by others and by other things. After the shooting, Warhol became obsessed with documenting his life through different media: magazine, art, films, audio recordings, diaries, an ongoing artistic gathering of the multiple selves that occurred at the moment of near-death.

Andy Warhol's childhood rheumatic fever stimulated his interest in automata, fashion, repetition. His solitude created a distant persona that the 1968 shootings intensified and focused Warhol on becoming a process and a part in the artworks themselves. Warhol's genius was Warhol himself, and his life through illness and trauma exemplified Slavoj Žižek's maxim: "Thou shalt love thy symptom as thyself."

At the beginning of his career, Warhol dropped the final "a" from his family name, Warhola (it had been erroneously omitted in a magazine article credit), and the "a" becomes that Lacanian "*objet petit a*" — Warhol's detachment from desire, from the ego, from anxiety and pleasure and his wish to be detached from his body, a cyborg or robot, a machine. If the absent *objet petit a* from his name indicates an unobtainable object of desire, or the desire to desire, Warhol believes in *The Philosophy* that "sex is more exciting on the screen and between the pages than between the sheets anyway. Let the kids read about it and look forward to it, and then right before they're going to get the reality, break the news to them that they've already had the most exciting part, that it's behind them already. Fantasy love is much better than reality love. Never doing it is very exciting. The most exciting attractions are between two opposites that never meet."

As the ambulances dispense Roland Barthes and Andy Warhol in the accident and emergency area to await their divergent fates, let us press on into the guts of the hospital itself, past people in the waiting area, nurses, doctors, care-workers, patients and visitors. As you may have realized by now, this is a strange hospital, one of ancient foundations and countless wards. Roberto Bolaño describes it in his poem "Victoria Avalos and I" as an arena of "the division and multiplication of pain / as if the cities we inhabit were / an endless hospital ward."

It stretches back in time; its foundations are in Ancient Greece or in the Anuradhapura Kingdom jungles of Sri Lanka. Its patients include artists and sculptors, novelists and poets, classical and contemporary musicians. The doctors who pound the corridors count among them such diverse persons as François Rabelais, Sir Thomas Browne, William Carlos Williams, Louis-Ferdinand Céline and Stanislaw Lem, ably assisted by the likes of Tobias Smollett and the young John Keats. Accompanying these physicians on their ward rounds will be their fictitious others: Charles Bovary, Yuri Zhivago, Herbert West, Ferdinand Bardamu, Bernard Rieux and Doctor Benway. And in the wards we will meet fictitious as well as real patients, the aforementioned John Keats, Franz Kafka (if we can track him down), D.H. Lawrence (tuberculosis), Bruce Chatwin, Michel Foucault, Edmund White (HIV/AIDS), Christopher Hitchens, Kathy Acker (cancer), plus Hans Castorp and the family in Edvard Munch's *The Sick Room* and *The Sick Child*. Our hospital has seen many diseases and illnesses, both real and imaginary, from the black death, polio, HIV/AIDS and MRSAs to Edgar Allen Poe's and William Burroughs' Red Death.

Although the subject matter is a serious one, I hope we can approach it in a similar manner to the way physician-writer-patient Chekhov looked upon his illness, as Janet Malcolm explained: "The shadow of mortality hovers over his texts; his characters repeatedly remind one another, 'We all have to die' and 'Life is not given twice.'" Chekhov himself needed no such reminders: the last decade of his life was a daily struggle with increasingly virulent pulmonary and intestinal tuberculosis. Yet, when he was dying, in the spa of Badenweiler, where he had stupidly been sent by a specialist, he wrote letters to his sister Maria in which he repeatedly complained not about his fate but about how badly German women dressed, "Nowhere do women dress so abominably [...] I have not seen one beautiful woman, nor one who was not trimmed with some kind of absurd braid." It is an arguable theory that Chekhov, Kafka and Mansfield did not write long novels because of their illnesses, from them, there was no *War and Peace* — 1,225 pages, Tolstoy died at the age of eighty-two — and it may have been a matter of getting it down in short stories and short novels than expending energy on longer projects.

We will not progress lightly, as all hospitals are arenas of pain and blood, of death and disease, of suffering and recovery. As we move into the corridors, I would like to begin our ward round with a quote from John Berger's *A Fortunate Man* (1967): "The primitive medicine-man, who was often also priest, and judge, was the first specialist to be released from the obligation of procuring food for the tribe. The magnitude of this privilege and of the power which it gave him is a direct reflection of the importance of the needs he served. An awareness of illness is part of the price that man first paid and still pays for his self-consciousness. This awareness increases the pain or disability. But the self-consciousness of which it is the result is a social phenomenon and so with this self-consciousness arises the possibility of treatment, of medicine."

As we move through the text and the hospital, each of us are these primitive medicine-men, ur-surgeons, housemen of all sexes, races, times and places, with our clipboards and beepers, our knowledge and lack of, as we explore the changes in self-consciousness of the people we encounter and the effect on their means and modes of creative productivity. Now we can begin our "slow stalk from bed to bed, pausing by each one, peering in the dimness at (our) patients." I hope we "relish the opportunity to take this somehow private look at each of (our) patients" as we stand "by their beds and watch their gentle respirations — sometimes if a hand is exposed we feel a pulse — but mostly we just stand there and watch." But let us hope that we find these rounds interesting, unlike Euan in Martin Bax's *The Hospital Ship* (1976), who "hated these great treks of white coats up and down wards; everybody chatting away, not looking at all at the patients who were not of interest medically, indeed shunning the half-curious, half-scared looks the patients threw at them." Bur rather we take Dr Bernard Rieux's example. After doubting his own medical skill and knowledge when faced with an unknown plague, Camus tells us, "Rieux pulled himself together. There lay certitude; there, in the daily round. All the rest hung on mere threads and trivial contingencies; you couldn't waste your time on it. The thing was to do your job as it should be done." Exactly. Let us attempt to conduct our rounds with clarity and honesty, as we do not wish our patients to believe we are dabbling in some arcane science, as in the case of patient-come-doctor Ferdinand Bardemu, who in *Journey to the End of Night* claims, "We saw our doctors every morning. They questioned us amiably enough, but we never knew exactly what they were thinking. Under their affable smiles as they walked among us, they carried our death sentences." In fear of being obtuse and dense, the case studies, I hope, will evade language and obfuscation of the type which Thomas Bernhard accuses the medical profession in *Wittgenstein's Nephew*, "Like all other doctors, those who treated Paul continually entrenched themselves behind Latin terms, which in due course they built up into an insuperable and impenetrable fortification between themselves and the patient, as their predecessors had done for centuries, solely in order to conceal their incompetence and cloak their charlatanry."

Let us approach our artists-patients more in the manner of Dr John Sassall of *A Fortunate Man*: "The recognition has to be oblique. The unhappy man expects to be treated as though he were a nonentity with certain symptoms attached. The state of being a nonentity then paradoxically and bitterly confirms his uniqueness. It is necessary to break the circle. This can be achieved by the doctor presenting himself to the patient as a comparable man. It demands from the doctor a true imaginative effort and precise self-knowledge. The patient must be given the chance to recognize, despite his aggravated self-consciousness, aspects of himself in the doctor, but in such a way that the doctor seems to be Everyman."

CHAPTER 3

My Death My Life

Oncology as Observation

Rather than dying from the eighteen straight whiskeys he had consumed at the White Horse Tavern in New York City in November 1953, Dylan Thomas' death was more likely caused by pneumonia complications. Thomas' doctor failed to diagnose the disease and administered morphine sulphate, which would have further problematized Thomas' breathing and accentuated the feeling that he was suffocating. In the early hours of 3 November, he lapsed into a coma and was taken to St Vincent's Hospital in Greenwich Village. The diagnosis on admission was acute alcoholic encephalopathy — severe damage to the brain caused by alcohol consumption. Six days later, Thomas died having never regained consciousness. The postmortem cited pneumonia with pressure on the brain and a fatty liver as the primary causes of death. Thomas was also a life-long asthma and bronchitis sufferer and his poems captured the sprung rhythm of breathing and the danger of it ceasing.

Thirteen years after Thomas' untimely death, I was in the Infectious Diseases Unit of South Middlesex Hospital, locally known as Mogden Lane Isolation Hospital. The admission date was 14/02/1966 and the discharge date was 23/02/1966. "Diagnosis: Lobar pneumonia, bilateral otitis media." Lobar pneumonia, which affects a large section of the lung, results from infection by the pathogenic bacterium *Streptococcus pneumoniae* and can be caused by *Mycobacterium tuberculosis*. I lied a lot when I was a child, I made up stories, which I told at length to whomever would listen, mostly my maternal grandmother. One of the lies I told her when I was about six years old was that I had TB, or TV as I called it before she corrected me. Until now, I wondered why I had told her that but, on reading my medical records, it could be that I overheard the doctors discussing my pneumonia and explaining to my parents that the tubercle bacillus was not the cause.

"Examination: T103. Obviously ill. Throat: Congested. Ears: Bilateral purulent discharge." Excuse me if you are eating your dinner while reading this. "RS: Evidence of consolidation left lower lobe. Investigations: Chest X-ray — consolidation left lower lobe. Throat culture: NAD. Ear culture: No growth. Course: Treated with ampicillin and cloxacillin. Made a good recovery. Chest film prior to discharge was reported clear. Discharged home." What were the signs and what were the symptoms of this disease? Fever and coughing, shortness of breath, but what distinguished those from my other maladies? How did my parents read my pneumonia as being distinct from my asthma or bronchitis? Maybe it was the "bilateral otitis media," an inflammatory infection of the middle-ear caused by bacteria or viruses travelling from the nasopharynx along the Eustachian tube, which, if you are wondering, is named after Bartolomeo Eustachi, the sixteenth-century scientist and author of *Anatomical Engravings*, one of the first books on human anatomy.

In *The Birth of the Clinic*, Michel Foucault writes: "In the medical tradition of the eighteenth century, the disease was observed in terms of symptoms and signs. These were distinguished from one another as much by their semantic value as by their morphology. The symptom — hence its uniquely privileged position — is the form in which the disease is presented: of all that is visible, it is closest to the essential; it is the first transcription of the inaccessible nature of the disease. Cough, fever, pain in the side, and difficulty in breathing are not pleurisy itself — the disease itself is never exposed to the senses, but 'reveals itself only to reasoning' — but they form its 'essential symptom', since they make it possible to designate a pathological state (in contradistinction to health), a morbid essence (different, for example, from pneumonia), and an immediate cause (a discharge of serosity). The symptoms allow the invariable form of the disease — set back somewhat, visible and invisible — to show through. The sign announces: the prognostic sign, what will happen; the anamnestic sign, what has happened; the diagnostic sign, what is now taking place." So the signs I presented to my parents became symptoms once I had reached the hospital, once I had entered the separate semantic order of doctors and their privileged position as healers and sages, the hidden processes of the disease available to them through technology. My hidden language, my lack of breath, my coughing, my fever translated into "pneumonia" and not "tuberculosis" or "pleurisy" — the killer of William Wordsworth, Erik Satie, Thomas Hardy and Edmund Husserl.

Gilles Deleuze (tuberculosis, thoracoplasty, lung cancer, emphysema) had a problem with doctors and their diagnostic signs, as he told Claire Parnet in the "Maladie" section of the DVD *Gilles Deleuze from A to Z*: "Personally it's not a matter of individuals because I often come across, like everyone, some very charming doctors, delightful, but it's a kind of power, or a way in which they handle power [...] I find it odious the way doctors manipulate power, and they are odious — as doctors, they are odious. I have a great hatred, not the individual doctors — on the contrary, they can be charming — but I have hatred for medical power and the way doctors use this medical power." My cough, my fever and my shortness of breath were not pneumonia until the doctors (after their tests, the X-rays, the cultures) named it. My parents must have described what had happened, the "anamnestic" sign, only for it to become the "diagnostic sign" in the hidden language of the medical profession and after it being revealed to reasoning by appliance and trials. The prognosis after the fact, "made a good recovery. Chest film prior to discharge was reported clear" is the transparent phenomena of the diagnosis.

The next page of my medical records is as dark as the first, and begins on 19/09/1967 with the words "asthmatic attack" and then what looks like "Pib Plus," a type of asthma inhaler, but to the right of that it has "betnovate," a topical corticosteroid cream that reduces inflammation and irritation caused by eczema or psoriasis. I associate this with my father, not myself. I have small patches of eczema, usually caused by stress. This summons John Updike and Nicholson Baker on the subject. Writing about the disease in his essay "At War with My Skin" (1989), Updike states that "because of my skin, I counted myself out of any of those jobs — salesman, teacher, financier, movie star — that demand being presentable. What did that leave? Becoming a craftsman of some kind, closeted and unseen — perhaps a cartoonist or a writer, a worker in ink who can hide himself and send out a surrogate presence, a signature that multiplies even while it conceals." Psoriasis marked Updike as a writer, informed his prose style and even influenced his literary fans, as Nicholson Baker explains in *U and I* (1991): "I put off the trip to the dermatologist that I knew was imminent, though, because I wanted to see whether my disease had it in itself to be worse, more consuming, than Updike's disease — not only in the structural arthritic symptoms, which I had learned to live with, but right on the surface. Whose prose cells divided more uncontrollably?"

On 24/01/68, two days after my seventh birthday: "Sprain rt ankle" and some frantic scribbling in square brackets. I imagine this is from a football injury, of which more later. The rest of the page is illegible apart from 17/05/68: "Infection…" illegible, followed in the drugs column with the gnomic "DQUK125." "Bronchitis" on 22/01/69, I appeared to have always visited the doctor on or around my birthday. "Influenza vaccine" and "DQUK125" twice. 20/10/69, what looks like "has hot appendix" and "chest still infected, CT," but CT scans were not introduced until the early 1970s, so CT must stand for something else, cardiothoracic surgery maybe?

I have always suffered from asthma, as far back as I can remember, with all its attendant vapour rubs and open windows, the inhalers and the nebulizers. Not, unfortunately, the eighteenth and nineteenth-century treatments using opium, chloroform, ether, ipecacuanha, coffee, belladonna and cannabis. Asthma, the constant and conscious awareness of the act of breathing, turns the body into a machine and the future into a negligible space, it is the first inkling that the body is fragmented, that the lungs and the mouth are separate. Mine was a body straight out of the central casting for Deleuze and Guattari's *Anti-Oedipus* (1972): "It is at work everywhere, functioning smoothly at times, at other times in fits and starts. It breathes, it heats, it eats. It shits and fucks." (Not quite yet.) "For every organ-machine, an energy-machine: all the time, flows and interruptions." Fragmentation, fracturing, flows and interruptions of breath, of linearity, of childhood.

"A black vomiting, a sudden and great flux of pale urine; nervous atrophy; a nervous or spasmodic asthma, a nervous cough; palpitations of the heart, the pulse often varying in quickness, strength and fullness, periodical headaches, giddiness, a dimness of sight, low spirits, melancholy and mania, the incubus or nightmare." No, this not from my doctor's notes from the end of 1969, but from the chapter "Hysteria and Hypochondria" in Michel Foucault's *History of Madness*.

Could any of my childhood psychological stress — I was an anxious young boy, competitive — have been manifested in physical symptoms? Classic Freudian hysteria. Or was I a hypochondriac seeking attention? Again that slippage, that fragmentation, that symptom used as a creative reimagining of the body. Or hypochondria as a storytelling device, an imaging of a crisis, the awakenings of the solipsistic mind or an attempted extension of infancy. "It is anxiety itself that is at issue, and the hypochondriac's fear is fundamentally a mistake, an error in his or her apprehension of the body and its relation to the world," Brian Dillon states in *Tormented Hope* (2009), his book on hypochondria and the arts.

Marcel Proust (1871–1922), hypochondriac and asthma sufferer, wrote in "L'Indifférent": "A child who since birth has breathed without being careful about it is unaware how central to his life is the air which swells his chest so gently that he does not even notice." Proust's first asthma attacked happened when he was nine years old, and he suffered from asthma, hay fever and pulmonary infections throughout his life, some real, some imaginary. He died of pneumonia and a pulmonary abscess so, like many of my illnesses, some of Marcel Proust's must have been real. Dillon on Proust's hypochondria: "Proust lived at a time when asthma and hay fever, the ailments that affect him most severely (and to which his later melodies may be ascribed as secondary or reactive consequences), were among the maladies commonly thought to express the struggle between mind and body, pathology and personality."

My doctor probably thought the same about my asthma and eczema and tonsillitis and bronchitis and sprains and breaks. But my memory doesn't have that Proustian recall, and so this narrator, "despite partial victories, fails in his project; that project was not at all to regain time or to force back memories, but to become master of speeds to the rhythm of his asthma." This mastering of speed to the rhythm of an illness is essential to the fact that people who are ill from an early age and live with their disease are more aware that we all face annihilation. But from that negative experience, there emanated a strength, a different way to look at the world. I was a sick little boy who enjoyed attention when I was ill but not when I felt healthy, then I wanted solitude, to be on my own, to arrange my soldiers into surreal armies, to create weird football leagues, to play football on my own. My most solitary activity was creating scrapbooks, a collection of images and scribbles, some words no doubt copied from an alphabet book. I remember thinking that this is what I wanted to do if I couldn't be a footballer — a selfish number ten, no doubt — I wanted to make books, and this came from the period of intense reading while ill. My mother has since told me that I was twice close to dying and that she and my father were once called in and told that I might not survive the night. This experience, recalled or not, changed my infant view of the world, as it would again thirty-seven years later, on both occasions, as if Marcus Aurelius were internalized in my post-traumatic consciousness, whispering from his meditations: "Remember how long you have been putting this off, how many times you have been given a period of grace by the gods and not used it. It is high time now for you to understand the universe of which you are a part, and the governor of that universe of whom you constitute an emanation: and that there is a limit circumscribed to your time — if you do not use it to clear away your clouds, it will be gone, and you will be gone, and the opportunity will not return."

Albert Camus' quote about football is famous enough to be carried on T-shirts: "Everything I know about morality and the obligations of men, I owe it to football." He actually said: "After many years during which I saw many things, what I know most surely about morality and the duty of man I owe to sport and learned it in the RUA." The RUA was the Racing Universitaire Algerios (RUA) junior team for whom Camus played in goal. At the age of eighteen, he was diagnosed with TB and remained bed-bound for months, and his lungs became so damaged he had to give up playing. Towards the end of *The Plague*, he wrote, "The plague had ended with the terror, and those passionately straining arms told what it had meant: exile and deprivation in the profoundest meaning of the words." On 7 December, 1971, I was back at the doctor's surgery with an injury to my knee. I had been playing football, alone or with other people, I cannot remember. Since, then I have had problems with my knees, plural.

For the rest of my time at junior school, until August of 1972, I visited the doctor — Dr Griffin, I can now see from the notes of that period — mostly because of chest problems, asthma, bronchitis, which were treated with generic drugs. It was also at this age that I started to write short stories and poems. The majority of the time, I came top of my class in "composition" and had received three gold stars for my non-fiction story "Bert Trubshaw — the man who drove [sic] Concorde," a no-doubt plagiarized account from journalists' reports in the newspapers. We lived only a few miles from Heathrow Airport and I would have seen the plane's first visit to Heathrow on 1 July, 1972. I'm surprised there's no date with the doctor on this day but it was a Saturday and so I'm sure I was as healthy as Bert Trubshaw.

That September, I started at the local comprehensive school, looking forward to the English classes and being in the football team. I had become a fan of Sven Hassel's brutal World War II novels about a group of maverick German soldiers. I loved

the covers with their double-sig rune lightning bolt in Sven
Hassel's surname. Until the age of eleven, I had only been on
holiday to the south coast and north-east coast of England
and had spent one-week in the Channel Islands where I had
become fascinated with the German fortifications and, in
particular, the German Underground Hospital on Guernsey,
which I wrote pages and pages of stories about, twisting
the facts so that they fitted in with my personal mythology
of the war. The Hassel novels took me all over Europe and
expanded my knowledge of France, Spain, Italy, Greece, the
Balkans, Germany, Finland and Russia. As Thomas Bernhard
noted in *Concrete* (1982) about the problems of travelling
while suffering from tuberculosis: "Not long ago I had asked
the specialist if I could contemplate travelling. Naturally,
anytime, he had said, but the way he said naturally struck me
as sinister. On the other hand, whatever condition we are in,
we must always do what we want to do, and if we want to go
on a journey, then we must do so and not worry about our
condition, even if it's the worst possible condition, because, if
it is, we're finished anyway, whether we go on the journey or
not, and it's better to die having made the journey we've been
longing for than to be stifled by our longing."

The Hassel books prompted my interest in history in general,
and in European geography. Before I started what we called
"senior" school, my parents bought me *The World of History*
and *The World of Science*; they were large and red and illus-
trated with colour drawings of historical and scientific events
and people. I spent most of that summer, when not playing
football, lying on my bed poring over these books, memorizing
the narratives by copying them out in a notebook. I even
copied some of the illustrations, a memorable one was an oil
painting I did of Hengest and Horsa striding through long
reeds somewhere near Ebbsfleet. At university, I discovered

that there is a Hengist in *Beowulf*, "yet Hengest / the death-stained winter / spent with Finn, / in a place with no fellowship at all," and Hengest also appears in another Old English epic poem, *Finnesburg Fragment*, recounting events of the Battle of Finnsburg when the Jutes, Frisians, Angles and Saxons settled in East Anglia. My surname derives from Finborough, and deep in the heart of Anglo-Saxon Suffolk are two villages, Little and Greater Finborough, with many a Finbow gravestone.

These synchronicities, obviously, only became apparent later in life, but what I read and studied that summer has stayed with me. Maybe because I was, for once, feeling healthy, and this was something a Dr P.E. Baldry MB, FRCP, Consultant Physician at Ashford Hospital had written to Dr Griffin on 8 August, 1972, "I am delighted to find that this lad who was almost a respiratory cripple from asthma is now symptom-free since going on to Intal Co. I suggest that he continues with this on a long-term basis using three capsules per day." Respiratory cripple? I suppose I was. Sickness had given me the time to read and study, to be selfish and disciplined, to create worlds. In *Correction* (1975), Thomas Bernhard states, "Time was no problem. This must be done systematically and most resolutely, yet solely, too, I thought, standing near the door, nothing, absolutely nothing, must be done in haste, I had plenty of time, because I was not quite over my illness, it was still manifest in every breath I took." My newfound health was thanks to the Intal Spinhaler. This contraption pierced a capsule of disodium cromoglycate, which decreased inflammation in the lungs and improved their function. Again, aware of the workings of your breath, you exhaled as much air as possible, put your lips around the plastic mouthpiece and breathed in, the rather bitter powder shot straight to your lungs. And it worked.

So midway through that summer between junior and senior school, I could breathe for the first time without thinking about breathing, and this allowed me to think about other things and, although I enjoyed playing football with other people and had started to have girlfriends, I would still rather spend time on my own, reading, writing, constructing my scrapbooks and looking through my father's art books. As Bernhard explains, this time in *Concrete*, "Sometimes we need someone, sometimes no one, and sometimes we need someone and no one. In the last few days I have once more become aware of this totally absurd fact: we never know at any time whether we need someone or no one, or whether we need someone and at the same time no one, and because we never ever know what we really need we are unhappy, and hence unable to start on our intellectual work when we wish and when it seems right."

Throughout that summer, I was torn between playing football (if I didn't get into the senior school's team my dream of playing for Brentford — another Griffin — would be over and I would be forced to become an artist — my second option), going for walks along the river with Karen Higginbotham (another K), or studying the paintings of Fra Angelico, Filippo Lippi, Piero della Francesca, Albrecht Dürer, Lucas Cranach the Elder and Matthias Grünewald. My second-favourite painting was Paolo Uccello's *Niccolò Mauruzi da Tolentino at the Battle of San Romano* (c.1438—1440), with its dead bodies and shattered lances, its white and pale horses, its grey armour, the crimson and gold flamboyant hat worn by the titular leader of the Florentine army. But my favourite painting, the one I studied closely for hours, was Albrecht Altdorfer's *The Battle of Alexander at Issus* (1529). I would use a magnifying glass to look at the colour plate, try to count the soldiers, analyze the clouds, look in my atlas to get the exact geographical location (on the Mediterranean coastal border of Turkey and Syria). Altdorfer was one of the pioneers of purely landscape painting but the work also has resonances from the earliest Renaissance paintings, through Bosch and the Danube School, and would inform my later interests in art, from the Surrealists (look at Max Ernst's *Europe After the Rain*) and contemporary artists such as the Chapman Brothers, their *Hell* and *Fucking Hell* could be a twenty-first century revisit to *Issus*.

I wouldn't have said I was a loner, I had girlfriends and friends, I was in a Sunday morning football team, I was looking forward to going to senior school and studying but preferred to do all the other things, the reading, writing, scrapbooking, drawing, analyzing paintings. But, mostly, I did not share with other people that I did all these things, I did them locked in my room or hidden somewhere over the expanse of land behind the block of flats we lived in, a bombed wasteland which still had the derelict remains of WWII pillboxes scattered throughout. These solitary acts occurred at around the same time as I had discovered another solitary act — masturbation. Staring at paintings is what Nancy calls, "the masturbation of the eye," and I transplanted that into a voyeuristic onanism, spying on women and girls from our third-floor flat. I would invent stories of saviour and seduction, seducing the girls, being seduced by the women, and I wrote stories about it and — as a football fan and fantasist — built a league table and kept count of how many times I masturbated about certain females. I made up a running commentary on my thoughts about the winners and losers at the end of that season, my girlfriend being perpetually in mid-table. In *The Temptation to Exist*, published in English for the first time in 1968, Cioran wrote of a poet, "tuberculosis and masturbation, that is his fate." Maybe asthma and masturbation was mine.

For now, with the Intal spinning its drugs deep into my lungs, I was healthy and, although I visited Dr Griffin on a few occasions between 1972 and the summer of 1976, my chest problems were diminishing; a few colds, nothing asthma-related. However, on 26 October, 1974, a new illness occurred in the records for the first time — "headache."

Jean des Esseintes, the anti-hero of Joris-Karl Huysman's *A Rebours* (1884), propounds a theory on the restorative and soothing aspects of smell, that our olfactory senses, if stimulated in the correct manner with a mixture of odours, a concoction of aromatics, may be put together in such a way as to trick us to believe we are at home rather than in some noisome hospital or sanatorium. A symphony of smells to replicate the atmosphere of our hometowns — the diesel fumes of buses, the meat-fat splash of doner kebabs, the ozone whiff of a million mobile phones; this would be a form of medical treatment, and des Esseintes argues that sufferers from tuberculosis would be beneficiaries of this pseudo-fragrance as they waited in the south of the country for death to consume them. They do not need the lavender and lemon infused fresh air of Provence or the Beaufort cheese and honey pungency of the French Alps because, as des Esseintes believes, "here, in an artificial climate maintained by open stoves, their lecherous memories would come back to them in a mild and harmless form, as they breathed in the languid feminine emanations given off by the scent factories. By means of this innocent deception, the physician could supply his patient platonically with the atmospheres of the boudoirs and brothels of Paris, in place of the deadly boredom of provincial life. More often than not, all that would be needed to complete the cure would be for the sick man to show a little imagination."

We all know the smell of a hospital. As des Esseintes creates unique perfumes from his array of orange-blossom, tuberose, vanilla, cassia, iris and new-mown hay, so most of us are able to recreate that peculiar and particular hospital effluvium. As

Mark, one of Denton Welch's visitors in *A Voice Through a Cloud* (1950), complains, "'Hospitals always fill me with horror. I can't bear the special smell they have. It isn't disinfectant; everybody makes that mistake. I think it's just plain floor polish made horrible by association.'" But it's more than that, it is the sterile smell of disinfectant mixed with the metallic reek of blood, the sewage stink of gastrointestinal discharges and diseased bowel movements, the putrescence of gangrene and abscesses, the noxiousness of singed hair mixed with the tang of tea and coffee, mass-produced meals, tomato soup and mashed potato, glucose, salts, amino acids, the sour breath, the eructations and flatulence of patients, doctors, nurses and visitors, yeasts and bacteria, necrotic flesh and vernix-covered new-born babies, colostomy and garbage bags, bromodosis and halitosis and talcum-powdered latex gloves.

It is the smells of our lives, from our birth until our death, hanging in the air, confined within the hospital walls, a miasma of memory and projection, a scent of our own temporality and temporarity, of our bodily fluids and their corruption, or as Thomas Mann has it in *The Magic Mountain*:

> "Dissolution, putrefaction," said Hans Castorp. "They are the same thing as combustion: combination with oxygen — am I right?"
> "To a T. Oxidization."
> "And life?"
> "Oxidization too. The same. Yes, young man, life too is principally oxidization of the cellular albumen, which gives us that beautiful animal warmth, of which we sometimes have more than we need. Tut, living consists in dying, no use mincing the matter — *une destruction organique*, as some Frenchman with his native levity has called it. It smells like that, too. If we don't think so, our judgment is corrupted."

"And if one is interested in life, one must be particularly interested in death, mustn't one?"

If one is interested in life, one must be fascinated with cancer in all its forms. The big C, once stigmatized and now fought on a military footing. There is a war against cancer, people battle cancer, there are campaigns to combat cancer, tumours are targeted, sufferers (such as the actor Angelina Jolie) take pre-emptive strikes (double mastectomy) against the risk of breast cancer. Cancer is the enemy within and people cope or do not cope with its onset in as many ways as there are cancers. But this is a smokescreen, a means of coping, of denying the corruption of the body. As one of the first patients we will meet, Hitchens, explains in *Mortality* (2012): "Unfortunately, it also involves confronting one of the most appealing clichés in our language. You've heard it all right. People don't have cancer: they are reported to be battling cancer. No well-wisher omits the combative image: You can beat this. It's even in obituaries for cancer losers, as if one might reasonably say of someone that they died after a long and brave struggle with mortality. You don't hear it about long-term sufferers from heart disease or kidney failure." Some doctors and scientists disagree and see the "fight" metaphor as crucial to a patient's chances of survival and that the "battle" commences when the "mammalian" core self or being — pre-linguistic, hardwired — moves into survival mode. Hitchens continues: "Myself, I love the imagery of struggle. I sometimes wish I were suffering in a good cause, or risking my life for the good of others, instead of just being a gravely endangered patient. Allow me to inform you, though, that when you sit in a room with a set of other finalists, and kindly people bring a huge transparent bag of poison and plug it into your arm, and you either read or don't read a book while the venom sack gradually empties itself into your system, the image of the ardent soldier or revolutionary is the very last one that will occur to you. You feel swamped with passivity and impotence: dissolving in powerlessness like a sugar lump in water." Deleuze and Hitchens agree.

Imagine that in the past five years, a catastrophic disease had wiped out some of our major cities. In 2010, there are no people to respond to the muezzin's call to prayer in Karachi, the loudspeakers in the mosque crackle and hum. In 2011, the giant pandas at Chongqing Zoo die of starvation, as do the Asian tigers, no keepers remain alive, the once-bustling streets are deserted. In 2012, Bangkok, its temples and canals, its red-light districts and shopping malls left empty of people, blind baby elephants roaming the forsaken streets, scrofulous macaques swinging below the Skytrain tracks. In 2013, London falls, the statue of Sir John Betjeman in St Pancras Station hails an empty hall and the Thames carries only driftwood and rubbish towards its deserted estuary. In 2014, New York City goes silent, there is nobody left to honk car horns, to laugh loudly in noisy bars, to hail taxis from street corners. In 2015, it is the turn of Mexico City, each of its inhabitants drops dead. Each year more than eight million people die of cancer. And each year, cities the size of Hanoi, Hyderabad and Rio de Janeiro would discover that they had contracted cancer. That's fifteen million people per year with the knowledge that they may be dying from the disease — a city larger than Istanbul under siege from fear, attacked by its own body.

There are over two hundred different types of cancer, ranging from curable cancers such as thyroid and melanoma to ones highly resilient to treatment like pancreatic, lung and colon. If discovered early enough, even the deadliest may be treatable, but some — pancreatic and stomach in particular — can be powerful and swift in their development and denouement.

The Latin word "cancer" derives — through the medical-encyclopaedist Galen (25 BC–50 AD) — from the Greek *carcinos* for "crab-like." Hippocrates used the simile to describe the appearance of dissected tumours. Evidence of breast, bone and skin cancer have been found in Egyptian mummies, and the first known written recording of the disease is to be found in the Edwin Smith Papyrus, a surgical text on battle trauma in Ancient Egypt c.1600 BC. The papyrus may be a copy of an even earlier text (2650–2600 BC) detailing the medical theories of Imhotep, one of the ur-doctor-divinities along with Asclepius and Hermes Trismegistus. If so, Imhotep understood the mortal seriousness of the disease, noting that he believed cancer to be incurable.

Diagnosed with prostate cancer in June 2006 and dying in April 2009 after the disease metastasized to his ribs and spine, in a *Penthouse* interview in 1970, J.G. Ballard could be describing the mechanics of his disease, "Well, the facts of time and space are a tremendous catastrophe, aren't they? Each day millions of cells die in our bodies, others are born. Every time we open a door, every time we look out across a landscape — I'm deliberately trying to exaggerate this — millions of minute displacements of time and space are occurring. One's living in a continuous cataclysm anyway — our whole existence takes place in the eye of a hurricane."

This is how cancer works, but instead of time and space it is our cells that are displaced, become abnormal and multiply uncontrollably. Just one of our one-hundred-million-million cells has the potential to become a cancer cell and start its revolution against the body, its own terminal journey. They are transponders, omitting different signals to the body's natural array. They are usually formed when a mutation occurs as the cells split; the genetic information becomes scrambled and forms rogue cells that then multiply exponentially to form tumours in organs and bones or liquid masses in blood and marrow. This process — I am sure you would like to discover — can be a matter of chance, or it may be an outside factor (the sun, cigarettes, etc.) or inheritance. As William Burroughs puts it, "This film is about cancer and that's a powerful subject."

Returning to Ballard's science fiction analogy of the body and its cancerous potential; with the universe in cataclysm, the landscape of cancer is one of mutant proliferation, a minute cell within us with the potential of corporeal apocalypse, a thing within us that is a billion copies of the original mutant. Our cells are differentiated, they auto-repair and then they die in order not to become cancerous, they self-suicide so as not to kill the body (*apoptosis*). Cancer cells do none of these things, they override these signals, deny them access, they know nothing but to replicate and spread. The bloodstream and lymphatic system can act as rivers for these crab-like mutants with their abnormal nuclei, the cells coursing through the body into their auto-created heart of darkness. "Hurry, hurry, don't be late for your death. Sickness, the poverty that disperses your hours and years, the insomnia that paints whole days and weeks gray, the cancer that may even now, meticulous and bloodspotted, be climbing up from your rectum," as our good doctor would describe it in *Journey to the End of Night*.

Cancer cells may remain static and small within the organ, tissue or bone where they first mutated — the primary tumour. They may have grown in size at the site but not yet spread. They may have moved into lymph nodes close to the primary tumour. Or they may have metastasized through the body into other organs and tissue. Best-case scenario, they are abnormal but are not yet replicating; in medical terms, they are called carcinoma in situ or in situ neoplasm (tumour) caused by dysplasia (bad formation) but are not, as yet, and may never be, cancerous.

Iain Banks, diagnosed with gallbladder cancer in 2013, describes the cancer process in his novel *The Quarry* (2013): "Cancer makes bits of you grow that are supposed to have stopped growing after a certain point, crowding out the bits you need to keep on living, if you're unlucky, if the treatments don't work." A few pages earlier in the novel, he details the onset of environmental cancer caused by smoking: "'Oh, give it here,' Hol says, taking both from him. She sticks the cigarette in her mouth, cups her hand and lights the rally, handing it back as she exhales. The cloud of smoke is shredded and dissipated by the gusting wind. I don't think she inhaled properly. I have a swooning moment, thinking of the smoke leaking into her lungs and a single molecule of carcinogenic compound settling in an alveolus and triggering cancer in one of her cells, starting a primary tumour that metastasizes throughout her body, killing her, taking her away as well."

Throughout the novel, Guy, suffering from lung cancer, rages at the disease, the embarrassment of illness, the indignity of dying, full of anger at what his body has done to him. He even names his killer — he calls it Rupert — but he mostly calls it "fucking cancer," and he raves, "'You might as well walk into a burning building and try to put out the fire through the medium of dance. But it means when you do lose your brave fucking battle — because it always has to be a brave fucking battle, doesn't it? You're never allowed to have a cowardly battle or just a resigned one; that'd be letting the fucking side down, that would… Anyway, they can secretly think, Well, fucker didn't think positively enough, obviously. If that had been me, *I'd* have thought so positively I'd have been fine; I'd be fit as a fucking fiddle by now and out publicizing my number one best-seller *How I Beat the Big C* and appearing on chat shows and talking with Spielberg's people about the fucking film version.' Guy coughs again. 'So you don't even get to die in peace; you don't even get to die without the implication that it's somehow your own fucking fault because you weren't fucking *positive* enough.'"

This was Banks' final novel, published late June 2013, just weeks after he died. Hitchens, who succumbed eighteen months earlier to oesophageal cancer, although agreeing with Banks on the fatuous romantic "battle" terminology surrounding the disease, nevertheless had a more restrained attitude to its effects and consequences.

When Hitchens discovered that he had oesophageal cancer he wanted to speak of it and speak of the fact that one of the things the cancer would affect was his ability to speak. Hitchens saw the humour in this, realized that his enemies and detractors would see this as retribution for his atheism and his attacks on totemic personalities such as Mother Teresa, Henry Kissinger and Bill Clinton. Cancer had played its own version of musical chairs with Hitchens and given him a form of the disease that seemed to mock his oratorical brilliance. Yes, the sunbather may develop melanoma, the smoker pulmonary carcinoma, and cancers do develop through environmental and occupational situations, but it appears as though Hitchens' specific cancer had targeted him and that speaking in public had caused the illness, as if Plato had been struck down with a malignant brain tumour or Billie Holliday silenced by laryngeal cancer. "The word 'metastasized' was the one in the report that first caught my eye, and ear. The alien had colonized a bit of my lung as well as quite a bit of my lymph node. And its original base of operations was located — had been located for quite some time — in my esophagus. My father had died, and very swiftly, too, of cancer of the esophagus. He was seventy-nine. I am sixty-one. In whatever kind of a 'race' life may be, I have very abruptly become a finalist."

However healthy we are, or think we are, we must have all imagined that moment. The blood in the stool that leads to a trip to the doctor's surgery, the referral to a specialist, the tests, the wait, the results. We have all already projected our cancer into our futures, have chosen our specific disease as if it were a pair of shoes that, although a tad flamboyant, fit us perfectly. The very fear of cancer causes hypochondria.

A pseudonymous friend of mine — let's call him John Player — smoked between forty and fifty cigarettes per day from the age of sixteen, through university, into work, until his late forties. John Player smoked a lot. He also, occasionally, smoked marijuana when he wasn't smoking normal cigarettes. His girlfriends smoked, his friends smoked, his colleagues at work smoked. He took so many cigarette breaks that the boss of the media company for whom he worked considered not allowing him to have a lunch break. He didn't want to stop smoking, he enjoyed smoking. He would smoke when he woke up, all through the day, and he would have a last one outside — weather permitting — on the terrace before he went to bed. In his dreams, he smoked. His life was an embodiment of the line from *Money* (1984) by Hitchens' friend Martin Amis, "'Yeah,' I said and started smoking another cigarette. Unless I inform you otherwise, I'm always smoking another cigarette" and from Amis' *The Information* (1995), "It was more that he felt the desire to smoke a cigarette even when he was smoking a cigarette. The need was and wasn't being met."

Yet John Player was healthy, he played football, ran, rode a bicycle, sang in a band. Then one night over a few beers, he told me about his Saturday night, how he and his wife had gone out with friends, he had smoked more than usual, which was quite a feat, and drank more than usual, and when the night was finished and they were at home, they smoked some weed and drank some rum. And John Player had explained how they had both ended up at the accident and emergency department of their local hospital suffering from what I would say was paranoid hypochondria but John Player had been sure was the onset of terminal lung cancer — he had found it difficult to breathe — while his wife was sure she had a brain tumour (the symptoms were dizziness, dropping things and not being able to walk properly). In their tobacco haze, their marijuana miasma, their alcoholic inebriation, they had summoned their greatest fear — cancer, and cancer meant not being able to smoke cigarettes or weed or drink alcohol. I am pleased to say that John Player hasn't smoked for five years (he's now a non-player), but this is only because he was diagnosed (after two years of cancer fears) with myalgic encephalomyelitis and the doctors warned him that he had to give up smoking. Again, Burroughs with his usual deadpan humour, "The doctor sniffs. He shakes his head with a terrible smile. 'I am referring your case to the coroner.'"

We could all be going about our daily business with cancer cells busily proliferating through our blood and lymph systems. We could all be in denial of this event. Or we could be living in fear of it, imagining the spread of the disease, fearing the horror that lurks within. Like John Self in Martin Amis' *Money*, our body is an unreliable narrator, it tricks us into thinking all is well, or awakens us to a pain that could be serious or fleeting. This duplicitousness — John Self is sure that he has a double who is trying to kill him — can either makes us hypersensitive to the body's signs, or shrug them off as unimportant, however often they occur and however painful these events are. It is the scale of our morbid imagination that makes us prone to hypochondria or denial, neither of which are any help when diagnosed with cancer.

Cancer becomes the omniscient narrator, the body is "it," the patient "he" and "she," there are twists and turns in the plot, hints of denouement, the patient always in danger of becoming a secondary character amidst the doctors and specialists, family and friends. Hitchens explains how this shift in the plot affected the journalist John Diamond, who wrote a weekly column for *The Times* chronicling the stages of his disease (throat cancer) and his attendant emotions and thoughts, "But after a year and more... well, a certain narrative expectation inevitably built up. Hey, miracle cure! Hey, I was just having you on! No, neither of those could work as endings. Diamond had to die; and he duly, correctly (in narrative terms) did. Though — how can I put this? — a stern literary critic might complain that his story lacked compactness toward the end..."

Like Hitchens, Diamond despised the warlike metaphors surrounding cancer; the title of his book on the subject *C: Because Cowards Get Cancer Too* (1998), reflects the mostly arbitrary nature of the disease. Hitchens also wrote about how the body "turns from reliable friend to more neutral to treacherous foe." In Diamond's case, his body became the ultimate unreliable narrator. Initially tests showed that the tumour in his neck was non-malignant, but Diamond discovered in a telephone call a few days later that it had become cancerous. The plot twisted further when, two months later, a secondary cancer developed in his tongue. If Hitchens was able to see the irony in his oesophagal cancer, John Diamond raged against his throat and tongue cancer, it stripped him of his power of speech, the tools of his profession, it made him sound, he said in a BBC interview, like "Charles Laughton in an underwater version of *The Hunchback of Notre Dame*." There was not only a double irony in the locations of Diamond's carinomas — his throat and tongue — he was married to the celebrity chef Nigella Lawson and became unable to speak and eat. He realized that the shift in narrator and the twist and truncation of his own story meant that "he thought of his two children. 'Fancy not seeing how that plot turns out,' he said."

In *But Beautiful* (1991), his book on jazz, Geoff Dyer reiterates John Berger, who wrote in "The Moment of Cubism" that, "the moment at which a piece of music begins provides a clue to the nature of all art." Dyer goes on to liken "the suggestive force of Berger's formulation, 'the incongruity of that moment, compared to the uncounted, unperceived silence which preceded it'" to the moment when jazz musician Keith Jarrett first touches the piano keys. But it is no great stretch of the imagination or the metaphor to link these quotes to the body's silence before the diagnosis of cancer. It is the moment when, rather than art beginning, death becomes more apparent, more present, in the corporeal and temporal meanings of that slippery word. And "the moment at which" a diagnosis is made provides a clue to the nature of all life and, in time, death.

The opening notes to Jarrett's "The Cure," the first brushstrokes of Edvard Munch's *Death in the Sickroom* or the first sentences of Fritz Zorn's *Mars* (1976) — "I'm young and rich and educated, and I'm unhappy, neurotic, and alone. I come from one of the very best families on the east shore of Lake Zurich, the shore that people call the Goldcoast. My upbringing has been middle-class, and I have been a model of good behaviour all my life. My family is somewhat degenerate, and I assume that I am suffering not only from the influences of my environment but also from some genetic damage. And of course I have cancer" — that moment when a note becomes a song, a sketch develops into a painting, a few words become a novel, is mirrored at the moment a single cell begins its uncontrollable growth until death, as the cell mutates and multiplies, so the artist's imagination transmutes and transmits.

This is about information, the body's signals. This is about narrative, the day-by-day increasing chance that life will end. This is about how as people and as artists we handle the information that may or may not transform that narrative.

Some patients, those in denial, those who discover that their cancer is terminal and only have a short period to live, are forced to use, in different ways, a form of negative capability in which they know they are dying and can either reject that notion or embrace it — or both — because the fact of death is unknowable. For these, the denialists and the short-term terminals, cancer remains a mystery without what Keats calls in a letter to his brothers Tom and George on 22 December, 1818 "any irritable reaching after fact and reason." In a sense, cancer brings to these patients instant old age; the body is beaten by itself, the bodies of these patients undergo what we all will and do go through but in fast-forward.

In the prologue to *The Emperor of Maladies: A Biography of Cancer* (2010), Siddhartha Mukherjee writes, "And cancer is imprinted in our society: as we extend our life span as a species, we inevitably unleash malignant growth (mutations in cancer genes accumulate with aging; cancer is thus intrinsically related to age). If we seek immortality, then so, too, in a rather perverse sense, does the cancer cell." The patient who denies the carcinomic mutation their body has undergone courts immortality. The short-term terminal patients live their final days, uncertain about their past while living with the mystery of how their body had not divulged the signs of its forthcoming termination any earlier.

Whereas Fritz Zorn and Iain Banks have their carcinomic characters raging against the disease, others, like Hitchens, employ what Keats would argue was a more Coleridge-like approach. Coleridge, Keats argued, "would let go by a fine isolated verisimilitude caught from the Penetralium of mystery, from being incapable of remaining content with half-knowledge." Hitchens, like Coleridge, sought fact and reason, he wanted answers; as a journalist, he wanted to investigate the disease, not experience it as an existential mystery. An epistemology of epidemiology.

Hitchens perceives cancer as banal, yet he understands the thoughts of the deniers and the short-term terminals because he experienced that "vertiginous feeling of being kicked forward in time: catapulted toward the finish line. Trying not to think with my tumour, which would not be thinking at all. People try to make it sound as if it were an EPISODE in one's life. ONCOLOGY/ONTOLOGY: Under the old religious dispensation, heaven would simply sentence you to be lavishly tortured and then executed. Montaigne: 'Religion's surest foundation is the contempt for life.'"

There is no Romantic awe at the sublimity of cancer, there is no moment when the disease transforms the patient into a Caspar David Friedrich character standing on a precipice staring out at the sea of fog which is/was his life. For Hitchens, cancer was corporeal not crepuscular, it was about cells and organs riddled with cancer cells, after all, as he wrote, "it's no fun to appreciate to the full truth of the materialist proposition that I don't *have* a body, I *am* a body."

For Hitchens, cancer was not a metaphor, it was life and death. In his reckoning, there was no allegorical reading, no satire on the institutions of control and power. Mukherjee explains cancer's pervasiveness and invasiveness not only in the lives of patients and their families and friends but also in the attempts to use it in artistic formats: "In Aleksandr Solzhenitsyn's novel *Cancer Ward*, Pavel Nikolayevich Rusanov, a Russian in his mid-forties, discovers that he has a tumour in his neck and is immediately whisked away into a cancer ward in some nameless hospital in the frigid north. The diagnosis of cancer — not the disease, but the mere stigma of its presence — becomes a death sentence for Rusanov. The illness strips him of his identity. It dresses him in a patient's smock (a tragicomically cruel costume, no less blighting than a prisoner's jumpsuit) and assumes absolute control of his actions. To be diagnosed with cancer, Rusanov discovers, is to enter a borderless medical gulag, a state even more invasive and paralyzing than the one that he has left behind."

Diagnosed with terminal prostate cancer in January 1995, the American psychologist and psychedelic-drug guru Timothy Leary died on 31 May, 1996. Kathy Acker (who we shall visit soon and who died of breast cancer the next year on 30 November, 1997) wrote to the critic McKenzie Wark, "Leary, as natural, is proclaiming colon cancer 'the new thing to explore.'" His about-to-happen death had been mediatized; there were newspaper articles, Leary's followers ran a website with updates on Leary's condition, the drugs he was taking — pharmaceutical and recreational. Television stations interviewed Leary, who expounded his new theories on cancer, dying and death. Leary had once been an exponent of life-extension science, a theoretical and medical means of prolonging human existence and retarding or reversing the ageing process, but the knowledge of his imminent death and cancer's ineluctable defeat of his theoretical eternal life focused Leary's mind on dying and the ethics and aesthetics of death. Whereas Banks, Hitchens and Diamond (in their own way) railed against the indignity of the disease and the aftereffects of radiotherapy and chemotherapy, Leary's narcissism denied the ravages of his cancer. In his biography of Leary, John Higgs quotes him as saying, "Dying is the most fascinating experience in life. You've got to approach dying the way you live your life — with curiosity, hope experimentation, and with help of your friends, I have set out to design my own death, or deanimation as I prefer to call it. It's a hip, chic thing to do, it's the most elegant thing you can do. Even if you've lived your life like a complete slob, you can die with terrific style." Where Hitchens saw cancer as a purely materialist form, Leary believed there was a transcendental aspect to the disease, not only was it actually transforming his body but that transformation was spiritual. If he had been a patient in our hospital, he would be handing out route maps to his own prayer room, the offering plate full of LSD microdots, a twelve-foot sculpture of his DNA double helix instead of a crucifix beaming neon from the psychedelic altar.

Leary's design for dying (he wrote a book with that title published posthumously in 1997) included a wish for his head to be cryogenically frozen after he had taken two doses of LSD. There were fears that Leary would commit some kind of peaceful suicide live on the internet, but neither this nor the cryonic suspension took place; instead, his family and followers videotaped his death. Leary's posthuman theorizing questioned the taboo subjects of cancer and dying, he viewed his death in an almost anti-Heideggerian sense, that it was something a human being *could* experience. Leary denied *Being and Time*'s "the possibility of no-longer-being-able-to-be-there," whereas cancer, in its inception, shows us that we "cannot outstrip the possibility of death." Indeed, Leary believed that his cancer was a "Being-towards-the-end," a means of maintaining oneself, hence the internet blog, the videotape, the rounds of interviews and his *Design for Dying*, a kind of postmodern New-New Testament.

In their own ways, Hitchens and Leary (and countless other cancer patients) were confronted prematurely with death, be it corporeally, aesthetically, or spiritually. The original cancer cell became the punctum of their Being-towards-death. I'll let Martin Heidegger, in rare prose clarity, explain our everyday experience of and with death in *Being and Time*: "People who are no acquaintances of ours are 'dying' daily and hourly. 'Death' is encountered as a well-known event occurring within-the-world. As such it remains in the inconspicuousness characteristic of what is encountered in an everyday fashion. The 'they' has already stowed away [*gesichert*] an interpretation for this event. It talks of it in a 'fugitive' manner, either expressly or else in a way which is mostly inhibited, as if to say, 'One of these days one will die too, in the end; but right now it has nothing to do with us.'"

But with cancer, death becomes a unique event encountered daily and hourly and occurring within-the-body. The disease and its treatment are extraordinarily conspicuous, despite Leary's claims for elegance. Hitchens explains in *Mortality* some of the bodily facts of living with and dying from cancer: "Nobody wants to be told about the countless minor horrors and humiliations that become facts of 'life' when your body turns from being a friend to being a foe: the boring switch from chronic constipation to its sudden dramatic opposite; the equally nasty double cross of feeling acute hunger while fearing even the scent of food; the absolute misery of gut-wringing nausea on an utterly empty stomach; or the pathetic discovery that hair loss extends to the disappearance of the follicles in your nostrils, and thus to the childish and irritating phenomenon of a permanently runny nose. Sorry, but you did ask…" This is not an interpretation, this is the ur-text of the body coping with cancer, uninhibited by the bodily signs of decay and deanimation. What Hitchens understands in his candidly titled memoir is that "very soon one will die, it is the end; and right now it has everything to do with me."

Contrary to Heidegger's ambiguousness in talking about death, some of us are aware of it on a daily basis, not only sufferers from cancer, tuberculosis, HIV/AIDS and other life-threatening diseases. Life itself for some writers, especially Cioran in *The Trouble with Being Born* (1973), is a disease: "Suddenly I was cold, so cold that I was sure there was no cure for it. What was happening to me? Yet this was not the first time I had been in the grip of such a sensation. But in the past I had endured it without trying to understand. This time I wanted to know, and now... I abandoned one hypothesis after the next: it could not be sickness; not the shadow of a symptom to cling to. What was I to do? I was baffled, incapable of finding even the trace of an explanation, when an idea occurred to me — and this was a real relief — that what I was feeling was merely a version of the great, final cold — that it was simply death exercising, rehearsing." Cancer is the dress rehearsal, enduring death, something we can no longer deny or believe to be inconspicuous. If we hold up a mirror to our lives, we do not see death staring back. But faced with cancer — to quote Hitchens quoting Saul Bellow — "death is the dark backing that a mirror needs if we are able to see anything." For Leary, knowledge of death is lived in denial, experienced spiritually as some kind of happening trip. For Heidegger, it is an impossible event that cannot be experienced. For Hitchens, it is a means of reflecting on life. For Cioran, it is relief — he died by natural causes at the age of eighty-four.

Back to Heidegger before — like one of Cioran's colds — the obfuscation returns, "The analysis of the phrase 'one dies' reveals unambiguously the kind of Being which belongs to everyday Being-towards-death. In such a way of talking, death is understood as an indefinite something which, above all, must duly arrive from somewhere or other, but which is proximally *not yet present-at-hand* for oneself, and is therefore no threat." Leary wrote that, "personally, I've been looking forward to dying all my life." Cioran experienced the recurring sensation of death's exercise. Death was a definite something that arrived from a definitive place (the body), cancer patients know (however spiritually in Leary's case, or pessimistically in Cioran's theories) that death is intimate rather than proximal and is very *present-at-hand*.

On New Year's Day, 1994, three years before his death from liver cancer, Allen Ginsberg gave a characteristically honest rebuke to any theory of Being-towards-the-end in a take on "Here We Go 'Round the Mulberry Bush," where he writes about shitting his pants when he got old and how lucky he was to be old.

Before his death from liver cancer in 1997, Ginsberg had numerous ailments including hypertension, hyperglycaemia, minor strokes and hepatitis C. Whatever Ginsberg suffered from, he wrote about it; likewise when he discovered that he only had a short time to live. Although Ginsberg's *Collected Poems-1947–1997* (2007) stretches to over 1,000 pages, in his later years, he produced very few poems annually but the knowledge of his imminent demise inspired, (and I will use that word in reference to Ginsberg's work because he theorized about the use of breath and line-length in poetry) yes, "inspired" him to write.

One cliché among the many surrounding the word "cancer" is the response to it in terms of vocabulary. People say, "I have no words" or "I cannot describe how I feel." Martin Amis explains this in *The Information* regarding a parent's response to the murder of a child, "Of the perpetrator or perpetrators the mother or the father of the dead will often say, *I have no words for them. Something like. Words cannot express what I feel for them. Something like, As for those who did this, I have no words for them. Or, There are no words for them.* By which I take them to mean: words are inadequate and also inappropriate. You cannot find the right words — so don't look for them. Don't look." And this is a response to the diagnosis of cancer. The body under physical attack falls silent, even friends and relatives reject the possibility of reassuring verbal language. As we have seen with Ginsberg and Hitchens, writers who discover that they have cancer DO have the words and use them in an attempt to express what they feel about it, but it is always with the knowledge that silence awaits, and the world and the words are embedded in, buried in, present nostalgia.

The next artist we shall visit on our rounds is the American writer Kathy Acker. Her novels, including *Blood and Guts in High School* (1984), *Empire of the Senseless* (1988) and *Great Expectations* (1983), foreground the female body, elide genres and use plagiarism as an integral textual tool. Acker not only experimented with the limits of the fictive form but also with her own body. As other texts were assumed into her narrative, so she covered her skin with tattoos. As elements of BDSM stud her novels, so she pierced her flesh. As she expanded the realm of her prose, so she developed her muscles through bodybuilding.

In her collection of essays *Bodies of Work* (1997), Acker wrote, "Imagine you are in a foreign country. Since you are going to be in this place for some time, you are trying to learn the language. At the point of commencing to learn the new language, just before having started to understand anything, you begin forgetting your own language. Within strangeness, you find yourself without a language." This is similar to how one feels when faced with the word "cancer." Cancer has invaded your body from within, it has made your body into a foreign country, one in which you no longer understand the language, recognize the signs or remember the topography. Your body is forgetting what it once was, now overwhelmed by the mutated cells. You are within the strangeness of the disease without a language to explain it, in Hitchens' case without the organs to explain it: "I lay at the point of death. A congestive heart failure was treated for diagnostic purposes by an angiogram that triggered a stroke. Violent and painful hiccups, uninterrupted for several days and nights, prevented the ingestion of food. My left side and one of my vocal cords became paralyzed. Some form of pleurisy set in, and I felt I was drowning in a sea of slime. In one of my lucid intervals during those days of agony, I asked my physician to discontinue all life-supporting services or show me how to do it."

Acker acknowledges this entry into the realm of strangeness in her essay "The Gift of Disease" (1996). (Whether or not there is irony in her title, Acker's appropriation of works and lines from other texts makes it difficult to tell, and the essay proves problematical in seeing any "positive" gift her cancer bestowed upon her, unless that gift was one of death.) In this essay published in *The Guardian* six months after the breast cancer diagnosis, nine months before she died, she began, "I am going to tell this story as I know it. Even now, it is strange to me. I have no idea why I am telling it. I have never been sentimental. Perhaps just to say that it happened. In April of last year, I was diagnosed of having breast cancer. I had had a history of breast lumps but, until this time, none of them had been malignant. A biopsy revealed that the mass involved was less than five centimetres in diameter." However much Acker lived with the possible realities of cancer — she had previous benign tumours — she experienced the cancer as "strange," but that is exactly what cancer is not. The *Online Etymological Dictionary* explains: "late 13c., 'from elsewhere, foreign, unknown, unfamiliar,' from Old French *estrange* 'foreign, alien, unusual, unfamiliar, curious; distant; inhospitable; estranged, separated' (Modern French *étrange*), from Latin extraneus 'foreign, external, from without.'" Hitchens described the tumour in his oesophagus as a "blind, emotionless alien." However blind and emotionless cancer may be it is not alien; it is local rather than foreign and it is intimately connected to you. Beginning unknown, it makes your body unfamiliar, it is essentially internal rather than external. In *Corpus*, Jean-Luc Nancy sees it as invasive,

"Cancer also arrives: a lymphoma, notice of whose eventuality (certainly not a necessity: few graftees end up with it), though signaled by the cyclosporin's printed advisory, had escaped me. It comes from the lowering of immunity. The cancer is like the ragged, crooked, and devastating figure of the intruder. Strange to myself, with myself estranging me. How can I put this? (But the exogenous or endogenous nature of cancerous phenomena is still being debated.)" It is you and not you. So why did two very dissimilar writers who both discovered they had cancer describe the disease as "strange" and "alien" when, in itself, it is neither?

If we look more closely at Acker's essay and bring into it some aspects of her work as a whole, we might be able to analyse the projection of cancer as other rather than as self. We will have to do this while struggling with something that rejects language and which causes its victims to reject their views of the self. Acker explains this to some extent in an essay she wrote about bodybuilding, "In a gym, verbal language or language whose purpose is meaning occurs, if at all, only at the edge of its becoming lost." In a short while, I might get Lacanian on your ass. But before that, I'd like to digress.

One day, about halfway through writing this book, sitting at my desk researching — I sit on the floor to write — I experienced a sharp pain in my right hip radiating inwards through my buttock, causing spasms in my gluteus maximus — that Roman legionnaire of human muscles. The pain didn't last for very long, maybe about five minutes. I rose from the chair, walked around the kitchen, went up and down stairs, made probably the hundredth cup of tea I had had that day, returned to my chair and carried on with my research into the medical history of Frida Kahlo. All that remained of the pain was a residual burning in the ilium region — "besieged by Saturn's flaming torch" — but the pain had disappeared and

I thought nothing of it, I must have been sitting awkwardly, strained a muscle while walking earlier.

The pain I had experienced was nothing compared to that suffered by Kahlo. In the 1925 bus accident, the injuries she sustained to her pelvis made it impossible for her to carry a foetus to its full term and she subsequently had a number of miscarriages and abortions. In *Henry Ford Hospital* (1932), she depicts herself lying naked on bloodstained sheets in a hospital bed in the aftermath of a miscarriage. From her abdomen float six red umbilical cords and at the end of each is a representation of her miscarriage. Directly beneath the bed is a purple orchid, a gift from her husband, but also signifying female genitalia (see Georgia O'Keeffe's flower paintings from 1925 onward). Kahlo corresponded with O'Keeffe and sent her a letter on 1 March, 1933. Worried about her fellow artist's health, Kahlo wrote, "I felt terrible when Sybil Brown told me that you were sick but I still don't know what is the matter with you. Please Georgia dear if you can't write, ask Stieglitz to do it for you and let me know how are you feeling will you?" and "If you are still in the hospital when I come back I will bring you flowers, but it is so difficult to find the ones I would like for you." Next is an industrial machine, Kahlo's opinion (similar to Deleuze's) of the indifferent cruelty of medical institutions. Above that is an anatomical model of a female torso, again reflecting the dispassionate side of the medical profession and how Kahlo thought she had been treated. To the right of the torso floats Little Diego — the foetus who will never be a boy — named after his father, the perpetually childish Diego Rivera. A snail follows the foetus, a sign of the slow agony of the miscarriage and the slow torture of Frida's body. Finally, beneath that image of inexorable suffering is the cause: the pelvis. If one looks at the detail of the pelvis in the painting, one can see a little notch in the top right of the ilium, and that is exactly where the embers of the burning sensation glowed still. On our rounds, we will visit Frida for a lengthier examination.

A few days later, the pain returned, this time more intensely, as if "fiery darts in flaming vollies flew," and I found it hard to sit, I found it hard to walk, I found it hard to lie down. The pain was sharp and burning simultaneously and it now went from the ilium region of my pelvis, through my gluteus maximus into my groin. When it wasn't painful, it was tingling, when it wasn't tingling, it was numb — or a combination of all three. Well, of course I did what I always did when faced with unknown aches and pains and numbings and tinglings, I ignored it and took some paracetamol and went back to working on this book. It would eventually go away — or so I thought, so I hoped.

For the next week, I would wake up with a pain in my right buttock — the stabbing variety seemed to rule the night. To relieve the pressure, I would turn over and, for a few minutes, that would work, until the weight of the right gluteus maximus — the now rebellious secutor gladiator with sword raised — ignited the flame once again. On my back, the pain became numb and then the tingling started, it was better than the stabbing pain but I can't sleep on my back, so I tossed and turned until the pain forced me to get up. So I had trouble sleeping, I also had trouble sitting and just to make the full set, I had trouble walking.

I phoned my doctor, the receptionist said I could have the next possible appointment — two weeks. I visited the pharmacy and described the symptoms — they prescribed paracetamol to be taken for two weeks, I had already been taking it for two weeks. I asked my friend who teaches Pilates, she suggested exercise. I had exercised. I walk miles every day. But I couldn't walk miles every day to exercise because my pelvis, arse and groin hurt so much that the only exercise I could manage was crawling upstairs on my hands and knees to get into bed in which I slept for a few hours only to get painfully out of bed after not enough sleep to crawl back down the stairs and sit at my desk, trying to research this book while waiting for the sharp and burning pain to return along with the attendant tingling and numbing sensations. There was only one thing left to do, turn to the one source of all medical knowledge — the internet. I would self-diagnose.

Now, I am sure you are asking yourselves, "What does the above have to do with cancer?" Please bear with me and you will discover the relationship. For weeks, I had denied that anything was wrong, it was, well, it was a pain in the arse but nothing serious, despite the fact that I couldn't walk or lie down for any lengthy period of time, which meant I couldn't exercise, which may have been a factor in not being able to sleep for the amount of hours I needed every night, which, in turn, may have contributed to the reason that my research had stalled because I felt too tired and too physically in pain to visit the British Library and Wellcome Library, or sit for any sustained time at the computer. But I did have time to type in the keywords and symptoms — pelvis, buttocks, burning, pain, tingling. There was my anti-hero, the scourge of Ilium, the rectilium gladiator thrusting his trident into my gluteus maximus — Sciatica.

This was real, this was not hypochondria, this was not denial, it was not strange or alien, it was pain caused by my sciatic nerve being compressed and/or irritated, causing me to be depressed and irritated. I had put a name to it. I was halfway to being cured. Finally, I got an appointment with my doctor, she asked me to perform a series of movements — raise my arms and rotate my torso clockwise and then anti-clockwise, move my head up and down, left and right and in a circle and finally touch my toes (well, nearly). She told me to return in a month if the symptoms were the same or had worsened and she would arrange for it to be examined. As I type, the pain has largely disappeared and there is just the occasional tingling sensation, mostly behind my knee and down into my calf muscle. Shame, I was looking forward to that magnetic resonance imaging session.

So I had a name for the pain, I had a consultation with my doctor, I even had a possible medical procedure, so none of this was any longer strange or alien. In *The Shaking Woman or A History of My Nerves* (2010), Siri Hustvedt wrote, "Every sickness has an alien quality, a feeling of invasion and loss of control that is evident in the language we use about it. No one says, 'I am cancer' or even 'I am cancerous,' despite the fact that there is no intruding virus or bacteria; it's the body's own cells that have run amok." This is a denial of the self, a self that has changed and yet remains the same. Pain has manifested within the body and overridden the mind, and the mind has countered with denial as protection. This is called anosognosia — the denial of illness — which can be a matter of indifference to the symptoms or the diagnosis or outright denial that anything has happened. Hustvedt cites a case where a woman had lost her sight after suffering a series of strokes in her occipital lobes and either denied her blindness or stated that she didn't care that she was (or may have been) blind.

As I found some relief in knowing that my pain was caused by a pinched sciatic nerve, so the naming of it altered my comprehension, and I knew it wasn't a cancer or deep-vein thrombosis. Hustvedt's search for the cause of her mysterious shaking was also a search for a name, something familiar or, at least, understandable: "It is human to want to pin things down and give them a name. No one really wants to live like Borges' hero, a person so attentive to the shifting plethora of the phenomenal world that the dog seen at three-fourteen deserves a name different from the one seen at three-fifteen. And yet, the story reminds us that all abstraction comes at a cost. Doctors need diagnoses, names for groups of symptoms, and so do patients. At last, I have a sign to hang on my disparate aches and pains or shakes and wobbles. Or do I?" Hustvedt's magnetic resonance imaging session discovered nothing that they could put a name to — at least she got to have an MRI. Familiarity with a disease makes it more readily integrated into the mind/body, moving it out of the alien other and into the self, or as Hustvedt puts it, "out of the third person and into the first." The disease always begins as other and may create a double of the sufferer, one whom embodies the self with the disease.

Earlier, in a counter argument to Hitchens' disavowal of the "battle" metaphor, I mentioned the mammalian brain's fight response, its move into survival mode. The autonomic nervous system and its branches, the sympathetic nervous system and parasympathetic nervous system, trigger the fight-or-flight response by releasing norepinephrine along with epinephrine (adrenalin), oestrogen and testosterone in order to ready the body for a threat to its survival. I would argue that the "fight" component Hitchens derided is manifested in the "flight" response to cancer, which is denial. And believing your cancer to be alien, to be strange, to be emotionless, is a form of denial.

So cancer is internal, part of the self (whatever that may be) and is formed by our own cells. It is, as Hitchens wrote of cancer patients, "self-centred and even solipsistic," it is fundamentally selfish and this is the clue to a patient's understanding of it. Cancer is essentially "self-ish," it is and isn't you, it is like you, it belongs to you, it has all the characteristics of you, but it is other. In analysing the metaphorical aspects of illness, Hustvedt quotes the psychoanalyst D.W. Winnicott, "Flight to sanity is not health. Health is tolerant of ill health; in fact, health gains much from being in touch with ill health with all its aspects," and explains that what Winnicott means by this is that, as Hitchens would agree, "health can tolerate disintegration. At one time or another all of us go to pieces, and it isn't necessarily a bad thing. The state of disunity may allow a flexible and open creativity that is part of being healthy." The flight into denial inaugurates a split, a double in which the healthy self tolerates its other.

Kathy Acker wrote a lot about doubles, other selves in sadomasochistic relationships, incestuous couplings, even some of her books were copies — *Great Expectations, Don Quixote, Empire of the Senseless* — plagiarism and parasitism, repetition as revolution, pornography as pedagogy; each book contained its double, it was literature as anti-literature, fiction as non-fiction. Kathy was both Kathy and not Kathy, her autobiographical self is not her biological self. In books such as *Childlike Life of the Black Tarantula by the Black Tarantula, I Dreamt I Was a Nymphomaniac: Imagining, Kathy Goes To Haiti, My Death My Life by Pier Paolo Pasolini, In Memoriam to Identity, Hannibal Lecter, My Father,* and *My Mother: Demonology,* it is as though Acker's core identity denies her autobiographical being; like Siri Hustvedt, she is "not the person saying or writing 'I remember.'" In an interview with Sylvere Lotringer, Acker states, "I became very interested in the model of schizophrenia. I wanted to explore the use of the word 'I', that's the only thing I wanted to do. So I placed very direct autobiographical — just diary material, right next to fake diary material. I tried to figure out who I wasn't and I went to texts of murderesses… I was doing experiments about memory." Memory, the narrative of the "I" is doubled, mirrored, even fractured, the body becomes likewise, discontinuous, disconnected. "Not only have I shirked facing my problems. I shall die at sixty before having formed any opinion concerning myself. I made a list of human characteristics: every time I had one characteristic I had its opposite," Acker wrote in *Great Expectations.*

After discovering she had breast cancer, Acker radically estranged her body — she underwent a double mastectomy.

After the surgery, on discovering that the cancer had spread to her lymph nodes, she refused further chemotherapy and, according to Jason McBride in an essay in *Hazlitt*, "The Last Days of Kathy Acker" (2015), "sought alternative treatment, surrounding herself with acupuncturists, herbalists, astrologers, psychics. Diligently, obsessively, she followed their post-op instructions for months: a diet entirely free of alcohol, dairy, and gluten; daily hours of yoga and meditation; regular powdered herbal supplements (which she lugged around, along with vitamins, in a full-sized suitcase). Under the guidance of Georgina Ritchie, a 'certified Louise Hay healer,' she even experimented with past-life channelling." As her narrative sought alternative realities to the "I" / "Me" universe, so Acker, against medical advice, sought alternative therapies as a means of escaping the "solipsistic" cancer-patient viewpoint. Acker's financial situation also played its part in her decisions; she could afford a double mastectomy ($7,000) but not chemotherapy ($20,000), plus she had no health insurance. Her political beliefs also influenced her decisions, "Breast cancer, in the realm of western medicine, is big business. The two largest industries in the US are weapons and medicine — cancer research and care are a mainstay of the latter," she wrote in "The Gift of Disease." She believed that cancer was business. This goes directly against men's reaction to cancer, as Mark Leyner explains through his oncologist David Samadi, "'You know, once they're diagnosed with cancer, they forget about the blueberries and come to me,' referring, I think, to men who, when contemplating cancer in the abstract, are willing to consider all sorts of alternative-treatment modalities, but when actually diagnosed with the actual disease in their actual bodies, want the fucking cavalry called in."

Acker distrusted the medical establishment in the same way she railed against patriarchal authority in her novels. This conversation with her doctor could have come straight from one of her novels:

> Me: Tell me about cancer and lymph nodes. If my cancer's so advanced, how come there wasn't any other cancer in the breast tissue? Aren't the lymph nodes the body's filter? Couldn't it be possible, since I've been on a super-high antioxidant diet ever since the lump was discovered, that the lymph nodes have been doing just what they're supposed to do? Couldn't they be registering cancer because they've been cleaning out the diseased cells?

> My surgeon: Unfortunately, studies — and I've read the best — all indicate that there's no connection between diet and cancer. The same is true with regard to environmental pollution. The truth is that we don't know what causes cancer.

Acker responded to her "alien" cancer by radically altering her body, she viewed chemotherapy and other medical intrusions as forms of torture or experimentation. She feared becoming that trope of the uncanny — a meat puppet. The alien cancer would have won, the microscopic perverted cells of her own body would reduce her to an automaton without purpose, without knowledge of why she existed in the first place, without that memory theatre that is "I". Acker had highlighted her own absence in her texts and the cancer had made her permanent absence a reality.

This classification of cancer as strange and alien can be studied in reference to the theories of the *unheimlich* in the writings of Freud and Lacan, and it is with the knowledge of one's own materiality that an attendant feeling of the uncanny emerges. In a sense, some patients' reaction to this materiality is a leap into the spiritual, the corporeal transformed into the incorporeal; we will see this in Bruce Chatwin's wish to be received into the Greek Orthodox Church before he died or Michel Foucault's near transcendental mysticism after being struck by a car in July 1978.

Acker wrote: "The reduction of all that one is to materiality is a necessary part of the practice of conventional western medicine. Actually, I was this one thought: I knew I wanted to live. To live was to stay alive and to not be reduced to materiality. There was no way I was going to go through chemotherapy. I never got in touch with that doctor again, except to pay his bill. My search for a way to defeat cancer now became a search for life and death that were meaningful. Not for the life presented by conventional medicine, a life in which one's meaning or self was totally dependent upon the words and actions of another person, even of a doctor. I had already learned one thing, though I didn't at the time know it: that I live as I believe, that belief is equal to the body." Where Hitchens and Proust used their illness and impending death as deadlines for their body of work, Acker and Chatwin saw a transcendent aspect to their illnesses, a going beyond the body, a need for belief rather than an acceptance of the body's limitations.

Being ill, whether it is because of a bad cold or that one is dying from breast cancer, places us firmly in the world of the "*unheimlich*" — the "unhomely," the "uncanny." Rather than a world of cleanliness, beauty and health, we are — through accident, cell mutation or viruses — transported to a realm of unpleasantness and repulsion. In Freud's analysis of the uncanny, he states, "the 'uncanny' is that class of the terrifying which leads back to something long known to us, once very familiar." That original feeling of helplessness as a child, the need to feel safe, to feel "at home." In Freud's investigation into the etymology of "*heimlich*," he discovers that as well as meaning homelike, friendly and intimate, it can also mean hidden, secret and concealed. So the word, in its second sense, contains its own opposite, its own double. *Unheimlich* meaning ghostly, eerie, the appearance of something that should have remained hidden, cloaked. So, for our purposes, *unheimlich* is the definition of dis-ease, something that has manifested itself from our body, our intimate physical home. While living in London after fleeing Nazi-controlled Vienna, Freud had thirty-three surgical procedures on the cancer in his mouth and jaw, but they were to no avail, the cancer worsened and became terminal. He requested that his physician assist him in an induced suicide; after three large doses of morphine, he died on 23 September, 1939.

In *The Uncanny* (1919), Freud goes on to quote from Ernst Jentsch's earlier definition of an occurrence of the uncanny: when a person has "doubts whether an apparently animate being is really alive; or conversely, whether a lifeless object might not be in fact animate." Exactly. That is the loci of sickness, the littoral borderline between life and death, animation and stillness, human and not human. Cancer, in all its manifestations, reminds us on a second-to-second basis of our existence in those uncanny margins. For sufferers of illness, the world as we know it, the "being-at-home," has broken down, our physical and symbolic attachment to the real becomes tenuous and our imaginary untrammelled existence becomes circumscribed by the definitions of our disease, our diagnosis and our prognosis. Something other has mutated our ability to categorize our existence, to feel at home in the world.

The *unheimlich* world is inhabited by doubles, doppel-gängers, those beings that are identical to us and our direct other, and Freud states that the themes of uncanny literature "are all concerned with the idea of a 'double' in every shape and degree, with persons, therefore, who are to be considered identical by reason of looking alike." In hospital, in a place that is home but not home, we are ourselves and we are not ourselves. Referencing Otto Rank, Freud states that the "'double' was originally an insurance against destruction of the ego, an 'energetic denial of the power of death,' and that the 'immortal' soul was the first 'double' of the body." The double is a safety mechanism, one that either takes on the pain and suffering of the body and mind or that creates a 'public' persona to deny the suffering and present a version of the self. However, as soon as the double appears, death skulks in its wake; as Mukehrjee writes, "This image — of cancer as our desperate, malevolent, contemporary doppelgänger — is so haunting because it is at least partly true. A cancer cell is an astonishing perversion of the normal cell. Cancer is a phenomenally successful invader and colonizer in part because it exploits the very features that make us successful as a species or as an organism."

Freud continues: "(In) the pathological case of delusions of being watched this mental institution becomes isolated, dissociated from the ego, and discernible to a physician's eye. The fact that a faculty of this kind exists, which is able to treat the rest of the ego like an object — the fact, that is, that man is capable of self-observation — renders it possible to invest the old idea of a 'double' with a new meaning and to ascribe many things to it, above all, those things which seem to the new faculty of self-criticism to belong to the old surmounted narcissism of the earliest period of all." As a hospital patient, one regresses to a primary narcissism, the bed becomes the focus of the institution's cycloptic panopticon; not only are the doctors, nurses and care staff watching, but you are being tested, charted, measured, diagnosed. Not only that, but you are more aware of yourself, your body, how your mind works, how the illness changes your thoughts, your physical capabilities — what Deleuze describes as "tuning into life." You are infantalized and create a double that is at once yourself and not you, that is the old you, supra-you, super-you. The double reveals the possible futures that — threatened by illness and possible death — the ego still desires. "Our knowledge of pathological mental processes enables us to add that nothing in the content arrived at could account for that impulse towards self-protection which has caused the ego to project such a content outward as something foreign to itself." Is the double the illness projected externally in order that it can be recognized, reconciled and even defeated? Whatever it is, illness is ego disturbance, that sense of helplessness Freud theorizes is essential to the feeling of uncanniness.

Specifically with terminal illnesses, there is that dreamlike recurrence of states and situations, that no matter which way we turn we end up back in the same place, the same town, piazza, room that is so familiar and yet not. The relapses, the remissions, the re-remissions are the uncanny representation of the repetitive/compulsive life of a stay in a hospital. Patients become institutionalized and may only see themselves as a double within the hospital, separate from yet bound to their pre-illness self or pre-pathological self.

Where Hitchens embraced medical science's attempts to assist with his strange and alien cancer, Acker sought alternative treatments. Both suffered from primary and secondary effects, both felt other than their own body, yet Acker's experience of cancer had similarities with Freud's inclusion of the "magical" in his examination of the uncanny: "Our analysis of instances of the uncanny has led us back to the old, animistic conception of the universe, which was characterized by the idea that the world was peopled with the spirits of human beings, and by the narcissistic overestimation of subjective mental processes (such as the belief in the omnipotence of thoughts, the magical practices based upon this belief, the carefully proportioned distribution of magical powers or 'mana' among various outside persons and things), as well as by all those other figments of the imagination with which man, in the unrestricted narcissism of that stage of development, strove to withstand the inexorable laws of reality." Acker wrote that she felt forced into the world of "mana" because, "I realized that if I remained in the hands of conventional medicine, I would soon be dead, rather than diseased, meat. For conventional medicine was reducing me, quickly, to a body that was only material, to a body without hope and so, without will, to a puppet who, separated by fear from her imagination and vision, would do whatever she was told." This returns us to the uncanny "wax-work figures, artificial dolls and automatons" as in the doll Olympia in "The Story of the Sand-Man" in *Tales of Hoffman*, the text Freud used as an example of uncanny literature.

As one of Acker's alternative healers, Georgina, explained to her: "The body remembers, especially traumas […] and holds these memories as scars, as wounds. Disease is when the body isn't in harmony, when there are areas of blockage in the body. So in order to lead someone to healing for I work verbally rather than Greg does, I go to the past. When a person goes through regression, childhood or past lives, that person is able to situate the trauma in the whole picture and so stop obsessing about it." She could have been quoting from Freud's essay on the uncanny, "For this uncanny is in reality nothing new or foreign, but something familiar and old — established in the mind that has been estranged only by the process of repression. This reference to the factor of repression enables us, furthermore, to understand Schelling's definition of the uncanny as something which ought to have been kept concealed but which has nevertheless come to light."

Acker's "healers" convinced her that the double or multiple selves were a part of the healing process, that "every person has two selves: a local and a transcendental. The transcendental self is the one who watches. I help a person get there, for if he can see or find how to heal himself." She wrote, "I experienced my body either as having several aspects or as several connected bodies, as soul, as energetic or emotional, and as physical. I saw that the organs, the tissues and the cells physically remember all that happened to and within the body. I experienced the body as an entity separate from all other entities only in its physical aspect."

Whether it is Hitchens' eloquent rationalism or Acker's alternative punk attitude, for both cancer sufferers, "the whole matter (was) one of 'testing reality,' pure and simple, a question of the material reality of the phenomena." The experience of illness, the pathology of everyday life, is uncanny, and "an uncanny experience occurs either when repressed infantile complexes have been revived," (birth, being buried alive, primary narcissism) "by some impression, or when the primitive beliefs we have surmounted seem once more to be confirmed," (death, the finite bounds of the self).

As a coda to this section, Freud could also be explaining the doctor's role in the patient's experience of the uncanny, "The writer has then one more means he can use to escape our rising vexation and at the same time to improve his chances of success. It is this, that he should keep us in the dark for a long time about the precise nature of the conditions he has selected for the world he writes about, or that he should cunningly and ingeniously avoid any definite information on the point at all throughout the book." Substitute "doctor" for "writer" and "the patient he diagnoses" for "the world he writes about" and "stay" for "book" and we come close to a description of a patient/doctor relationship. Acker — as she did in her approach to literature and the Western canon — rebelled against this narrative. As she explained, "The hardest part of my cancer was the walking away from that surgeon and from conventional medicine. Belief in conventional medicine, in what our doctors tell us, is so deeply engrained in our society that to walk away from conventional medicine is to walk away from normal society."[1]

Freud states, "Concerning the factors of silence, solitude and darkness, we can only say that they are actually elements in the production of that infantile morbid anxiety from which the majority of human beings have never become quite free." I will finish this section with a quote from J.G. Ballard's autobiography *Miracles of Life*, published in 2008, a year before he died of prostate cancer, for him to illuminate the pages above in the strange surgical glare of his prose: "I moved into the care of Professor Jonathan Waxman, in the Cancer Centre at Hammersmith Hospital in west London. Professor Waxman is one of the leading prostate cancer specialists in this country, and he rescued me at a time when I was exhausted by the intermittent pain and the fears of death that blotted everything else from my mind. It was Jonathan who convinced me that within a few weeks of the initial treatment the pain would leave me and I would begin to feel something closer to my everyday self." Ballard, that surrealist chronicler of the uncanny (see *The Crystal World*, *The Drowned World*, *Hello America*) and its attendant doubles (see "Zone of Terror"), acknowledges that his cancer made him different from his everyday self; it made him feel *unheimilich*, far from home, and confirmed what he experienced in writing *Crash* where he appears as himself, as a fictional double. As he explains in a 2003 interview in *Age*, "In all of us there are elements of contradictory, sometimes rather unwelcome ghosts, doubles of ourselves." Those shadows on the

---

1   All of the above quotes about Acker's cancer are from her essay "Outward from Nothingness," originally published in *The Guardian*, 18 January, 1997.

X-ray, those spectral masses on the CT scans, those flickering ghosts in the MRI.

In *The Emperor of Maladies*, Mukherjee writes: "Cancer was a disease of pathological hyperplasia in which cells acquired an autonomous will to divide. This aberrant, uncontrolled cell division created masses of tissue (tumors) that invaded organs and destroyed normal tissues. These tumors could also spread from one site to another, causing outcroppings of the disease — called metastases — in distant sites, such as the bones, the brain, or the lungs. Cancer came in diverse forms — breast, stomach, skin, and cervical cancer, leukemias and lymphomas. But all these diseases were deeply connected at the cellular level. In every case, cells had all acquired the same characteristic: uncontrollable pathological cell division."

The Hungarian author Frigyes Karinthy chronicled the symptoms, effects and treatment of a non-cancerous brain tumour in his autobiographical *A Journey Round My Skull*, first published in 1939. Fritz Zorn's *Mars*, a book detailing the existential crisis he underwent after discovering he had malignant lymphomas, was published shortly before his death from cancer in 1976. What follows is a tale of two tumours.

After suffering from auditory hallucinations, the sound of a train in a café in Budapest, Karinthy realizes that, although he knows he is not going mad, "something else must be wrong..." His internal world has shifted; his perceptions have altered. What is to blame? From the first manifestation, Karinthy lights out in search of the cause with patience and humour. For a forthcoming selection of his short stories, he chooses the title *The Laughter of the Sick* and argues against the claim that "art was largely a pathological condition." Conversely, he believes art is "evidence of an exceptionally vigorous state of health." He fears that this unknown ailment will hinder his writing, postpone his other artistic endeavours. The invading (from within) tumour necessitates a questioning of the self and the processes of the self — "I am a writer" not "I am a man with a tumour." Deleuze and Guattari focus on this symptom in *A Thousand Plateaus*: "*Cancerous tissue*: each instant, each second, a cell becomes cancerous, mad, proliferates and loses its configuration, takes over everything; the organism must resubmit it to its rule or restratify it, not only for its own survival, but also to make possible an escape from the organism, the fabrication of the 'other' BwO on the plane of consistency. Take the stratum of signifiance: once again, there is a cancerous tissue, this time of signifiance, a burgeoning body of the despot that blocks any circulation of signs, as well as preventing the birth of the asignifying sign on the 'other' BwO." I would like to create another acronym here, a furtherance of Deleuze and Guattari's BwO (Body without Organs): BwAO (Body with Another Organ), the tumour — be it malignant or benign.

The thing inside of us must be escaped from and to do so means a reconfiguration of our knowledge about our bodies, a resubmission to our body's inherent disconnectedness to what we believe and think it to be. The body/mind dualism is complicated by a third entity. The tumour is an extension, a menace to both the body and mind, it destratifies our duality, insisting on a third plane of being, one that threatens proliferation and occupation. The BwAO is "the cancerous BwO of a fascist inside us."

Throughout the book, Karinthy references Hitler's Germany and the Nazi presence in Vienna where he has to go for treatment. Vienna is the metonym for this invasive occupation. Tumours enact an annexation not only of the spaces of our body but the processes of thought; they reconfigure our perceptions and disassemble our means of articulation. As Karinthy puts it, "The mirror opposite me seemed to move. Not more than inch or two, then it hung still. In itself, this would never have worried me. It might have been a mere hallucination, like the roaring trains. But what was happening now?" Realizing that this is not his writerly imagination in a feverish mode, he continues, "And yet everything, myself included, seemed to have lost its grip on reality." The plane of consistency falters, the café's tables, customers, water-jug and match-box all look familiar, "yet in some eerie and alarming way they had all become accidental," they were terrifying caricatures and "happened to be there purely by chance, and might just as well be anywhere else." This is an unilluminated and menacing extension of perception's stratifications of the real, and concomitantly Karinthy's plane of consistency restratifies itself, metastasizing the body's inherent disconnectedness: "I did not feel certain I was there myself, or that the man sitting there was I. There seemed no reason why the water-jug should not be sitting in my place on the seat, and I standing on the tray. And now the whole box of tricks was starting to roll about, as if the floor underneath it had given way. I wanted to cling on to something. But what was there to cling to? Not the table or the seat, for they, too, were rocking about like everything else. There wasn't a fixed point anywhere... Unless, perhaps, I could find one in my own head. If I could catch hold of a single image or memory or association that would help me to recognize myself. Or even a word might do."

This moment of disconnectedness is fleeting yet seems to take a lifetime, and although he experiences no physical pain, the event is one of torture. Karinthy struggles to maintain his plane of consistency, his grip on his body and mind, and realizes that if he fails "the next instant would see me no longer the captain of the ship. No more should I be in command of the myriads of tiny atoms, cells and organs over which I had been king since birth." The invasion has begun, the body has started restratifying itself, re-organ-izing. Karinthy experiences "that rebellious multitude," a Cioran-esque "horror of the flesh, of the organs, of each cell, primordial horror, chemical horror. Everything in (him) disintegrates, even this horror. In what grease, what pestilence the spirit has taken up its abode! This body, whose every pore eliminates enough stench to infect space, is no more than a mass of ordure through which circulates a scarcely less ignoble blood, no more than a tumor which disfigures the geometry of the globe." Within that moment, Karinthy perceives his body as an inert mass, common matter with him deposed as master.

Pre-empting *A Thousand Plateaus*, Karinthy doesn't know whether he has it within his means "to make the selection, to distinguish the Bw[A]O from its doubles: empty vitreous bodies, cancerous bodies, totalitarian and fascist." The symptoms and aftereffects cause an *unheimlich* event in Karinthy's reality; the present and future no longer exist, they have coagulated, they have become violently destratified, as Hitchens experienced, the present hurtling fast-forward to the future, the future collapsing in on itself, becoming common matter.

As Hitchens and Acker comprehended their cancers as alien presences, so Karinthy fears that something has invaded his body. He tours the wards of a lunatic asylum and encounters the inmates. One man is infected by a fungus that has attached itself to the membranes of his throat, divided and infected his brain where it metastasizes and leaves him in drooling agony. The next man is suffering from cysticercus, a tapeworm in the brain, attacking his central nervous system. The third suffers from acromegaly, an excess of growth hormones due to disturbances in the function of the pituitary gland. With illness comes hypochondria, as if the metastasizing of the body's cell structures causes a collateral response of symptomatic paranoia in the patient. From *A Thousand Plateaus*: "The

Bw[A]O: it is already under way the moment the body has had enough of organs and wants to slough them off, or loses them. A long procession. The hypochondriac body: the organs are destroyed, the damage has already been done, nothing happens anymore […] The paranoid body: the organs are continually under attack by outside forces, but are also restored by outside energies. ('He lived for a long time without a stomach, without intestines, almost without lungs, with a torn oesophagus, without a bladder, and with shattered ribs, he used sometimes to swallow part of his own larynx with his food, etc…')."

Observing these patients is a form of creative hypochondria, a means of progressing the narrative of Karinthy's illness; each "case" is an artistic examination of what is not the diagnosis, like a private eye dismissing possible suspects in a detective novel. Writing on hypochondria and its relationship with creativity, Brian Dillon also uses Deleuze's case studies and states, "That is not to say, argues Deleuze, 'that great authors, great artists, are all ill, however sublimely, or that one's looking for a sign of neurosis or psychosis like a secret in their work, the hidden code of their work. They're not ill; on the contrary, they're a rather special kind of doctor.'" Karinthy suffers from "professional hypochondria" both as a writer and as an ex-medical student; his doctor reminds him that "every medical student imagines he's got all the diseases going. He gets small-pox and cholera and phthisis and cancer."

Before we continue with Karinthy's journey around his skull, I would like to examine the existential masturbatory hypochondria of Fritz Zorn's *Mars*. Fritz Angst, born on 10 April, 1944, six years after Frigyes Karinthy died of a stroke while holidaying at Lake Balaton in Hungary, assumed the pen-name Fritz Zorn as author of *Mars*. This punkish pseudonym (the book was published in German in 1976, followed by a post-punk version in the UK in 1982) shifts his surname from anxiety to anger; the title is taken from the Roman god of war and, like war, the book is mostly humourless. I remember buying it when it was first published, one of those Picador volumes I collected. Its cover was a swirling red mass; it could have been blood, a close-up of a syringe. But it could have also been the surface of Mars painted by J.M.W. Turner. I bought it because the back cover promised me something "in the tradition of Sartre's *La Nausée* and Camus' *L'Étranger*." It also went rather well with my burgundy vinyl trousers. I must have read it — in those days I read everything through to the end, whether I liked it or not. On re-reading, I find it sub-Sartre, quasi-Camus, a memoir of spoiled anguish and punkish attitude, interesting, nevertheless, in its assertion that neurosis may cause cancer.

Zorn (Angst) died on 2 November, 1976, the day after he heard that *Mars* was to be published, he was thirty-two. He spent most of his life on Zurich's Goldcoast, on the southeastern shores of Lake Zurich. He taught at a Zurich Gymnasium and was a published author. His tumour developed in his neck, a malignant lymphoma, a proliferation of cancerous blood-cell tumours in the lymphatic system. Karinthy's response to the first symptoms of his tumour is the inevitable need to know the cause, but Zorn shrugs and experiences the disease as inevitable; it will kill him or it might not, it is physical yet also a manifestation of all the hurt, fear, neuroses and paranoia of his (rather privileged if boring) upbringing. "There are two points I would like to make about my cancer. On the one hand, it is a physical disease from which I will most likely die in the near future, but then again I may win out against it and survive after all. On the other hand, it is a psychic disorder, and I can only regard its onset in an acute physical form as a great stroke of luck. By this I mean that in view of my unfortunate family legacy, getting cancer was by far the cleverest thing I have ever done in my life." Whereas Karinthy sought enlightenment and cure, Zorn wallows in apathy and blame, using the disease as inspiration for vitriol and regret.

His childhood was one of conformity and non-commitment; his parents lived bland lives and Zorn fears that he is trapped in a world that is falsely perfect but recognizes that, like the body, there may be something within that is malignant. It is as if Zorn were a hypochondriac from birth, seeing disease in every gesture, every unspoken word, willing, almost, a sickness to devour him, to make him different from his bourgeois parents, "Perhaps the point can be pressed more accurately this way: Extreme instances of improper education (and my own case was an extreme one) can be so harmful that they result in neurotically generated diseases, such as cancer." Do they?

This is a rather antiquated view of cancer's origins. Mukherjee notes that "nineteenth-century doctors often linked cancer to civilization: cancer, they imagined, was caused by the rush and whirl of modern life, which somehow incited pathological growth in the body. The link was correct, but the causality was not: civilization did not cause cancer, but by extending human life spans — civilization unveiled it."

Going further back in the biography of cancer, Zorn is closer to the Greek physician Galen (129AD-c.200AD), whose extension of Hippocrates' theory of the four humours hypothesized that cancer was caused by black bile (melancholia) and so "depression and cancer, the psychic and physical diseases of black bile, were thus intrinsically linked." Rather than seeing a third plane of existence (the cancer both of and separate from the body), Zorn conflates the psychic with the physical, the cancer becomes a metaphor for his neuroses. Although Zorn's cancer was lymphatic, his "anger" and "anxiety" are closer to the symptoms of stomach cancer. Mukherjee again: "For centuries, gastritis had rather vaguely been attributed to stress and neuroses. (In popular use, the term dyspeptic still refers to an irritable and fragile psychological state.) By extension, then, cancer of the stomach was cancer unleashed by neurotic stress, in essence a modern variant of the theory of clogged melancholia proposed by Galen." Zorn agrees, "Every wealthy Zuricher has heart trouble or an ulcer, but he doesn't have sense enough to draw any conclusion to the fact." Having been raised to contract cancer, Zorn believed he was in a unique position to understand the evil in his life.

From childhood, Zorn maintained that it was his fate to get cancer, for his physical body to mirror his psychic state, for his anxiety to transform into anger and then bodily tumours. In *History of Madness*, Foucault reminds us that, "in the eighteenth century a unity would be found, or rather an exchange would be accomplished, when that cold, black humour became the dominant colour of the delirium, its full value by contrast with mania, dementia and frenzy, its principle of cohesion." Zorn is almost delirious in his illness, in the reification of his neuroses into nodules, "I don't know if I will survive this illness. If I do die of it, it will be correct to say that death was the ultimate goal of my education." Zorn's principle of cohesion is the knowledge that he has cancer because it was willed, it is the plane of consistency in his dying life. Foucault again: "While Boerhaave still defined melancholia as 'long, stubborn delirium without fever, during which the patient is obsessed by a single thought', within a few years Dufour had moved the weight of definition to the 'fear and sadness', which were now taken to explain the partial character of the delirium." Zorn's life, according to his writings, was one of fear and sadness and these components of melancholy, of black bile, caused his cancer, caused his obsession with the singularity of living with cancer, of dying from cancer. Where Karinthy followed a narrative drive for understanding through contemporary medical science and experimentation as a goal of his education his will to wellness, Zorn's memoir inexorably pushes him towards death, towards the fulfilment of his existential (and erroneous) theories.

Karinthy seeks out doctors, psychoanalysts, experts in brain surgery. Zorn is a loner, he doesn't mix with other children, he is snobbish, people were "outsiders" or "other people". He wrote that, "(m)y body was alien to me, and I didn't know what in the world to do with it. I was quite at home in that dubious world of the 'higher things,' but I was afraid of the brutality and primitiveness I sensed lurking in the physical world." He lives a psychic life believing his body to be ugly, that it already harbours something brutal within it, some tumour lurking in the unthinkable "thisness" of his physical body. He recognized no tie between his body and the rest of the physical world, he banned the word "body" and other words for bodily parts from his vocabulary, he denied his body and became insular and his body became a source of embarrassment and fear. Foucault continues: "This explains why melancholics prefer solitude and avoid company, which in turn increases their attachment to the object of their delirium or their dominant passion, whatever that might be, while they appear to remain indifferent to all other things. This fixing of the concept was not the result of a new rigour in observation, nor any discovery in the domain of causation, but of a qualitative transmission going from a cause implied in the name to a significant perception among the effects."

One of the effects of Zorn's delirious-melancholic-hypochondriac-neurosis is his fear of pain, particularly pain caused by doctors, "the doctor's sharp instrument mustn't stab through my skin. It mustn't penetrate into me. Since I had shielded myself from life and the outside world in all other things, I could not tolerate any kind of breach in the skin that helped protect me from the outside world. The skin is the physical symbol of the vulnerable inner life's protection against a hostile world." Yet again, Zorn uses metaphor to deny the body's actuality, which contrasts directly with Karinthy's viewing of experimental brain surgery and acceptance that pain is a component of something known to him as "I." Cancer operates by disrupting the entire economy of the body and Zorn (a complete Descartean) believes that his anger and melancholy and his thinking of untoward things, namely, the life he led before the onset of a malignant lymphoma, have caused his impending death from cancer.

As early as page sixty in these tales of two tumours — one in the skull, one in the lymphatic system, one benign (although Karinthy is unaware of this), and one malignant (Zorn seems pleased that this is the case) — it is clear that the two writers fall into the two categories of optimist and pessimist, of positivist and existentialist. Nietzsche summed up this kind of sick person in *Human, All too Human* (1878): "They are the most grateful animals in the world, also the most modest, these convalescents and lizards again half turned towards life: — there are some among them who allow no day to pass without hanging a little song of praise on the hem of its departing robe. And, to speak seriously: to become sick in the manner of these free spirits, to remain sick for a long time and then, slowly, slowly, to become healthy, by which I mean 'healthier', is a fundamental cure for all pessimism (the cancerous sore and inveterate vice, as is well known, of old idealists and inveterate liars). There is wisdom, practical wisdom, in for a long time prescribing even health for oneself only in small doses." A nihilist hypochondriac would know the difference. Whereas Karinthy seeks to observe, learn from and then escape his tumour, Zorn absorbs it into his being, the cancer is he and he the cancer. For Karinthy, a cure is a turn towards life; for Zorn, life is a perpetual cancerous sore caused by the inveterate vice of growing up in bourgeois

Switzerland. Whereas Nietzsche stayed at Sils-Maria on Lake Sils for health reasons, Zorn experiences lake Zurich's Goldcoast as deleterious to his well-being. Nietzsche hoped through the writing of *Thus Spoke Zarathustra* (1883) to find a cure for, an antidote to or even an evolution from humanity's sickness, Zorn saw himself as a symptom of existential malaise and illness.

As a perpetual invalid and philosophical patient, in *Human, All Too Human* Nietzsche vacillates between optimism and pessimism, and the reactions of Karinthy and Zorn to their tumours illustrate this: "The chemical process and the strife of the elements, the torment of the sick man who yearns for an end to his sickness, are as little merits as are those states of distress and psychic convulsions which arise when we are torn back and forth by conflicting motives until we finally choose the most powerful of them — as we put it (in truth, however, until the most powerful motive chooses us)." Karinthy explores various medical treatments to put an end to his sickness, the aural hallucinations, the dizziness, the headaches, while Zorn wallows in the states of distress and psychic convulsions caused by his cancer. Both are torn by examining the physical and psychological effects of the tumours, Karinthy choosing life and Zorn being — as he believes it — chosen by death. In *The Space of Literature* (1955), Blanchot, writing about Rilke's leukaemia in relation to his poetry, helps us explain how Karinthy's optimism and drive to find a cure acknowledges death and how Zorn, by embracing death as some form of revenge on life, views cancer as a stage of life. "Rilke appeals to the image of vegetable or organic maturation only in order to turn us toward what we prefer to stay clear of — in order to show us that death has a kind of existence, and to train our attention upon this existence, awaken our concern. Death exists, but what form of existence does it have? What relation does this image establish between him who lives and the fact of dying? One might believe in a natural link; one might think, for example, that I produce my death as the body produces cancer. But that is not the case: despite the biological reality of the event, one must always reflect, beyond the organic phenomenon, upon death's being. One never dies simply of an illness, but of one's death."

Cancer is the embodiment of death, it is not a metaphor for it; it is the organic maturation of the body unto death, death as existence. Hitchens, Acker and Zorn all lived with cancer and died from it. Hitchens wrote wryly and precisely about the biological reality of the event, the side effects, the effects on his family and friends, the effects on his enemy. Acker attempted — as she did in her fiction and essays — an alternative solution beyond the organic phenomenon, and Zorn railed against death's being, against his cultural and familial background that he believed was linked to his cancer. Karinthy's investigation into his aural hallucinations and then the discovery of his tumour was also an examination of life and the fact of dying.

Gilles Deleuze — who suffered from lung cancer — wrote in his essay "Louis Wolfson; or, the Procedure," collected in the book *Essays Critical and Clinical* (1993), that "the struggle between knowledge and life is the bombardment of the body by atoms, and cancer is the riposte of the body. How can knowledge heal life, and in some way justify it? All the world's doctors — those 'green bastards' who come in pairs like fathers — will never be able to cure the cancerous mother by bombarding her with atoms." However much Acker and Karinthy thought they knew their bodies, however much Zorn believed that social fate and cultural anxiety affected his body, and however often Hitchens responded to his illness with clever retorts, cancer had the last word, the final riposte. Knowing one has cancer does not heal it — see Acker's redundant and ultimately fatal exploration of alternative therapies, Zorn's megalomaniacal neurosis and blame. The atomized body is atomized more by the proliferation of cancer cells until it breaks down under its own internal bombardment. Deleuze continues: "The question, however, lies elsewhere, since it concerns the body in which he lives, with all the metastases that constitute the earth, and the knowledge in which he evolves, with all the languages that never stop speaking, all the atoms that never stop bombarding. It is here, in the world, in the real, that the pathogenic intervals are opened up, and the illegitimate totalities are made and unmade. It is here that the problem of existence is posed, the problem of his own existence. What makes the student sick is the world, not his father-mother. What makes him sick is the real, not symbols. The only 'justification' of life would be for all the atoms to bombard the cancer-Earth once and for all, and return it to the great void: the resolution of all equations, the atomic explosion." The major problem with cancer is that it is our own body that is bombarding us; when cancer is present our bodies become illegitimate totalities focusing our thoughts directly on the "problem of existence" before we return to the great void. Zorn justified his cancer through blame, Acker through her resistance to control and need for a spiritual aspect, Hitchens through his need to know and his disbelief in God.

When the cancer becomes terminal, the effects are apocalyptic. In *Corpus*, Nancy writes: "The intruder exposes me to excess. It extrudes me, exports me, expropriates me. I am the illness and the medicine, I am the cancerous cell and the grafted organ, I am these immuno-depressive agents and their palliatives, I am these ends of steel wire that brace my sternum and this injection site permanently sewn under my clavicle, altogether as if, already and besides, I were these screws in my thigh and this plate inside my groin. I am turning into something like a science-fiction android, or else, as my youngest son said to me one day, one of the living-dead." The body's healthy cells have been replaced by cancer cells that the body does not recognize as harmful and intrusive; like the aliens in *Invasion of the Body Snatchers*, they are zombies, bent on mimicry and overthrow. Nancy again: "We are, along with the rest of my more and more numerous fellow creatures, the beginnings, in effect, of a mutation: man begins again by passing infinitely beyond man. (This is what 'the death of god' has always meant, in every possible way.) Man becomes what he is: the most terrifying and the most troubling technician, as Sophocles called him twenty-five centuries ago, who denatures and remakes nature, who recreates creation, who brings it out of nothing and, perhaps, leads it back to nothing. One capable of origin and end."

Nancy perceives cancer as a metaphor for humanity's effects on the Earth; in this, he echoes Cioran's "Trees are massacred, houses go up — faces, faces everywhere. Man is *spreading*. Man is the cancer of the earth." Cancer is a quasi-homonym turned quasi-synonym; it is of us and not, it is creation and destruction, our life and death is the play between the two, between the cellular and the mutation of it. Cancer is the dividing line between the signified and the signifier, which takes over control of both and turns itself into the indispensable part of the mechanism. Cancer cells replace healthy cells by a mutant rather than metonymic displacement because of the very abundance and mobility (in metastases) of the substitutive cancer. The body becomes polysemic under the attack of cancer cells, it proliferates its own meaning and being. The body becomes unspeakable through what is lurking inside and that code-name to unlock life is death. The unspeakable word, after all, is cancer.

Just as I was finishing the first draft of this chapter, I received a telephone call from my mother informing me that my father — already in remission from prostate cancer and having had surgical procedures on malignant melanomas — had been told that he had stage-four bowel cancer. A few days later, on 10 January, 2016, I heard the news that David Bowie had died of liver cancer two days after his sixty-ninth birthday and the release of his album *Blackstar*. I shall return to these two events in the Conclusion.

CHAPTER 4

The Broken Column

Orthopaedics as Opinion

On 6 October, 1890, doctor-writer-tuberculosis-sufferer Anton Chekhov wrote to his mother Evgenia, "I am very well, if you don't count a twitch in my eye which seems to be bothering me often just now, and which always seems to give me a bad headache. My eye was twitching yesterday and today, so I am writing this letter to the accompaniment of an aching head and a heaviness throughout my body. My haemorrhoids also remind me of their existence." Pain does that, it reminds us of our being and headaches focus that attention while simultaneously blurring our perception of it. In *On Nietzsche* (1944), Georges Bataille writes, "This is the moment when the individual finds out that he or she has become time (and, to that extent, has been eaten away inside), and when, on account of repeated sufferings and desenions, the movement of time makes him or her a sieve for its flow — so that, opened to immanence, nothing remains in that person to differentiate him or her from the possible object."

At the time of writing the letter, Chekhov was coming towards the end of his six-month visit to Sakhalin, a large island off Russia's Pacific coast, close to Hokkaido. He had travelled across Siberia to reach the island and had spent four months there recording data on the penal colonies that dotted the harsh landscape. The violence and inhumanity he witnessed would also have reminded him of his existence as he chronicled his observations in letters to friends and family and in *Sakhalin Island*, his published report.

Although his letters are candid masterpieces of detail and humour, Chekhov claimed, in an 11 October, 1899 letter to Grigory Rossolimo, that he suffered "from an affliction known as autobiographophobia" and that "being forced to read, let alone write, any details about myself is the purest torture. I have put down a few bare dates on a separate sheet of paper to send you, but that's the best I can do." Chekhov's letters contradict this claim; they are as intriguing as his short stories and plays, dealing as they do with social minutiae, medicine, disease and creativity. So, as Chekhov's haemorrhoids reminded him of their existence, let's flip his claim and investigate headaches in the next section of my autobiographophilia.

Over the next eighteen months, from October 1974 until March 1976, I visited the surgery nine times because of headaches. On 5 March, 1976, Dr Griffin prescribed Panadeine, a compound analgesic of codeine phosphate and paracetamol; obviously, the aspirins were not working, nor the cannabis I had been smoking for the previous year or so. On the note, there is also a referral to a Dr Gross at Ashford Hospital.

I remember these headaches very well and fear their return. When out walking, if light reflects off of something and flashes in my vision, I still think, forty years on, "Oh, no, here comes another pain-filled day." Here is what Dr M. Gross M.D. F.R.C.P., Consultant Neurologist, had to report to my new doctor, Dr Aswani, on 26 July, 1976: "This boy came to see me recently and told me that he had been getting headaches for the last 18 months. These became worse about two months ago since when they have been occurring almost every day. They are, however, lasting rather less time, even though they are more severe." I do not remember the increase in frequency but the headaches more often than not occurred on a Thursday morning when I had double English, definitely not on a Tuesday afternoon when I had physics and chemistry. I realize now that my life was very similar to Oliver Sacks' Case 18 from his book *Migraine* (1970), "This 24-year-old man had suffered from frequent nightmares and somnambulistic episodes to the age of 8, attacks of periodic, usually nocturnal, asthma until the age of thirteen, and classical and common migraines thereafter. The classical migraines would come, with considerable regularity, every Sunday afternoon."

The waking up, the breakfast, the walk to school, all in a world that appeared to have Vaseline on the lens, where birds miaowed and dogs honked and the chocolate bar I bought tasted of tomato soup. Sound familiar? In class, I wouldn't put my hand up if I knew the answer to a question — very unlike me — my shoulders and arms and hands and all my joints felt like they were made of osmium, my mouth felt full of cotton-wool gobstoppers. After half an hour of this, my sight would be affected. Dr Gross: "The headache may be bifrontal or right frontal only and a relatively short duration, lasting perhaps half a minute, when they're sharp in character. If bifrontal they may be preceded by visual disturbance, which he describes as a haziness if he looks directly at anything, but without teichopsia." As the attack started, I would get a series of lightning-strike pains in my forehead, agonizing darts that nearly brought me to tears. What was worse was that these moments of pain would be a sign that a completely different torment would soon begin and it would last hours.

I am not sure how effective my consultation with Dr Gross was, but by "haziness" I meant all the signs of classic scintillating scotoma and negative scotoma during a migrainal aura. Sacks elaborates, "The term scintillating scotoma denotes the characteristic flickering of luminous migraine spectra, and the term negative scotoma denotes the area of partial or total blindness which may follow, or, on occasion, precede scintillating scotoma." After the intense jolts of pain had vanished, I experienced bright flares and a blind spot occurred in the central vision of my right eye. A little while after that, my sight would begin to ripple, like shifting sand, like a sidewinder snake on shifting sand, nothing was fixed, everything shimmied — the haziness. My left eye had (what now I think resemble) fractal blooms or the spreading of a glob of blood-red liquid on the microscope slide in *Don't Look Now*. My scintillating scotoma were not as fanciful as one patient who, Sacks notes, "described small white skunks with erect tails, moving in procession across one quadrant of the visual field." Someone should write a book on migraine and the artwork of Vincent van Gogh, Claude Monet and George Seurat — scintillating scotoma is also known as the Seurat effect.

By the summer of 1976, not only was I a punk but I had become obsessed with the poems and letters of Arthur Rimbaud, so I am disappointed that the poet had written, "And how it contains, big with sap and rays of light / The vast swarming of all embryos," at the age of sixteen, which describes my scotoma better than I could have done at the same age. There is also a connection between the prodrome events of my migraine, Rimbaud and Baudelaire's experiments with synaesthesia and Sacks' "systematic enumeration of the full range of aural symptoms."

Charles Baudelaire's *Les Fleurs du mal*, published in 1857, contains the poem "Correspondances" ("Correspondences"), in which "Sounds, fragrances and colours correspond." Baudelaire suffered from migraines, insomnia, neuralgia of the right eye, he was sometimes seen walking the Parisian streets with his head wreathed in bandages and believed he was suffering from "cerebral contagion." The headaches and other illnesses could have been symptoms of syphilis, opium and alcohol addiction or a result of all three. In 1866, a stroke left him paralysed and he died the next year aged forty-six.

Four years later, the seventeen year-old Arthur Rimbaud, a devotee of Baudelaire's work, wrote "Voyelles" ("Vowels"), in which "A" is black, "E" white, "I" red, "U" green, and "O" blue, each sound has a colour, the "A" a "black hairy corset of shining flies," and the "U", "cycles, divine vibrations of green seas." Earlier the same year, he may have given his readers a clue as to the source of this when he wrote in "Accroupissements" ("Squattings"), "When the sun, bright as a scoured cooking-pan / Darts a migraine at him and blinds his vision." Correspondences, synaesthesia, I experienced both of these in the lead-up to the onset of migraine.

Sacks lists similar categorical symptoms of migraine aura: "(a) Specific visual, tactile, and other sensory hallucinations. (b) General alterations of sensory threshold and excitability. (c) Alterations in level of consciousness and muscular tone. (d) Alterations of mood and affect. (e) Disorders of the higher integrative functions: perception, ideation, memory, and speech."

A contemporary of Rimbaud and a fan of Baudelaire, Nietzsche would have recognized Dr Sacks' categories. Nietzsche's first migraine event occurred when he was fourteen years old, roughly the same age that I suffered my first attack, but, unlike mine, his remained with him throughout his life. Writing to his sister Elisabeth from Bayreuth on 1 August, 1876, Nietzsche complained, "Things are not right with me, I can see that! Continuous headache, though not of the worst kind, and lassitude. Yesterday I was able to listen to *Die Walküre* but only in a dark room — to use my eyes is impossible! I long to get away; it is too senseless to stay." The increasing severity forced him to leave Bayreuth, after which he quarrelled and broke with Richard Wagner, and returned to Basel University from where he was given a year's sick leave. Maybe it was listening to *Die Walküre* and *Das Rheingold* that was giving Nietzsche migraines. I am sure pumping out records by the Sex Pistols and The Clash was not helping my attacks. In a letter to his sister on 3 February, 1882, Nietzsche almost blamed Wagner for his headaches, "My Wagner mania certainly cost me dear. Has not this nerve-shattering music ruined my health? And the disillusionment and leaving Wagner — was not that putting my very life in danger? Have I not needed almost six years to recover from the pain?"

On 27 January, 1877, Nietzsche wrote to his mother that "my head still seems to be short of blood" and from Lugano on 13 May he tells Malwida von Meysenbug: "Human misery during a sea journey is terrible, and yet actually laughable, which is how my headaches sometimes seem to me when my physical condition may be excellent — in brief, I am today once more in the mood of serene crippledom, whereas on the ship I had only the blackest thoughts, my only doubts about suicide concerned where the sea might be deepest, so that one would not be immediately fished out again and have to pay a debt of gratitude to one's rescuers in a terrible mass of gold. As a matter of fact, I knew very precisely what the worst part of sea sickness was like, from the time I had been tormented by violent stomach pains in league with headache — it was a memory of half vanished times." In *Correction*, Thomas Bernhard had a similar idea, "Happiness can even be found in the so-called acceptance of pain."

In his letter, Dr Gross continues to Dr Aswani, "When the headache is at its height he has to lie down and has vomited. When severe, the bifrontal pains may last several hours, during which he cannot concentrate on his work. He is apparently a tense boy and becomes readily uptight to use his own phrase and occasionally rather depressed. There were no other very significant symptoms." Oliver Sacks counters,

"Migrainous headache is frequently complicated by the simultaneous or antecedent occurrence of other types of head-pain. Characteristic tension-headache, localized especially in the cervical and posterior occipital regions, may inaugurate a migraine headache, or accompany it, particularly if the attack is marked by irritability, anxiety, or continued activity throughout its duration." And "if the patient is fortunate, vomiting may terminate not only his nausea but the entire migraine attack; more commonly, he will fail to secure relief from vomiting, and suffer instead an excruciating aggravation of concurrent vascular headache. When florid, nausea is far less tolerable than headache or other forms of pain, and in many patients, especially youthful ones, nausea and vomiting dominate the clinical picture and constitute the crowning misery of a common migraine."

Migraine was first published in 1970, so it is clear to me that Dr Gross did not know his Sacks from his elbow. I had all the classic and common signs of migraine, yet he did not seem to believe me or tie the symptoms together. He explains, "I have also seen his father recently for headaches which I thought were due to tension, but there is no history of migraine in the family. Examining him, there were no abnormal neurological general signs." My father does not remember this. As soon as an attack occurred, I sought darkness. My teachers were very understanding and sent me home. If a migraine (because that's what they obviously were) came on during my drama class, the teacher would massage my head, which I think helped, but I had a crush on her, so it may also have hindered. I would get home (I can't remember how) and crawl into bed with the covers over my head. The pain was agonizing and the nausea came over me in jellied waves. The attacks lasted for a few hours until I vomited, or made myself vomit, and then the pain would disappear. Nietzsche had similar episodes and, like Dr Gross, did not believe them to be neurological in origin, "There were extremely painful and obstinate headaches which exhausted all my strength. They increased over long years, to reach a climax of which pain was habitual, so that any given year contained for me two hundred days of pain. The malaise must have had an entirely local cause — there was no neuropathological basis for it at all. I have never had any symptoms of mental disturbance — not even fever, no fainting." Nietzsche wrote this letter to Georg Brandes on 10 April, 1888 from Turin; on 3 January, 1889, in the same city, he suffered a mental collapse and was confined in a mental asylum in Jena. However, on 6 January, 1889 he wrote to the art historian Jakob Burckhardt, "This autumn, as lightly clad as possible, I twice attended my funeral" and asked "Are we happy? I am God, I made this caricature," claiming, "I too was crucified at great length last year by the German doctors."

When a migraine attack occurred, I wished I had a separate body, a caricature of myself, one in which I could function without the pain and nausea. I told Dr Gross (German doctor?) that I "could not concentrate on my work." What work? I was 15. It was the start of the summer holiday. By this date, I had dabbled in writing my own poems, imitations, of course, of Patti Smith, Rimbaud, Baudelaire, Paul Eluard and others whose books I had bought (or had bought for me by L, a generous and rich girlfriend) from Compendium Books in Camden Town, London. One of the poems, self-published in a magazine *In A Glass* (I edited the one edition, 1976) was called "Tick-Tock" and included the lines:

Inner models of timeless hours.
Without Within motionless space,
open but closed yet allowing a passage, to where?
An antediluvian bird haunts

the vertebral column enclosed in open walls
Beauty stands by closed doors,
you cannot enter here
4am is that the time, space movement of
a womb, a labyrinth that cozens time,
Is it space that sculptures a caress of the sphere.
The trace of the moment
holds the Logos in its empty frame.
an external room, a multiple plane,
Doors closed, open to the darkness,
they're all there
Who? Where? What.
An object, a neck, a bare neck, the same substance,
A second a minute, an hour is not contained in silence.
Help ... suffocating, stop squeezing
life life where is life
Still, all is still, yet, I hear scampering over the roof the black
the black,
Still, all is still.
Outer. Inner, no definite view of the whole.

Reading this forty years later, it is inescapable to me that this poem is very poorly written, immensely derivative, unflinchingly pretentious and a record of my migraine events. The poem, for that is what it very nearly is, recounts the chaotic state of an impending attack, the mind without and within, unstable and unsettled. There is no certainty of its course, "a passage, to where?" Sacks writes, "in this unsettled state one may feel hot or cold or both," ("Is it cold or is it hot"). He continues, "bloated and tight, or loose and queasy; peculiar tension, or languor, or both," (Help ... suffocating, stop squeezing"). Sacks explains further, "there are head pains, or other pains, sundry strains and discomforts, which come and go" ("An object, a neck, a bare neck, the same substance"), and where, "Everything comes and goes, nothing is settled, and if one could take a total thermogram, or scan, or inner photograph of the body, one would see vascular beds opening and closing," ("4am is that the time, space movement of / a womb, a labyrinth that cozens time, / Is it space that sculptures a caress of the sphere"). He concludes, "peristalsis accelerating or stopping, viscera squirming or tightening in spasms, secretions suddenly increasing or lessening — as if the nervous system itself was in a state of indecision," ("Still, all is still, yet, I hear scampering over the roof the black the black, / Still, all is still. / Outer. Inner, no definite view of the whole"). "Tick-Tock" is my fifteen year-old self's self-analysis of the organized chaos of migraines, their hallucinatory effects ("antediluvian bird haunts"), their dream quality — this could be a daymare with its, in Sacks' terminology, "feelings of dread, horror, paralysis and duration," ("Doors closed, open to the darkness," "I hear scampering over the roof the black the black," "Without Within motionless space" and "Inner models of timeless hours.").

Let us turn to the last two sentences of Dr Gross' letter to Dr Aswani, "I think there is probably a migrainous basis for some of his headaches, but he is clearly also tense and it may well be that the tension is playing a considerable part in the genesis of his headaches. I have arranged for him to have one or two tests and have given him a supply of Librium to take 5 mgms TDS." And scribbled on the bottom right in pen, "PS X-ray of skull negative." He had already mentioned that I was "readily uptight," and I was. I actively enjoyed getting into fights but this also brought on depression, yet again signs of a migrainous genesis, as Sacks explains, "Feelings of depression will be associated with feelings of anger and resentment, and in the severest migraines there may exist a very ugly mixture of despair, fury and loathing everything and everyone, not excluding the self." This was 1976, not the overmedicating Nineties and Noughties, so I was shocked that he had prescribed Librium, a benzodiazepine used as a sedative for people suffering from anxiety and stress. It is now used to treat "new daily persistent headache" syndrome, first diagnosed in 1986, which mimics chronic migraine and chronic tension-type headache. Librium is also used to manage alcohol-withdrawal syndrome but, at the age of fifteen, I was only drinking two bottles of Newcastle Brown a night and maybe a Party Four at the weekends.

Five milligrams of Librium (TDS) three times daily to treat my chaotic state of equilibrium and disequilibrium. The X-ray of my skull was negative, which I take to mean that they found no fractures or tumours and therefore no physiological reason for my headaches. So Dr Gross had ruled out a neurological and a physiological reason for the excessive pain I was experiencing on a daily basis. What I do remember is the feeling of lightness and clarity in the period after I had vomited, and I used these occasions to write. Sacks states, "Thus it will be possible for us to approach a migraine not only as a physical event, but as a particular form of symbolic drama into which the patient has translated important thoughts and feelings; if we do this we will then be faced with the task of interpreting it as we would interpret a dream, i.e. discovering the hidden meaning of the manifest symptoms." The act of vomiting, a primitive rejective reflex, led to a state of bliss, a state which Nietzsche also experienced, as he wrote in *Ecce Homo* about the composition of *Daybreak* (1881): "The consummate brightness and cheerfulness, even exuberance of spirit which this same work reflects can coexist in me not only with the most profound physiological debility, but even with an excessive feeling of pain. Amid the torments brought on by three days of unremitting headache accompanied by the arduous vomiting of phlegm, I possessed a dialectician's clarity par excellence and very cold-bloodedly thought through things for which, in healthier circumstances, I am not enough of a climber, not cunning, not cold enough." I do not remember taking the Librium, maybe I sold it to my friends, but the migraines stopped the next year and there are no further mentions of headaches and no repeat prescriptions for it. The dark pages continue but they are now spidered with Dr Aswani's inky scrawl, mysterious acronyms — BOR, occult alphanumeric formulations — T974 p/65 and gnomic pronouncements "Bad that birthday." Birthday again.

There are various other notes: one from Ashford Hospital accident and emergency department on 19 January, 1979. I can't decipher the handwriting but I remember fracturing my wrist while working backstage at Richmond Theatre. I was drunk and fell off the back of a chair, snapping my hand back as I hit the floor. I went home after work and woke in the morning in agony. I am not sure this is what Nancy had in mind but "along with this excrescence comes the always possible imminence of a fracture and of a spontaneous outpouring of the word itself from veins of sense, where it was circulating with other words. Body, like a piece of bone, a pebble, a stone, a granule, falls right where we need it," and my body seemed to fall right where and when I didn't need it. It had become a piece of bone that broke and fractured, a pebble that didn't skip across glassine lakes, a stone that was kicked along streets, a granule that became stuck in the teeth of the world.

In July of that year, the note reports, "Respiratory catarrh and infection," and in August, "Lifting today, strained back, part locked." If I wasn't coughing and wheezing, I was grumbling and groaning. In 1980, there are notes on more back strains and sore tendons (not sure where). In 1981, I find "vomiting bile and a little blood," but that could have been due to the copious amounts of speed and cocaine I was consuming at the time.

In 1982, in fear of my girlfriend leaving me because of the drug taking and the drinking, I moved to Liverpool to be with her, fostering an idea of going to university. The first two notes from my new doctor in Liverpool read, "25/01/83. Chesty cough and generalized difficulty of breathing, asthma/bronchitis." And "27/06/83. Wheezing. Cough. Shallow and scattered breath." Well, that's what it looks like. Followed by prescriptions for Ventolin inhalers. I was twenty-two years old, I knew my body and its illnesses and accidents more intimately, more anatomically, than the majority of men my age. I had experimented with most illegal drugs that were available: marijuana, speed, LSD, cocaine and heroin. I was a nascent alcoholic and worked hard at my potential. I was about to begin university in September 1983 to read English Language and Literature and, apart from a few notes on Ventolin prescriptions, there are no records for the period up until I left university in 1989.

I do not recall being ill in that six-year period, apart from an ear infection in 1986 when sitting my finals. I remember it being particularly severe while I was revising for the exam on Chaucer. I also remember that the pain, intense and deep, while it affected my balance, focused my studies. Tuned me in to life. "Hem wolde he sleen in torment and in payne." I couldn't go out to the pub, I couldn't hear my flatmates when they spoke to me, I couldn't reply because I had no idea how quietly or loudly I was speaking. I became a revision machine — as Deleuze and Guattari put it, "The issue is no longer to adapt, even under violence, but to localize: Where is your place? Even handicaps can be made useful, instead of being corrected or compensated for. A deaf-mute can be an essential part of a 'humans-machines' communicational system." That was me. The violence of the pain localized my thought into a communication system of theories on the works of Geoffrey Chaucer.

Alphonse Daudet, in his exquisitely tormented *In the Land of Pain* (1930), opens his confessions about suffering from syphilis — and the attendant medical treatments — with the tag "Suffering is instructive." He follows with what might have been one of my conversations with a friend or girlfriend, "'What are you doing at the moment?' 'I'm in pain.'" I was always in pain, whether from not being able to breathe or from some ache and soreness from an injury or an infection. But these moments of affliction and discomfort had allowed me to read and to think, to draw and to write. But did they? As the horrific effects of the disease worsened, Daudet revised his own thoughts on pain and suffering, questioning, "Are words actually any use to describe what pain (or passion, for that matter) really feels like? Words only come when everything is over, when things have calmed down. They refer only to memory, and are either powerless or untruthful. No general theory about pain. Each patient discovers his own, and the nature of pain varies, like a singer's voice, according to the acoustics of the hall." That's very good.

Pain changes like the sun on water; asthma pain is different from ear-infection pain is different from migraine pain is different from pancreatitis pain. Maybe words only came after the pain, not during. As with work written under the effects of LSD or heroin, the revisited pages are mostly gibberish, sentimental, irrational (sometimes all three). As each writer discovers their own style, however much they struggle and suffer with the anxiety of influence, patients locate their own pain thresholds under the influence (or not) of medication. Daudet points out that, "Pain is always new to the sufferer, but loses its originality for those around him. Everyone will get used to it except me." However much we try, we cannot describe pain to others. It is unfortunate that doctors do not have Mr Spock's telepathic mind meld to experience the pain of the patient first-hand, and we have all wished our hospital visitors could, just for ten seconds, have an idea of the hurt we are going through. Towards the end of his syphilis notebooks, Daudet concludes, "Pain blots out the horizon, fills everything. I've passed the stage where illness brings any advantage, or helps you understand things; also the stage where it sours your life, puts a harshness in your voice, makes every cogwheel shriek. Now there's only a hard, stagnant, painful torpor, and an indifference to everything. *Nada! ... Nada! ...*"

Daudet came to see disease and pain as anti-creative, almost disembodied, the "indifference" is also pain's indifference. If we think of Daudet and of Kahlo, Welch and D.H. Lawrence, as Elaine Scarry notes in *The Body In Pain*, "Perhaps only in the prolonged and searing pain caused by accident or by disease or by the breakdown of the pain pathway itself is there the same brutal senselessness as in torture." And she agrees with Daudet that "it is the intense pain that destroys a person's self and world, a destruction experienced spatially as either the contraction of the universe down to the immediate vicinity of the body or as the body swelling to fill the entire universe. Intense pain is also language-destroying: as the content of one's world disintegrates, so the content of one's language disintegrates; as the self disintegrates, so that which would express and project the self is robbed of its source and it subject." ·

Heute ist Immer Noch, it reads on the back of the painting — Today still goes on. After a year of pain, operations and medication, Kahlo painted *Self-Portrait in a Velvet Dress* in late September 1926; it was her first exploration of her self through paint, the primary portrayal of her role as woman, artist and subject, the mirror gaze of her ongoing torment through a fixed and steely stare — a reflection on reflection. A year earlier, on 17 September, 1925, eighteen year-old Frida and her boyfriend, Alejandro Gómez Arias, were riding a bus through the centre of Mexico City on the way to her home in the suburb of Coyoacán.

Rain had misted the windows of the buildings around el Zócalo and they looked like they were melting as the young bus driver hurtled through the busy streets, dodging horse-drawn wagons, automobiles, bicycles and brightly coloured trolley cars sporting adverts for cigarettes and a new brand of beer called Corona. Frida and Alex were seated on a bench that ran along the interior sides of the bus, they had been to the market stalls where they had bought a candy-striped *balero* and a parasol, which Frida had subsequently lost, and were sitting together chatting about school, their friends, literature and art. Other *Chilangos* rode the bus: a woman with her shopping basket, a man in blue overalls holding a ratchet seated next to an indigenous woman suckling her baby under a shawl, while a young boy looked out of the window at the ebb and flow of the city's traffic. There was an American, who resembled Buster Keaton, wearing a suit and hat and clutching a bag of money, sat on one side of Frida who, at this age, was wearing typical 1920s fashion: a pale dress cinched with a belt, blue stockings, black heels and a flowing scarf the colour of a coyote — or so the 1929 painting *The Bus* depicts.

It was an average day among ordinary people, however socially allegorical the painting may be, and the passengers were unaware of the trolley car bearing down on them just outside the entrance to the San Juan market. Although moving slowly, the two-car electric trolley broadsided the wooden-clad bus, the momentum crushing it against a wall. The concertinaed vehicle imploded, causing glass, large splinters and metal framework to cut through flesh and bone, to penetrate and impale, to maim and kill. Someone on the bus must have been carrying a bag of gold powder — the figure of the *gringo* with his bag of money — because the mangled scene was covered in the stuff, blood mixed with gold, just like the red velvet dress Frida is wearing in the 1926 self-portrait, as if her flesh had been turned inside out, gold brocade on a bruise-coloured background, her skin pale from a year of hospital stays and enforced bed rest, the melancholy sea/sky behind as solid as the wall the bus had struck, a wisp of a cloud in the top right corner, an awareness of expiration used as inspiration.

A metal handrail had lanced Frida, entering through her left hip, shattering her pelvis, penetrating her abdomen and exiting through her vagina; "the way a sword pierces a bull" is how Hayden Herrera describes it in her biography *Frida* (1983). Somehow all of her clothes had been stripped off and she lay on the glass-littered pavement covered in blood and gold, while people surrounded her, some in shock, some trying to help the dying teenager, others crying "*La bailarina! La bailarina!*" Little did they know what had happened to her body — not just in the aftermath of the crash — but twelve years earlier, when she was just six years old, when her pain first began, when she realized that her imagination could create a world within which she could investigate and manipulate her peculiar self-obsession.

We'll leave Frida stretched out on the billiard table to which she has been carried, her naked body now covered by her boyfriend's coat, her screams drowning out the approaching ambulance siren, the offending handrail, pulled free of her broken body by an unknown man, lies glistening on the pavement, and let's leap forward in time to Friday, 7 June, 1935, to Brighton Road, running through the small village of Hooley, where a twenty year-old artist is cycling from his home in Crooms Hill, Greenwich, to Leigh in Surrey to visit his aunt and uncle. It's mid-afternoon, the sun paints liquid light on the road, and with the smells of the surrounding countryside in his flared nostrils, Denton Welch is about to experience his own particular traffic accident.

Born in Shanghai on 29 March, 1915, Maurice Denton Welch lived in China until he was nine years old, when he was sent to England to attend school. Most of his childhood was spent travelling between China and England, visiting his parents' luxury house in Shanghai (his mother died in 1927) and back to a number of preparatory and boarding schools, like Repton School in Derbyshire, which he attended from 1929 to 1933. Denton came from a wealthy mercantile family, and he and his two older brothers (another — Tommy — had died when a child) were expected to work in their father's business; however, Denton had other plans.

In April 1933, he started a three-year course at the Goldsmith School of Art in New Cross, London, where he took lessons in printmaking, graphic design, still life, figure drawing, perspective and anatomy, refining his artistic skills and his interest in antiques, architecture and art history. At the start of the summer holidays in 1935, Denton left his rooms in Greenwich and rode across Blackheath on his way to pay a surprise visit to his aunt and uncle who lived in the village of Leigh in Surrey, his uncle was the vicar there. The journey would encompass many of Denton's hobbies; bicycling, travel, art — he sketched church architecture, did brass and stone rubbings and had an interest in funerary art. He also had chance meetings with strangers — two nuns who, rather than genuflecting before a cross in a Roman Catholic church, looked like they were about to be spanked for their sins and a couple of giggling tea-room waitresses in an eighteenth-century house in Beckenham — self-conscious of his frizzy hair, large forehead and pigeon-egg eyes, and not comfortable in the presence of young women, Denton's paranoia insisted that the young women must be laughing at him.

After strolling through the house, imagining how he would redecorate it, maybe have a mural on one of the walls, a version of the fantastical botanical painting he was working on at the time, one of his giant flowers having eaten the giggling girls — Denton had a love of horror — he wheeled his bike onto the main road and cycled towards Bromley. Although Denton was a seasoned cyclist, he usually stuck to country lanes and paths; he was not used to busy traffic-laden roads, and so stuck close to the verge. Careful yet day-dreaming of afternoon tea, he pedalled on as cars overtook him. Did he wobble and fall into the road as he fantasized about Earl Grey and scones? Did a flash of sunlight blind him momentarily, causing him to swerve in front of a car? Or did a vehicle clip him as it accelerated past, throwing him from his bicycle, the back wheel rolling over his body, crushing his bones and organs? Whatever happened during that traffic accident, the effects of it would make Denton into a writer; he would use the pain, immobility, memory and bitterness to write journals from which he would create his novels — *Maiden Voyage* (1943), *In Youth Is Pleasure* (1985) and *A Voice Through a Cloud* (1950) — the chronicle of his accident and its aftermath.

Denton's pyjamas littered the road, his toothbrush nestled in the grassy verge, his favourite ivory comb chipped and glinting in the sunlight. Somewhere between consciousness and oblivion, with great Turneresque clouds pulsing through his brain, Denton heard a voice, a policeman's voice. Or was it a surgeon? Was he about to perform a ritual operation? Was Denton dying? Was he being born? In some ways, both. Maybe it was a hallucination caused by trauma, a figure of Denton's fertile imagination. Slowly, the voice became more distinct. It was a policeman and he was asking Denton questions: What was his name? Where did he live? Where was he going? Denton tried to answer but he couldn't, the clouds had become a storm of pain and sickness, of blood and urine. He spoke in a glossolalia of hurt and fear as the uncomprehending policeman summoned an ambulance.

The hit-and-run car had caused extensive bruising to most of his body, a broken ankle, a fracture of the spine — like Frida, Denton was paralysed from the chest down for three months and had to wear an orthopaedic cast, trauma to the bladder had caused an infection that had spread to his kidneys. The complications from these injuries and infections caused headaches, high blood pressure, haemorrhages and partial impotence. In 1948, four years before he died as a result of his injuries, Denton wrote in one of his journals in his characteristic bittersweet prose, "Nothing can make up for the fact that my very early youth was so clouded with illness and unhappiness. I feel cheated as if I had never had that fiercely thrilling time when the fears of childhood have left one and no other thing has swamped one."

While on holiday, fifteen year-old Orville Pym — Denton's fictional double in *In Youth Is Pleasure* — buys a Chinese saucer from an antique and junk shop, it is decorated with pomegranates, rococo red foliage and has funereal mantling surrounding an "incongruous European coat of arms." The object costs him sixpence because it is cracked. Likewise Denton Welch, whose broken body sprawls on the roadside waiting to be transported to Lewisham Hospital. Over the next thirteen years, Denton would attempt to heal his injuries through writing and painting, like a piece of Kintsugi — broken Japanese pottery fixed with gold, silver, or platinum — he used writing as a precious metal (mettle) to burnish his memory and to gild his experience and observations.

Ten years and thousands of miles apart, two ambulance sirens compete in an intercontinental Doppler-effect war as they race towards our fictional hospital. The hospital is new, state-of-the-art, postmodern. And it is ancient, rudimentary, pre-anaesthetic. Its doctors are sawbones, quacks, croakers and butchers, and they are neurosurgeons, anaesthesiologists, oncologists, urologists — François Rabelais and Sir Thomas Browne, Henry Vaughan and John Keats, Friedrich von Schiller and Tobias Smollett, Georg Büchner and Louis-Ferdinand Céline, Anton Chekhov and Mikhail Bulgakov, John William Polidori and W. Somerset Maugham, William Carlos Williams and Walker Percy, Stanisław Lem and Leonid Tsypkin — all resplendent in their starched white coats. And the waiting nursing staff range from Phoebe to Florence Nightingale to Catherine Barkley to Hana caring for her lone English patient. There are male nurses also, including one who calls himself The Wound-Dresser and recites his poetry as he moves from ward to ward, Walt Whitman.

The ambulances are approaching; the nurses and care staff ready the beds in the intensive care units and the orthopaedic wards. The surgeons and anaesthetists don their personal protective equipment. Scalpels, scissors, forceps, pliers, clamps, mallets, chisels, retractors, rongleurs and suction tubes glisten under the overhead lights. Frida and Denton, semi-conscious, morphine coursing through their veins attempting to dull the pain, trying to silence the over-excitable nerve cells. Their splintered bones, their riven skin, their pierced vaginas, their paralytic bladders. Neither of them know it yet but these traffic accidents will change their lives, transform them into artists, creativity born from near-death experiences, their future subject matter appearing in an instant of pain and horror, affecting their lives, their art and their sexuality as only J.G. Ballard could describe in his novel *Crash*, "These wounds formed the key to a new sexuality, born from a perverse technology. The images of these wounds hung in the gallery of his mind, like exhibits in the museum of a slaughterhouse." But wait, there are three beds readied in the wards. Frida and Denton will make strange ward mates, but who will be the third who will convalesce beside them?

Nobody really knows what happened. As with most things in this man's life, events are not so much shrouded in clichéd mystery but wrapped in layers of self-mythology, inauthenticity, others employed to shield and to dissemble, to misdirect and to muddy. There are facts, of course there are, so let us begin with those because, when the fame kicks in, the records begin to resemble multi-layered deposits of story, lies and near truths that require the skills of an analytical archaeologist.

Born in Duluth, Minnesota, on 24 May, 1941, Robert Allen Zimmerman spent his childhood in the iron-mining town of Hibbing. In *Chronicles: Volume One* (2004), he describes how he lived amongst "gravel roads, marshlands, hills of ice, steep skylines of trees on the outskirts of town, thick forests, pristine lakes large and small, iron mine pits, trains and one-lane highways." He grew up doing the things most boys do: riding bikes, swimming, fishing, shooting BB guns, he went to drive-in movies with his family, to stock-car races, to carnivals and freak shows, to country and western concerts, all the while biding his time, waiting for a move to the city, first to the Twin Cities of Minneapolis-St Paul and then on to New York City.

He had spent his late teenage years performing folk songs in coffeehouses and busking the streets solo and with others. After a musical apprenticeship singing Woody Guthrie songs, he hitchhiked east and arrived in New York City in January 1961. He was not quite twenty years old and later that year recorded his first album, *Bob Dylan*, on Columbia Records in March 1962. Over the next four years, Dylan became prophet, poet and politician of the nascent counterculture, a turned-on protest singer who, at the 1965 Newport Folk Festival had discarded his double-O Martin acoustic guitar for a sunburst Fender Stratocaster, prompting accusations of being a traitor. A year later, on 19 July, 1966, Dylan was gunning his 1964, 500cc Triumph Tiger 100 motorcycle along Striebel Road just outside of Woodstock, New York. It was a warm day, the sun glinted off the red and silver petrol tank, a breeze barely ruffled the trees and Dylan's unkempt hair. He was on his way to his home in West Saugherties — or to have his motorcycle serviced — after visiting his manager Albert Grossman in Bearsville to discuss the details of yet more tours, yet more demands on Dylan's time, patience and privacy. Or was he on his way to score some heroin, as rumours of his addiction would have us believe? Did he hit a patch of oil? Did his brakes lock? Did, as playwright and actor Sam Shepard states, the sun get in his eyes? Whatever happened threw him from his bike, he landed on the baking road, he had injured his neck and cut his face. For the past four years, Dylan had lived the life of a gold and platinum and double-platinum rock star, he had toured unceasingly, most recently in the UK, and had, at the age of twenty-five, written some of the most iconic and influential songs of the early Sixties, "Blowin' in the Wind," "A Hard Rain's a-Gonna Fall," "The Times They Are a-Changin'," "Subterranean Homesick Blues," "Mr Tambourine Man" and "Like a Rolling Stone" among them.

Unlike the accidents of Kahlo and Welch, which had profoundly affected them physically, psychologically and artistically, Dylan's motorcycle nightmare was minor, his injuries negligible, if they ever really existed, if the crash had ever actually happened, if it wasn't a means by which to escape the demands that celebrity placed on the young singer-songwriter. But let's agree with the scant facts and focus on what did and didn't happen that sunny afternoon near a town that, three years later, would mark the end of nearly a decade of radical art and politics with a concert by musicians that included Dylan's close friend Joan Baez and his old backing group The Band.

Why didn't his wife, Sara Lowndes, who was following the bike in her car, call an ambulance? Some reports say that he was attended to at Middletown Hospital, over an hour's drive away, but there are no records of him being treated there. So, while our drivers waited in the ambulance station at our hospital — Ernest Hemingway working out with his punch bag, Harry Crosby studying his new tattoo and Jean Cocteau sketching the pair of them — we have to wonder why their services were not called for, why Bob Dylan never went to hospital and why that spare bed along from Frida and Denton will, for the time being, remain empty?

Most of Dylan's biographers believe that he was taken to his personal doctor's surgery. Ed Thaler lived in Middletown, so that may clear up that part of the mystery. He convalesced for a few days and Grossman was forced to cancel scheduled tours and recordings. Subsequently, Dylan had ultrasound treatment, wore a neck brace and claimed to have chronic back pain. Dylan stated in *Chronicles*, "I had been in a motorcycle accident and I'd been hurt, but I recovered. Truth was that I wanted to get out of the rat race. Having children changed my life and segregated me from just about everybody and everything that was going on. Outside of my family, nothing held any real interest for me and I was seeing everything through different glasses," and later elaborated in a 1984 interview in *Rolling Stone*, "When I had that motorcycle accident… I woke up and caught my senses, I realized that I was just working for all these leeches. And I really didn't want to do that." So how did this change Dylan's life? Did it transform his music, his politics and his view of the world, as Frida and Denton's accidents had changed theirs? Was it a transmigration of the body through suffering? Or was it another false chapter in the self-mythological journey that is the Bobyssey or its attendant volume of secrecy and media warfare — the Dylan-ad?

In Philip Roth's novel *Nemesis*, the teacher Bucky Cantor explains that "Polio is polio — nobody knows how it spread. Summer comes and there it is, and there's nothing much you can do." Set in 1944, *Nemesis* explores the effects of a polio epidemic on the inhabitants of Newark, New Jersey. Polio, as Roth points out, is "a paralytic disease that left a youngster permanently disabled and deformed or unable to breathe outside a cylindrical metal respirator tank known as an iron lung — or that could lead from paralysis of the respiratory muscles to death." This occurs in the worst cases and, back in 1944, fear was intensified because the medical world was unsure how the disease spread within communities and caused localized epidemics; there was no medicine to control it, no vaccine to prevent it and although it seemed to target young people, it also affected other age groups — Franklin Delano Roosevelt became a victim at the age of thirty-nine.

Did mosquitoes and flies spread the disease? Or stray cats and dogs? The polluted miasma that settles on cities during the summer months? Poor sewage and drainage systems? Was it spread in the water? Over-exertion, sweat, sharing drinking fountains, dirty clothes? Was it passed on by Italians? Jews? The poor? Did it come from infected milk, hot dogs, pigs or even dollar bills? No one knew. Theories and conspiracies spread as fast as the disease. In the period the novel covers, the epidemic is small compared to the 1916 infestation of Newark in which there were 1,360 cases and 363 deaths, a contribution to the wider total of over 27,000 cases and 6,000 deaths in north-eastern America. We know now that poliovirus is transmitted through ingesting infectious faeces and, in some cases through salival transfer. It causes influenza-like symptoms and infection of the gastrointestinal organs. The vast majority of people who are infected by the virus recover with no serious after effects. Paralytic polio occurs in a small number of cases when the virus invades and inflames the central nervous system, resulting initially in muscular pains, headaches, problems with defecation and urination, stiffness and the deterioration of reflexes. The virus may then cause paralysis of the chest and lungs and wasting of muscles and tendons, leading to problems with breathing, swallowing and the withering of limbs.

In George McKay's essay, "Crippled with nerves: popular music and polio, with particular reference to Ian Dury" in *Popular Music* (2009), he records how five years after the polio epidemic Roth chronicles in *Nemesis*, a seven year-old boy contracted the disease, possibly from swimming in an open-air pool in Southend-on-Sea. From 1949 to 1954, after spending five months in full body plaster, he recuperated in various hospitals and schools for the disabled but had to wear callipers in his atrophied right leg and was subsequently bullied and teased. Ian Dury went on to become a successful New Wave musician in the late 1970s, 80s, and 90s, and died of colorectal cancer in 1996. He campaigned for equal rights for the disabled and the eradication of polio, and did so through music that mixed punk-jazz and pub rock with lyrics that fused trauma with comedy.

Dury used his disability as inspiration, as a means of shocking the public into the realization of false body imagery manifested in the media, as a way of confronting the physical and sexual abuse prevalent in institutions such as schools, hospitals and care homes. During the early 1960s, Dury attended Walthamstow College of Art, where one of his fellow students was the artist and director Peter Greenaway, among their tutors was the artist Peter Blake. And from Dury's polio,

Greenaway's filmic disquisition on the erotics of amputation and Peter Blake's pop art we can "by a commodius vicus of recirculation" return to the Mexico City suburb of Coyoacán, where a six year-old Frida Kahlo is in a darkened room struck down with polio.

It is 1913, three years before the 1916 epidemic in the north-eastern United States, and the once vibrant and cheeky schoolgirl is now confined to her bed, her body wasted after nine months' confinement. The symptoms started with a pain in her right leg, which her doctors and parents washed in walnut water and wrapped in hot towels. This enforced solitude turned her thoughts inward; no longer could she play outside in the garden, ride her bike, explore the gardens, so she created or "experienced" an imaginary friend, someone who could maintain the narration of an outer life, a double. Frida created this childhood doppelgänger by breathing on a window, drawing a door in the vapour and escaping through it to visit her imaginary friend. The window was her first canvas, her finger the brush, her breath the paint, the subject matter — her double as it would remain in her paintings throughout her life.

The polio had atrophied and shortened Frida's right leg, and she underwent courses of physiotherapy. She wore clothes that covered her lower body in an attempt to stop the bullies calling her "peg leg," but still rode bicycles. To help with her convalescence, she joined in sports as she had done before contracting polio. But the virus had changed her; although she played with her friends, scored goals in soccer matches, boxed with the bullies and won first prize at swim meets, she had replaced the outside world with a core inner space and her friends with an imaginary companion. The door from her home to the streets and parks of Coyoacán had metamorphosed into a transient and erasable entrance to a fantastic world where she could exist without pain, without the constant trauma of surgery, where seconds were thousands of years and where her portraits and landscapes were particularly Kahlo-esque.

The trauma suffered as a six year-old and then again as an eighteen year-old doubled Frida's incentive to use her suffering as subject matter, but also to extend her loneliness and solitude to a perfect double, where her always imminent and immanent destruction is sublimated by a being-out-of the-world with whom she is able to produce representations of her inner turmoil as visual art, and where she experiences care and concern — she creates a "they" — to distance herself, observe, interrogate and produce, and to confide and dissolve in.

Painted in the last months of 1939, *The Two Fridas* was completed in December on the day Frida received a letter documenting the details of her divorce from Diego Rivera. They had been married for ten tempestuous years and they remarried a year later in 1940. The largest of Frida's paintings, 173.5 x 173 cm, *The Two Fridas* is a double self-portrait fusing traditional Mexican art, naïve art and Surrealism — she had recently visited Paris and been championed by André Breton (one of our doctor-poets). The painting was to be shown at the International Exhibition of Surrealism in Mexico City in 1940, although Frida rejected the label "surrealist" — her paintings were real and had nothing to do with dreams. The dual Fridas could be two alternative points of the representational — a dream Frida and a real Frida, an imaginary Frida and an authentic Frida, a Mexican Frida and a Western Frida, or they could be Frida and Frida, the double Frida locked inside, now shown beside herself, like an impossible matryoshka doll. But which one fits inside which?

The two Fridas sit side by side on a bench, like lovers, they hold hands as if about to exchange vows, Frida might now

be separated from Diego Rivera but she will never be parted
from her double. The Frida on the observer's left wears an
old-fashioned white dress with a lace bodice and embroidered
flowers and birds around its hem. The Frida on the right
wears a traditional Tehuana dress and holds in her left hand
a small oval portrait of Rivera — Diego also as double — as
child, as lover and as perpetual man-infant. But what is that
in the symmetrically opposite right hand of Frida in the white
dress? If we look closely, we see that it is a haemostat, surgical
forceps used by doctors to control bleeding. But some of the
blood has dripped on to Left-Frida's white dress, indicating loss
of (or the regaining of) her virginity (see the imagery of the
1946 painting *The Little Deer* and the virgin myths of the white
hart), of the numerous operations she had undergone in that
region of her body, of abortions and miscarriages. When we
look more closely at the flowers and birds, we see that these
too are made from blood, regardless of the fact that we want
them to represent nature, freedom and beauty, not blood
vessels, arteries and veins. If we look back at the egg-shaped
portrait of Rivera we can see that something extends from it
and rises up Frida's body. The picture is positioned directly just
above Frida's womb, wraps around her left arm and enters a
heart — what is shocking about this painting is that the heart
is depicted outside of Frida's body and is massive and red and
pumping. It is not a Disney heart, the heart of Valentine's cards
or the tree engravings of lovers; no, this is an anatomically
correct (if oversized) heart with its subclavian arteries, vena
cavas, atriums, ventricles, septum and aorta. It's palpable,
one can almost hear it beat, its brachiocephalic and carotid
artery reach up towards Frida's mouth as if to give voice to
its life and strength. This is a heart out of Leonardo da Vinci's
anatomical sketches rather than Jim Dine's pop-art scribbles;
this is the anatomist Andreas Vesalius rather than Hallmark.

The artery emanating from the oval (ovarial) portrait of Rivera takes blood from this pumping heart across the divide between the two Fridas, across the backdrop of a stormy sky with its black and grey clouds, around Left-Frida's lace-ensconced neck and bifurcates, one branch leading down into her lap where it is clamped by the haemostat, the other feeding yet another disembodied heart. But this is not a large, red, pumping muscle of a heart; this one is broken and decaying, its ventricles ripped apart as is the lace bodice surrounding it. The two Fridas sit impassive as one heart feeds another in order to maintain it — the clamped artery is the end of a recycling motion, the blood pumping back into the broken heart and back into the healthy heart and down again to re-energize the idea of Diego Rivera: the abortion of a husband, the miscarriage of love and fidelity, while all the time the splashed blood creates its own artworks, its own portraits.

Bones, blood and organs are common in Kahlo's paintings: the hearts of *The Two Fridas* (1939); the devastated spine in *The Broken Column* (1944); the blood in *Henry Ford Hospital* (1943) and *A Few Small Nips* (1935); the skeletons in *Four Inhabitants of Mexico* (1938), *The Wounded Table* (1940) and *The Dream* (1940); the abortions and miscarriages in *Frida and the Abortion* (1932) and *My Birth* (1932), which resembles a fusion of Max Ernst's *Men Shall Know Nothing of This* (1923) — on the back of which he had written, "The picture is curious because of its symmetry. The two sexes balance one another" — and Francis Bacon's *Three Studies of Figures on Beds* (1972). The viscera and vomit of *Without Hope* (1945) portrays Frida in her sick bed, in tears and gushing forth a great font of blood, slabs of meat, chickens, sheep, fish, sausages, brains and a *calavera* — a decorated sugar skull. The vomited objects, representing the horrors of her body and the aftermath of surgery, hang over the easel suspended above her bed that

Frida used to paint her pictures on while incapacitated, but it is also the fragile frame of her bones upon which are hung slabs of scarred and diseased meat.

Frida painted *Without Hope* in 1945, the year her health worsened; she had severe pains in her foot and spine, contracted a dose of syphilis, had a number of blood transfusions and spinal taps, been encased in plaster corsets for months at a time and had undergone more surgery. Both *The Two Fridas* and *Without Hope* externalize trauma, both physical and psychological; Frida becomes the observed and the observer, the subject and the artist, the broken person reflected in a perfect canvas, the dying animal transformed into an immortal work of art. Pathology as another form of narcissism. The outward gaze of the artist is also an inward gaze, all painting, all poetry, all novels, all symphonies and three-minute punk songs are versions of Basil Hallward's portrait of Dorian Gray. It can be argued that all artists are pathological narcissists. And we will encounter more of them.

Published in 1944, a year after Frida painted *Without Hope*, Denton Welch wrote in *In Youth Is Pleasure*, "Then suddenly he had a vision of the river flowing swiftly beneath the old toll bridge. It was swollen with the filth of ten thousand cities, sweat, excrement, blood, pus poured through the stone arches. The filth curled into marble patterns, streaked into horrible arabesques." This is a fantastical memory from a childhood holiday but could also be the hellish landscape of a hospital ward in *A Voice Through a Cloud,* the one in Lewisham Hospital in which Denton found himself after the road accident "as raw as a piece of butcher's meat." The ward in which nurses as "stern and unbending as Roman matrons" refused to believe his bladder was bursting and he was relieved only when a male nurse fitted a catheter. Shocked at the man touching his penis,

Denton soon forgot this transgression when he was finally able to urinate. Morphine calmed him but not for long. His body had cuts and grazes all over it, particularly on his chest and groin, and these were covered with bloody dressings, some soaked in iodine. One of the nurses, it seemed to Denton, relished ripping them off.

From ankle to knee, Denton's left leg had been splinted and wrapped in bandages. The nurse unwound the material and Denton saw a plum, mustard and cerulean leg appear, the ankle swollen immensely, the flesh yielding "in just the way that a wine jelly yields to the pressure of a spoon." In the X-ray department, Denton soils himself and throws the offending "pellet" out of the window. He fears that he is incontinent. Wheeled back through the hospital after the X-ray, Denton witnesses what look like people being tortured but realizes it is his overactive imagination creating scenes more reminiscent of Kafka's "In the Penal Colony."

Back in the ward, Denton has to deal with "other people" and their need for narrative, "What's your story" What's happened to you?" But Denton doesn't feel ready, he "knew nothing was real but pain, heat, blood, tingling, loneliness and sweat." The hallucinogenic imagery of his childhood holiday had become real in the horror of his body and his surroundings; he thought himself disgusting, like all the things he loved, and then the pain sucked him under and he "wanted to die and not be tortured any more."

After a night of pain and sleeplessness, Denton decides to alleviate some of the pain by taking off his bandages, holding the splint tight and in place. He hides the unspooled material under the sheets, momentarily relief from the suffering, the flesh bursting like a burned sausage. After the sister discovers what he has done, he is reprimanded, his leg re-splinted and wrapped in even tighter dressings, he is sedated and "after a little while I began to float away and the pain began to float away, too. I imagined the pain as diamond dew evaporating in the morning sun. This time my mind was filled with the thought of dew; its jewel-like wetness, its faint ghostly steam as it rose and disappeared in the air..." If, as Nick Land states in his essay "Meat (or How to Kill Oedipus in Cyberspace)" (1995), "the machinic unconscious tends only to flee, across a primary-process topography that is shaped by pain-gradients and escape thresholds," then Denton Welch mapped that topography in a lucid and bejewelled prose, using suffering as elucidation and memory as an escape into the present. If pain is the motivator for escape, memory of pain is the motivator to relive that experience through words — again as in Kafka's "In the Penal Colony," Denton as a writer becoming the Officer, the Condemned and the Explorer, torturer, torturee and observer.

Nick Land again: "What registers for the secondary process as memory, experience, data-acquisition, is for the primary process, scarring, damage, sticky micro-softed irritations." Memory is the scream of agony echoing to the present, the body, once turning to black jelly, now not quite whole, re-membering its near liquescence or, as Denton Welch fan William Burroughs puts it in *The Place of Dead Roads* (1983), his novel of a sexual virus sweeping the planet, "In filthy hovels needy Marbles are close to molting, the shell eaten through in patches, pus leaking out... flesh under there has lost all immunity... skin is long gone..." Denton's body brings the suppurating ego to the surface and forces it to gaze back and analyze its fleshy double, the corpse/corpus in Jean-Luc Nancy's words, "Ego forever articulating itself — *hoc, et hoc, et hic, et illic...* — the coming-and-going of bodies: voice, food, excrement, sex, child, air, water, sound, color, hardness, odor, heat, weight, sting, caress, consciousness, memory, swoon, look, appearing — all *touches* infinitely multiplied, all *tones* finally proliferating..." The senses which provide us with our perception of the world are thrown into disarray, the ego oscillates between differing selves, bodily secretions take on their own sentience, the sound of our bodies, the smell of our memories, the "I" looks at itself, its self.

As in the writing of our good doctor Louis-Ferdinand Céline, the use of ellipsis by Welch, Burroughs and Nancy is pathological. The ellipsis is the continual beeping of the medical monitor, not the final full stop, period. In his *Journals*, Denton sees them as points of survival; he says that since his accident, "sweeps of piercing sadness came over me. I was lost in the dark world, in the lighted streets alone, waiting to die…" Burroughs understood this from the moment he killed his wife Joan and through the continuing junk sicknesses — dysentery, haemorrhoids, hepatitis, jaundice, malaria, neuralgia, rheumatism, sciatica, uremic poisoning and intestinal worms. As Dr Benway in *Naked Lunch* (1959) explains, "We could seal up nose and mouth, fill in the stomach, make an air hole direct into the lungs where it should have been in the first place…" And Jean-Luc Nancy, recovering from a heart transplant only to contract a lymphatic cancer from the prescribed drugs, asks in *Corpus*, "Instead, treatments that deport to further strangenesses. They fatigue, they ruin the stomach, or there's the howling pain of shingles… Through it all, what 'me' is pursuing what trajectory?"

The "I" becomes scrambled between the medical event and the period of recovery, the linear movement of a life halts, oscillates, is thrown off course. The ellipsis… marks the pause, the place where things change, the ego freezes and the superego is thrown into disarray as blood, urine, pus and faeces break down inhibitions and prohibitions. In *Journey to the End of Night*, Louis-Ferdinand Céline, through his anti-hero doctor Dr Ferdinand Bardamu, notes: "I was asked to admit a writer… He was cracked… You know what he'd been shouting for over a month? 'They're liquidating!... They're liquidating!...' That's what he was shouting all over the house! He was a case all right. He had crossed over to the far side of the intelligence!... His trouble was that he simply couldn't liquidate... An old stricture was poisoning him with urine, stopping up his bladder... I had to relieve him drop by drop with a catheter... it took hours... But the family insisted that the cause of it all was his genius... I tried my level best to convince them that their writer's trouble was in his bladder, they clung to their idea... that he'd blown his top in a moment of excessive genius... In the end I had to fall in with their opinion... you know what families are like... You'll never get a family to understand that a man, related to them or not, is nothing but suspended putrefaction... No family will pay bills for suspended putrefaction..."

In Frida Kahlo's case, the self, split in two, psychologically (and almost physically) created a double, sometimes perfect, sometimes undergoing trauma in place of the injured Frida. This double immobilized and reified the "suspended putrefaction," enabling the artist to carry on with her compulsive self-referential painting, despite numerous complications and operations, until her death from a pulmonary embolism and/or suicide by painkiller overdose on 13 July, 1954.

Likewise, Denton Welch replaced the artist "I" with the writer "I." Although he continued to use his artistic skills, his crippled bladder, crushed leg and spinal tuberculosis transformed the active painter into a sedentary writer and he became obsessed with re-living his life, the years before the accident, in autobiographical fiction he took from his *Journals*, "I think that the murderous part of writing, the trying to force thought into a form that can be shared by others, is something that one shirks and turns away from with sick distaste in the morning. But it will never stop gnawing. There is always the longing to put the thoughts into the crude mincing machine." The mincing machine is the car, the operating theatre, the memory. This mincing creates liquidation and its reformation into something solid — a novel, a painting — before putrefaction begins.

Burroughs writes in the introduction to his autobiographical novel *Queer* (1985): "I am forced to the appalling conclusion that I would never have become a writer but for Joan's death, and to a realization of the extent to which this event has motivated and formulated my writing. I live with the constant threat of possession, and a constant need to escape from possession, from Control. So the death of Joan brought me in contact with the invader, the Ugly Spirit, and manoeuvred me into a lifelong struggle, in which I have had no choice except to write my way out." I am forced to the appalling conclusion that Kahlo and Welch would never have become the artist and writer we know without the automotive accidents and the extreme trauma they both suffered. They lived with the constant threat of an early death — Denton Welch died at 2pm on 30 December, 1948 at the age of thirty-three — both Frida and Denton required painkillers throughout their short lives, both transformed their lives into art and used trauma and pain as tools of creativity.

As Burroughs continues: "I have constrained myself to escape death. Denton Welch is almost my face. Smell of old coins. Whatever happened to this knife called Allerton, back to the appalling Margaras Inc. The realization is basic formulated **doing**? The day of Joan's doom and loss. Found tears streaming down from Allerton peeling off the same person as a Western shootist. **What are you rewriting?** A lifelong preoccupation with Control and Virus. Having gained access the virus uses the host's energy, blood, flesh and bones to make copies of itself. Model of dogmatic insistence never never from without was screaming in my ear, 'YOU DON'T BELONG HERE!'" Frida and Denton had escaped death by rewriting (repainting) copies of themselves, "basic formulated doing." Their "I" screaming "YOU DON'T BELONG HERE!" But resolutely creating new selves through creative will power.

Before we go back to the "trauma" of Dylan's motorbike accident, I'll leave the final words to Frida from her last diary entry:

Thanks to the doctors
Farill - Glusker - Parres
and Doctor Enrique Palomera
Sanchez Palomera.
Thanks to the nurses to the stretcher hearers to the
cleaning women and attendants at the
British Hospital
Thanks to Dr. Vargas
To Navarro to Dr. Polo
And to my will
Power.
I hope the exit is joyful and I hope never to return.
FRIDA

And to Michael De-la-Noy, one of Denton's biographers, "'He had just kept himself alive by will-power,' Eric had said, 'He'd recovered so many times that the only time I realized something was seriously wrong was when I tried to lift him up, and he was a complete dead weight.'"

What exactly happened on that warm summer day in late July 1966 is left open to speculation. Bob Dylan expanded on the details of the accident in a 2012 interview with Mikal Gilmore for *Rolling Stone* but never really explained how the crash happened, where he was taken afterwards, the extent of his injuries or how long it took him to convalesce. What he did say only added more layers — or cloaks — to the Dylan myth, "Transmigration is not what we are talking about. This is something else. I had a motorcycle accident in 1966.1 already explained to you about new and old. Right? Now, you can put this together any way you want. You can work on it any way you want. Transfiguration." Dylan believed he had been transfigured since the accident, that he was a different person from the singer-songwriter of *Highway 61 Revisited* (1965) and *Blonde on Blonde* (1966), that something transcendental and fundamental occurred during and/or after the crash that turned him into the writer of the albums *John Wesley Harding* (1967) and *Nashville Skyline* (1969).

Is it out with the old and in with the new? Or is it an escape from the corporatization of music into a purer form of songwriting? Or is it a desire to find the self after years of being "Bob Dylan." He goes on to explain to the interviewer about a Hells Angel whose name was Bobby Zimmerman and how he died in a motorcycle accident, and reads from a book *The Life and Times of Sonny Barger and the Hell's Angels Motorcycle Club* by Sonny Barger, the two co-authors — Kent and Keith Zimmerman. He says, "I'm not like you, am I? I'm not like him, either. I'm not like too many others. I'm only like another person who's been transfigured. How many people like that or like me do you know?" Dylan puts his transformation down to the accident and the correspondences he found in a book about Hells Angels — the ultimate outsider motorcycle riders.

If his injuries were not as serious as those of Kahlo or Welch, they did mean he could step back from the relentless touring, take time with his writing and contemplate who he was, who he is. In a 1984 interview published in *RE/Search 8:9*, Ballard documents the after effects of an automobile accident as reported in a book about crash injuries: "Because one's dealing with fundamental entities like one's own musculature, one's own sort of highly conventionalized response to one's own body, one's tenancy in time and space, things we take for granted and which are really completely arbitrary. That we are all shaped the way we are is totally arbitrary — a fact we take for granted. Something like a car crash with its various injuries to, say, the face shouldn't be a subject of fascination, nor the opposite (anybody interested in these things is obviously perverted) [...] The human body may crash, so let's look at it anew. Texts like that are a way of seeing the human self anew which is very difficult to do."

Whatever the extent of Dylan's injuries — contemporary reports claimed that it was a near-death experience — it is certain that Dylan suffered cuts to his face, bruising to his back and fractured vertebrae in his neck, had to wear a neck brace and stayed at his doctor's house for six weeks convalescing. He admitted in another *Rolling Stone* interview in September 2013, "I was pretty wound up before that accident happened. I probably would have died if I had kept on going the way I had been."

Did he lock the brakes? Hit an oil patch? Was he just a poor rider? He told the writer Sam Shepard in an interview for *Esquire* in 1987 that "it was real early in the morning on top of a hill near Woodstock. I can't even remember how it happened. I was blinded by the sun for a second... I just happened to look up right smack into the sun with both eyes and, sure enough, I went blind for a second and I kind of panicked or something. I stomped down on the brake and the rear wheel locked up on me and I went flyin'." What happened after the accident caused a reciprocal gaze, the blinding sun becoming an inner core of self-reflective energy. Dylan's injured body, now convalescing, urged him to slow down, to contemplate, in Ballard's words from *Crash*, "the mere existence of our own sort of musculatures, the particular skeletal morphology of the mammal, not to mention the whole vast system of inventions and dampers and blocks and subterfuges of various kinds — elaborate mental languages and visa systems that operate on all sorts of borders of the brain, which is in itself an incredibly elaborate structure — if you could only shine a light through the whole of it, existence would seem as bright as the sun! As shocking as a blast of sunlight, or a blare of noise." Through trauma, mere existence turns into — transforms into — sheer existence, the pre-accident frenetic Bob Dylan, invented, mythologized, dampers and blocks in order to obscure who he really is, becomes the post-accident Bob Dylan, a man who views life as a more personal experience. Having been blinded by the sun and having the trauma of the injuries shine a light through his existence he was, according to *Chronicles*, "seeing everything through different glasses."

Coupled with this transfiguration through trauma, Dylan underwent a period of convalescence and care and he explained to Sam Shepard that he "spent a week in the hospital, then they moved me to this doctor's house in town. In his attic. Had a bed up there in the attic with a window looking out. Sarah stayed there with me. I just remember how bad I wanted to see my kids. I started thinking about the short life of trouble. How short life is. I'd just lay there listening to birds chirping. Kids playing in the neighbour's yard or rain falling by the window. I realized how much I'd missed. Then I'd hear the fire engine roar, and I could feel the steady thrust of death that had been constantly looking over its shoulder at me. (Pause) Then I'd just go back to sleep." This convalescence and care was just as important to Dylan's transfiguration as the trauma and pain. In *The Trouble with Being Born* (I should have stolen that title for this chapter), Cioran states, "Each time you find yourself at a turning-point, the best thing is to lie down and let hours pass. Resolutions made standing up are worthless: they are dictated either by pride or by fear. Prone, we still know these two scourges, but in a more attenuated, more intemporal form." Dylan's ego had time to settle, his fear of death attenuated, the frenzy of time and the claustrophobia of celebrity space became reduced to a bed in an attic.

Convalescence is an overcoming, a will to health, a means to self-critique; if that sounds Nietzschean, then I'm on the right track. As Sarah Mann-O'Donnell argues in her article "From Hypochondria to Convalescence: Health as Chronic Critique in Nietzsche, Deleuze and Guattari" (2010), "This flickering continuum of convalescence between illness and a not yet arrived at health manifests as becoming in Nietzsche, and it is instrumental in his revaluation, in the *Menschliches* preface, of all three terms." The three terms being illness, health and becoming. Or re-becoming, convalescence being the point of transfiguration — the revaluation. For the next eight years, Dylan would undergo a chronic convalescence, he refrained from touring and significantly slowed his album releases. Nietzsche wrote in *Ecce Homo* that through convalescence "I discovered life anew, myself included, I tasted all the good things, even the small ones, as no other could easily taste them — I turned my will to health, to *life*, into my philosophy." Dylan's escape into solitude, however accidental, was a means towards convalescence from the illnesses of his hectic lifestyle (rumours abound of amphetamine and heroin abuse in the months leading up to the crash) and is also a detachment from the "sickness" of the corporate world, the commodification of "Bob Dylan." As Nietzsche further explains, "I need *solitude*, in other words convalescence, a return to myself, the breath of free, light, playful air."

It was after this confinement, a 1960s rock-folk singer's version of Proust's permanent convalescence, that Dylan was able, through the potentialities of health, to re-examine the direction and form of his music. On his way to full recovery from the accident, Dylan spent time over the next two years — 1967 to 1968 — at a house called Big Pink in West Saugerties near Woodstock, recording songs with members of The Band. He had said in a *Rolling Stone* interview in November 1969 that, "I had a dreadful motorcycle accident which put me away for a while, and I still didn't sense the importance of that accident till at least a year after that. I realized that it was a real accident. I mean I thought that I was just gonna get up and go back to doing what I was doing before… but I couldn't do it anymore." He didn't return to the pre-accident Dylan because these jamming sessions were to become *The Basement Tapes*, a legendary collection of cover versions and original songs.

In 1965, as Greil Marcus explains in *The Old, Weird America* (1997), "Bob Dylan seemed less to occupy a turning point in cultural space and time than to be that turning point. As if culture would turn according to his wishes or even his whim; the fact was, for a long moment it did." But that moment was cut short by the accident, by Dylan's withdrawal from a cultural turning point to a personal critical mass in which he underwent a shift in his individuation.

After their accidents, Kahlo and Welch lived lives of pain, they both suffered numerous operations and died years later from complications caused by the initial trauma. Even Dylan's neck still hurts when it's wet and cold because, for all three, for artist, writer and musician, "under the goad of pain, the flesh awakens; lucid and lyrical, it sings its dissolution. So long as it was indistinguishable from nature, it rested in the oblivion of elements: the self had not yet seized upon it. Suffering matter frees itself from gravitation, no longer particles in the universe, isolates itself from the somnolent sum; for pain, an agent of separation, the active principle of individuation, denies the pleasures of a statistical destiny," as Cioran characteristically puts it in *A Short History of Decay* (1949).

All three accidents dissolved the self and reassembled it; the wounds bring awareness, bearing with them an analytical insight, the injured person literally looks inward, within the body, they are now distinguishable from the crowd and seize upon that to isolate themselves from a statistical mass. In a sense, they have defeated destiny, defeated time, and *The Basement Tapes*, as Marcus describes, sucked "everything into itself suffering nothing to exist out of its own, temporal frame of reference — these old-timey albums were bereft of any nostalgia. If they were a look back they were a look that circled back, all the way around to where the singer and whoever might be listening stood."

Kahlo's self-reflective paintings with their pre-Columbian motifs, Welch's obsessive retelling of his childhood, the time before the trauma, a self-mythical world that only reiterates his present self, and Dylan's *Basement Tape* songs, with their dissolution of time and genre, are anti-nostalgic because, writes Cioran, "to live in expectation, in what is not yet, is to accept the stimulation disequilibrium implied by the very notion of the *future*. Every nostalgia is a transcendence of the present. Even in the form of regret, it assumes a dynamic character: we want to force the past, we want to act retroactively, to protest against the irreversible. Life has a content only in the violation of time. The obsession of elsewhere is the impossibility of the moment; and this impossibility is nostalgia itself." Suffering, the permanence of pain, the ongoing trauma, the memory of the accident rules out a defined future and places the self at the always-never event of the moment. That perpetual oscillation between past event and present desire to capture it is the essence of all three artists' creativity.

I'll leave the last diagnosis to that poet of pain, that philosopher of suffering, Cioran, and his *A Short History of Decay*: "Of all the bonds which link us to things, there is not one which fails to slacken and dissolve under the influence of suffering, which frees us from everything except the obsession of ourselves and the sensation of being irrevocably individual. Suffering is solitude hypostatized as essence."

CHAPTER 5

Description of a Struggle

Sanatorium as Speculation

In the autumn of 1989, I moved to New York City, initially to help a friend start up a bookshop. In my first week there, I called Allen Ginsberg, whom I had met a year earlier while researching William Burroughs' material at Columbia University. Allen said to drop by, so I walked the couple of blocks over to 437 East 12th Street between 1st and A. Strolling down it, I remembered these lines from Burroughs' novella *Blade Runner*: "*The siege of St. Vincent's at 12th Street.* Doctors, nurses and orderlies fight the rioters with scalpels, saws and bedpans. Ether bomb explodes in a corridor, stopping the rioters long enough so a doctor can pass patients down a laundry chute to safety. The hospital is on fire. A Chinese orderly throws copper into a vat of nitric acid, releasing nitric oxide. This is a delayed-action poison. Rioters who inhale the fumes collapse an hour or two later."

The right side of Allen's face drooped, the muscles lax and depending, as if that side of his face belonged to W.H. Auden. This was due to two minor strokes he had had in 1969 and 1975 — at the time, diagnosed as Bell's Palsy or Raymond Céstan syndrome. Despite him being constantly on the move, criss-crossing America, giving readings, protesting against censorship, teaching at Naropa, or travelling the world, Allen was not a well man. As I have mentioned, he had diabetes and hypertension (snap) and he was probably living with the effects of the hepatitis he had caught in April 1960 from an unclean needle a doctor had used to treat what Allen called, in a letter to Lawrence Ferlinghetti, "a rare disease of the ass," a non-malignant tumour that had appeared while he was in Bolivia searching for yagé. Allen also smoked and suffered from chest and breathing problems, bronchitis and colds; he had kidney stone attacks, a hiatus hernia, Peyronie's disease (caused by trauma to the penis) and in later life stress arrhythmia and congestive heart failure. Not that I could tell Allen was ill, he had more energy than I had and he was thirty-five years older. He would eventually die a swift death on 5 April 1997, aged seventy, from liver cancer.

I spent two years in New York City, living in Harlem for six months and then on 13th Street between 5th and 6th Avenue. I don't remember being ill during that time. I don't remember using my asthma inhalers. The only time I visited a clinic was to have my ears syringed, and I paid an exorbitant fee for the pleasure. I have had "trouble" with my ears ever since I was a baby, but I have a theory about why my ears became blocked in New York City. That theory — and it's not a medical one — is noise. My ears were blocked with car horns and sirens, with the constant insectoid buzz of people and with words, words from the poets I listened to at readings, from their words on the page I read aloud, from the words of my own poems that I read to whomever would listen, things like "where the colloquies live, with the pulsar pulse / of humans trilling in the underground's apodictic pubes / ears taught & sand trapped, a slump of attention / born in acute ribbons encapsulating playbacks." My experience of New York manifested itself in the labyrinthine turns of my inner ear, it entered as sound waves and slowly liquidized and then jellified and then solidified into amber-coloured wax that blocked the city's invasion and then became infected and painful as if to remind me where I was.

To continue with my health experience and for you to hear the acoustic illusions of my associative pathobiography, we will now travel back to 1992 and look at Nietzsche's dog. How do we gain control over the inner formulas of our illnesses? Is the body/mind fissile or is it immiscible? Is it a problem or is it a false dichotomy? Visiting my father, who had been taken to hospital after a fall and in the final stages of bowel cancer that had metastasized and moved to his kidneys and liver, I was shocked by his confused state. My brother said the doctors had no idea why my father was acting the way he was — previous to entering hospital, he was his normal self, I had spoken to him by telephone on the Sunday before his accident and, apart from a more than usual feeble voice, he sounded like he usually did. My brother thought it might be the pain medication, we both knew what morphine could do to the brain, but the doctors insisted this was not the case, he wasn't being given any form of analgesics. My father recognized me when I arrived but soon started talking in non sequiturs about blues and greens and reds, about a woman with fuzzy hair and how he could see things, lizards, on my mother's shoulder. He had told my mother that he had had conversations with two of his best friends, both of whom were long dead. When I left, I kissed him on the head as I would do to a baby. I had never done that before.

Was it shock that had sent his mind skittering across subjects like a passage from a Burroughs novel? "Insect hairs thru greypurple flesh. Of the scorpion people. The severed heads. In tanks of sewage. Eating green shit." Had the cancer cells migrated through the blood-brain barrier and caused metastatic lesions on his brain? The doctors had no answer. Nor did I. I asked my father if he was in pain and he said he wasn't, he just wanted to go home to die. How did he grasp his illness? How did he get a purchase on his mortality? Was he really not in any pain or was he not able to communicate it as pain if it was a constant state?

In *The Gay Science*, Nietzsche claims, "I have named my pain and call it 'dog' — it's just as faithful, just as obtrusive and shameless, just as entertaining, just as clever as every other dog — and I can scold it and take my bad moods out on it the way others do with their dogs, servants, and wives." As I was dictating this quote, my speech to text device heard and transcribed "shameless" as "Seamus," so now Nietzsche's dog has a name. Apt in that "Seamus" means "one who supplants" and Nietzsche, in naming his pain "dog," is attempting to supplant the reality of pain and illness with an idea of it, a metaphor for it. Maybe my father's fixation with colour was a way of describing how he was feeling, a synaesthesia of pain.

In early July 1992, I had just finished working as an executive editor at The British Council and was in Regent's Park about to play a game of football. I had just bought a pair of new Adidas boots and was eager to test them out. I played as a support striker, a left-sided inside forward, a number ten. It was late afternoon, people were walking home from work through the park. We kicked off. I had a few touches of the ball, nothing special, until, five minutes into the game, I found myself with my back to goal on the edge of the penalty area, a defender behind me attempting to stop me from turning. I dropped my shoulder to turn right and felt the defender shift his position that way and so I turned left and readied to shoot, except I didn't because my left knee had not turned with me. There was an instant of acute pain and, what others told me afterwards, a loud pop. I passed out and came around in the ambulance taking me to UCH. Consultant orthopaedic surgeon Dr Kenneth Bryant F.R.C.S. wrote in a letter to my then doctor, "I saw this patient here today, he was referred on to me from University College Hospital where he attended two days ago following a dislocation of the left patella at football." But I had done a lot more than that.

The third of Jean-Luc Nancy's "Fifty-eight Indices on the Body" states, "A body isn't empty. It's full of other bodies, pieces, organs, parts, tissues, knee-caps, rings, tubes, levers, and bellows. It's also full of itself: that's all it is." For Ginsberg, for Kahlo, for Hitchens and Mansfield, this plenitude of parts, these pieces that fail but bring attention to themselves and to their apart-partness, become synecdoches.

Deleuze is writing about naturalism here but he could as well be writing about patellas, or lungs, or pancreases, "And the fragments are torn from objects which have effectively been formed in the milieu. It might be said that the originary world only appears when the invisible lines which divide up the real, which dislocate modes of behaviour and objects, are supercharged, filled out and extended." The fragment (patella) is torn within and synchronously from the object (body), this causes the invisible lines which divide up the real (pain, trauma) to supercharge the originary world of the sufferer. For the next eighteen months, my knee remained in a constant state of disrepair, regardless of the "acute rehabilitation measures" of physiotherapy and hydrotherapy. My patella, and whatever was occurring behind it, was the fragment torn from the object. My knee became the centre of everything. I could not walk properly, I had to stop and use my right leg to shuffle my body ninety degrees to turn a corner. I walk everywhere, I might as well have been strapped to the bed. Sex was difficult. Getting up and down stairs nearly impossible. My knee was me. I was my knee. My knee had been dislocated and it continued to dislocate my modes of behaviour, my body and my mind. I was bored, and as Cioran observes, "Boredom dismantles the mind, renders it superficial, out at the seams, saps it from within and dislocates it." My dislocated knee had become synecdochal and now stood for my body and my mind, which were also dislocated.

After months of lobbying and moaning and visits to the doctor, on 23 February, 1994 I underwent arthroscopic surgery on my left knee to ascertain the cause of my continuing pain and immobility. The surgeon, Mr El-Tawil, notes "MUA." (manipulation under anaesthesia) "+ pivot shift; +++ Lachman's" (to diagnose anterior cruciate ligament injury) "AM & AL" (anteromedial and anterolateral) portals. "Supracondylar pouch OK. Medial compartment. OK. Intercondylar notch — most of ACL." (anterior cruciate ligament) "torn. Lat." (lateral) "compartment OK. Closure steristrips; IMPRESSION: Torn. ACL." After all that algebra, I was given a course of co-dydramol and sent home the same day, happy that I had been right all along and was going to have the same operation and, more importantly, the same scar that Paul Gascoigne had from his rash foul and subsequent injury in the 1991 FA Cup final. Coincidentally, as I type these words, it is FA Cup final day today.

These notes from an orthopaedic surgeon at the Royal Free Hospital in Hampstead fix my knee as the centre of my identity, the portals allow me access into the body, as Nancy suggests: "We need a corpus of *entries* into the body: dictionary entries, language entries, encyclopedia entries, all the body's introductory *topoi*, registers for all its articles an index for all its places, postures, planes, and recesses. A corpus would be the registration of this long discontinuity of entries (*or* exits; the doors always swing both ways). A seismograph with impalpably precise styluses, a pure literature of breaching bodies, accesses, excesses, orifices, pores and portals of all skins, scars, navels, blazon, pieces: and fields, body by body, place by place, entry by entry by exit." It's all there in that passage — the incision into the knee, the precise stylus of the scalpel, entries and exits (portals and steristrips), the synecdoche of the pores to the body, the apart-partness of here/there, the breathing in and out of the chronic asthmatic, the dislocation of body and place. So I was set for my anterior cruciate ligament reconstruction surgery but, of course, it wasn't going to be a simple route to the operating theatre.

"For all of us have a basic, intuitive feeling that once we *were* whole and well; at ease, at peace, at home in the world; totally united with the grounds of our being; and that then we lost this primal, happy, innocent state, and fell into our present sickness and suffering," writes Olive Sacks in *Awakenings* (1970), his study of patients with sleeping sickness. I am not sure I have ever felt whole and well or at peace and at home in the world. My sickness and suffering have been ever-present.

Before I could undergo the operation, my blood pressure soared. I visited the Hypertension Clinic at The Royal Free Hospital, the notes read, "the above young man was found at a job interview to have a blood pressure of 190/110, I later found it to be 170/110," and "I know this young man has missed an appointment with you because of his severe hypertension. His BP remains consistently high at 180/100 sitting on 180/120 standing." By May 1994, after two months of medication, my blood pressure was under control and the operation could go ahead.

On 17 May, 1994 I was admitted to The Royal Free for the operation to reconstruct my left anterior cruciate ligament, the notes record that Dr James is happy for me to have the operation, that my blood pressure is 170/110 and that I look well. The next day, under general anaesthetic (that weird smell of Malibu I get as I'm about to go under) and then the surgeons did this: "L. Ant. cruciate ligt. reconstruction (bone.,pat.ligt.,bone, (Dr El Tawil) MIDLINE ant. incision; 11 mm, diameter nid-patellar ligt; graft carefully taken 30 mm, length of patellar graft and 40 mm length; 11 mm, diameter tibial tunnel; 10 mm diameter femoral tunnel; Notchplasty was done, graft aligned. 7 x 05 mm screw fixed with femoral graft; 9 x 30 mm tibial screws with graft under tension at 900 flexion; closure i layers; clips to skin, no drain." Cool. On the 25th, I was sent home to lie on the sofa and read, my leg encased in a blue frame with all sorts of clamps and bolts holding my knee in place. What could go wrong?

My body had taken on a new form, a somatic transformation, the knee brace and stainless steel pins and screws giving my leg a robotic look, a trans-human cast and, therefore, the knees articulatory relation to my whole body meant that it was not an isolated injury and trauma but one that affected my entire organism, the double articulation of my knee and my thoughts about my knee. Those thoughts over the next few days accumulated and accelerated because I could see under the levels of blue foam surrounding the site of my operation that the skin was turning purple, was swelling and the pressure inside building. I took as many painkillers as I could but with no relief. My knee felt like it was on fire. On the 27th, I ordered a taxi to take me back to the hospital and was admitted immediately with a severe case of cellulitis caused by the streptococcus bacteria. After a five-day a course of flucloxacillin, I was back home, reading and writing.

On 9 August, 1994 Dr S.A.H. Jafri MB BS MRCPI noted that, "hypertensive investigations showed a large cardiac shadow on routine chest X-ray," but that my "urea, creatinine, blood glucose, serum lipid profile and urinary catecholamines were all normal." He then goes on to state that, "the results of echocardiogram suggested impaired relaxation of right and left ventricle but with good systolic function." My blood pressure on that day was 140/80. This was the same reading as William D. Toff, Clinical Fellow in Cardiology, had registered in July and had prescribed enalapril, bendrofluazide and nifedipine, drugs that I still take every day.

For the next eighteen months, besides the hypertension, asthma and problems with my ears, I was relatively healthy, so much so that on 12 March, 1996 I underwent a full medical for a life-assurance application and came out with a pass, my blood pressure was 130/70 and I received an all-clear from my GP. Although I did find a question that obviously had a dubious answer, "What do you know of the patient's smoking, drinking or other habits?" The doctor wrote, "Non-smoker. No alcohol excess." I have never smoked. As Deleuze explained to Claire Parnet, "the aim of writing is to carry life to the state of a non-personal power" (as in Denton Welch). "In doing this it renounces claim to any territory, any end which would reside in itself. Why-does one write? Because it is not a case of writing. It may be that the writer has delicate health," (as in Nietzsche, Lawrence, Welch, Deleuze) "a weak constitution. He is none the less the opposite of the neurotic: a sort of great Alive" (in the manner of Spinoza, Nietzsche or Lawrence or Chatwin or Ginsberg), "in so far as he is only too weak for the life which runs in him or for the affects which pass in him. To write has no other function: to be a flux which combines with other fluxes — all the minority-becomings of the world." And he goes on, "The line of flight is creative of these becomings" (as in Stevenson, Nietzsche, Lawrence, Mansfield), "Lines of flight have no territory. Writing carries out the conjunction, the transmutation of fluxes, through which life escapes from the resentment of persons, societies and reigns" (see again Stevenson, Nietzsche, Lawrence), "Kerouac's phrases are as sober as a Japanese drawing, a pure line traced by an unsupported hand, which passes across ages and reigns. It would take a true alcoholic to attain that degree of sobriety." Indeed.

Of his two periods spent in a sanatorium for tuberculosis sufferers, Roland Barthes (1915–1980) writes that, "at the time, tuberculosis was truly a way of life, I would almost say an election." It is true that tuberculosis, for a number of suffering artists, was a must-have accessory, the beard and dark glasses of today's Brooklyn hipster writers, albeit a more deadly one.

Is it possible to think of John Keats (1795–1821) without thinking of "consumption"? The Brontës had an equal talent for tuberculosis and for writing, Charlotte (1816–1855), Emily (1818–1848), Anne (1820–1849) and their brother Branwell (1817–1848) all succumbing to the disease. Robert-Louis Stevenson (1850–1894) became as famous as his characters, Long John Silver and Dr Jekyll and Mr Hyde, while travelling in France, the USA and the Pacific to find a place and an air to ease the debilitating effects on his health. Anton Chekhov (1860–1904), doctor and writer, remained in denial about his tuberculosis; afraid to have the disease confirmed by his medical colleagues, he travelled widely and worked incessantly. The New Zealand-born writer Katherine Mansfield (1888–1923) wrote the majority of her glitteringly banal short stories after being diagnosed with extrapulmonary tuberculosis in 1917. Who could disassociate stories such as "The Hunger Artist" and "A Country Doctor" from the consumptive figure of Franz Kafka (1883–1924)? Kafka was also diagnosed with tuberculosis in 1917, but his was laryngeal tuberculosis. Without the disease, D.H. Lawrence (1885–1930) would not have wandered the world seeking a place of respite from the illness, he would not have written *Aaron's Rod*, *Kangaroo*, *The Plumed Serpent* or his travel books. George Orwell (1903–1950), author of "Books v. Cigarettes" (1946), suffered from bouts of bronchitis, pneumonia and respiratory problems throughout his life, yet his main works were written after tuberculosis had been confirmed. Likewise, Gilles Deleuze (1925–1995) had a history of respiratory complaints including bronchitis, emphysema, asthma, lung cancer and tuberculosis. His apartment on the third floor of the building on Avenue Niel probably stank of cigarettes, wet dog, old books, maybe with an underlying note of coffee and chervil. Was the window already open? Probably not. Saturday, 4 November, 1995, the temperature near freezing, Deleuze reads from an old essay on Samuel Beckett, "An exhausted man is much more than a weary man. Does he exhaust the possible because he is himself exhausted, or is he exhausted because he has exhausted the possible? He exhausts himself by exhausting the possible, and inversely." Exhaust, inspiration, expiration. He then flicks through *Anti-Oedipus*, "I asked myself what it meant to exist, to be alive, what it meant to be conscious of oneself breathing, and I remember that I wanted to inhale myself in order to prove that I was alive and to see if I liked being alive, and if so why."

It is fanciful to think that this timeline of literary sufferers somehow transmitted the disease to each other, but tuberculosis was and is highly contagious and no doubt Keats' spit, Chekhov's cough, Kafka's sneeze, Lawrence's songs and Orwell's (double) speech infected some other person, artist or not. Tuberculosis is spread mostly by bacteria (*Mycobacterium tuberculosis* — once known as "tubercle bacillus," hence TB) in air droplets, which, when they reach the pulmonary alveoli, infect the lungs. As in the case of Kafka, the disease can also affect most other organs of the body, including the bones. However, the majority of tuberculosis cases are of the pulmonary variety and result in coughing, the expectoration of sputum and/or blood and may result in haemorrhaging, scarring of the organs, necrosis and eventual death.

The timeline shows that tuberculosis was a lethal and indiscriminatory disease until the end of the nineteenth century, claiming 25% of world deaths. The Brontës may not have helped this by living in such close, inclement and unsanitary conditions at Haworth parsonage. Even in the twenty-first century, it is estimated that the disease kills 1.5 million people per year, overtaking HIV-related deaths as the leading cause of death from infectious diseases, with up to 33% of the world's population being infected with the tuberculosis bacillus but remaining asymptomatic. In the past decade, new drug-resistant strains of tuberculosis have been discovered, some totally resistant, despite the improvements in public health and the development of antibiotics and vaccines.

The disease, under its various guises — tuberculosis, consumption, phthisis, scrofula, Pott's disease and the white plague — developed some time during the Neolithic period, at the birth of civilization as we know it: Mesopotamia, the Fertile Crescent, Minoan Culture, Egyptian mummification and the beginning of writing in Sumer. That beginning of writing brings us back to Roland Barthes and his sanatorium stays, which will act as an introduction to a visit to our own long-term illness ward.

In *Anglo-English Attitudes* (1999), Geoff Dyer writes of Barthes that his sanatorium stays "were especially important, removing him from the mainstream of academic advancement and allowing him to begin developing his own highly subjective version of theory." Because of its contagiousness and lethal transmission, tuberculosis meant long periods of enforced solitude and bed rest, it also meant in the cases of Stevenson, Mansfield and Lawrence months and years of travel to find a beneficial climate. In Thomas Mann's novel *The Magic Mountain*, its protagonist Hans Castorp visits a tubercular cousin at the Davos sanatorium in Switzerland for a three-week stay, is diagnosed with the disease and remains there for seven years. These enforced time-outs lead to contemplation, the past is reappraised in a perpetual present, a buffering zone where, Mann writes, "all the days are nothing but the same day repeating itself — or rather, since it is always the same day, it is incorrect to speak of repetition; a continuous present, an identity, an everlastingness — such words as these would better convey the idea."

This repetition, this experience of having "never lived in the world since" entering the sanatorium is analogous with Tom McCarthy's theory of buffering in *Satin Island* (2015), in which humans "require experience to stay ahead, if only by a nose, of our *consciousness* of experience — if for no other reason than that the latter needs to make sense of the former […] to narrate it both to others and ourselves and, for this purpose, has to be fed with the constant, unsorted supply of fresh sensations and events." It is as if the texts of Mann's *The Magic Mountain* and McCarthy's *Satin Island* and *Recessional — or, the Time of the Hammer* (2016) inter-infect the other, intra-infect the other, like the Brontës in their parsonage. Back to Mann, who coughs: "They bring you your midday broth, as they bought it yesterday and will bring it tomorrow; and it comes over you — but whence or how you do not know, it makes you quite giddy to see the broth coming in — that you are losing a sense of the demarcation of time, that its units are running together, disappearing; and what is being revealed to you as the true content of time is merely a dimensionless present in which they eternally bring you the broth." Back to McCarthy, who sneezes: "But when the narrating cursor catches right up with the rendering one, when occurrences and situations don't replenish themselves quickly enough for the awareness they sustain, when, no matter how fast they regenerate, they're instantly devoured by a mouth too voracious to let anything gather or accrue unconsumed before it, then we find ourselves jammed, stuck in limbo: we can enjoy *neither* experience *nor* consciousness of it. Everything becomes buffering, and buffering becomes everything." This "contagious relish" of texts is, McCartney sings in *Recessional*, "coloured by shades of eternity and entropy or run down, illness-time is time that is drifting towards death. But it is also, in classic Freudian fashion, time that is homing in on pleasure." The pleasure of the abstracted life of and in the sanatorium. As an aside, it's interesting to note that McCarthy's *Recessional* was published in Zurich, Switzerland, and that the majority of the sanatoriums our tubercular writers spent time in were in Switzerland, Mann's Davos being the largest and more closely documented.

Repetition, buffering and abstraction are apparent in the works of all of our literary consumptives and, as we move into the sanatorium, we will examine the patients and their work, notably their letters and journals, for signs of these time-altering causes and effects. As Barthes writes (Barthes never "says") in *Roland Barthes by Roland Barthes* (1977) of recurrent tuberculosis, "it had no other signs than its own interminable time and the social taboo of contagion; for the rest, one was sick or cured, abstractly, purely by the doctor's decree; and while other diseases desocialize, tuberculosis projected you into a minor ethnographic society, part tribe, part monastery, part phalanstery; rites, constraints, protections."

So as we leave the cancer ward, walk through reception, navigate the revolving doors, we take a path lined with benches adorned with nameplates to remember those who rested there, and open an old wooden door that allows us into a garden adorned with flowers and spotted with bath chairs where we will meet briefly other members of the "minor ethnographic society," this "tribe" in the grounds of the "part phalanstery / part monastery" that is our sanatorium.

Hippocrates states, "In persons affected with phthisis, if the sputa which they cough up have a heavy smell when poured upon coals, and if the hairs of the head fall off, the case will prove fatal." And this could refer to Deleuze, "Persons who become affected with emphysema after pleurisy, if they get clear of it in forty days from the breaking of it, escape the disease; but if not, it passes into phthisis." Hippocrates believed the disease was hereditary, Aristotle disagreed and thought it contagious, "In phthisis is the contagion due to the fact that phthisis makes the breath weak and laboured, and those diseases are most quickly contracted which are due to the corruption of the breath, as is seen in plagues?" Having a look around the garden, the tartan blankets on the skinny legs of the bath-chair inhabitees, their sunken cheeks, their wan pallor, their blood-spotted handkerchiefs, we can be in no doubt that that particular Ancient Greek philosopher got it right.

As we look around the garden, our tribe is split into smaller tribes; the writers hanging out with writers, the musicians forming trios, quartets, quintets and chamber orchestras (yes, there is enough of them), the artists trading gossip and swapping consumptive models. We put on our surgical masks, wander along the paths and recognize some of these tubercular patients. Underneath the white flowers of the blackthorn tree (like an inverted tubercular lung) Honoré Balzac (1799–1850), cafetiere of coffee at his feet, cup in hand, is in conversation with Scotch-whisky swigging Robert Burns (1759–1796) and a cigarillo-puffing Albert Camus (1913–1960). Skulking around the doorway, Charles Bukowski (1920–1994) shares a six-pack of Miller with Dylan Thomas (1914–1953) and Stephen Crane (1871–1900). Around a mosaic table, blankets on wasted legs, cups of tea in hand, bespattered handkerchiefs trailing out of pockets or tucked up the sleeves of their dressing gowns, Henry David Thoreau (1817–1862) discusses the garden and its inhabitants with the hawk-nosed Friedrich Schiller (1759–1805), the bewhiskered John Ruskin (1819–1900) and Alfred Jarry (1873–1907), who is wishing he were swilling a few beers with Bukowski and co.

There is a chorus of coughs and sneezes, blood and sputum is spat on to daisies and dandelions, which may or may not contain Mycobacterium tuberculosis, but these players have already lost their game of contagion roulette. Some will die of the disease, others, like Camus and Thomas, will suffer different fates, one in a car crash, the other, as we observed earlier, from pneumonia and a fatty swelling of the brain.

Sitting apart from the men, the frail and dark Elizabeth Barrett Browning (1806–1861), sips on her laudanum, places her hands together and from her bath-chair, whispers, "O blissful Mouth which breathed the mournful breath," her words become faint and then we hear, "call them back / Back to Thee in continuous aspiration!"

Aspiration, the action or process of breathing, the means of contracting tuberculosis; inspiration, the act of drawing breath into the lungs, the drive to create something, poetry. In 1837, Barrett Browning would seek refuge from her consumption in Torquay but returned to London a year later to occupy the upstairs room of 50 Wimpole Street, where she wrote many poems and, typical of tuberculosis sufferers such as Chekhov and Lawrence, wrote thousands of letters, corresponding with many writers, artists and politicians of the day, including John Ruskin, Thomas Carlyle, Elizabeth Gaskell (author of *North and South* and biographer of Charlotte Brontë) and Leigh Hunt (critic and poet, friend of Keats and Shelley). On 2 August, 1830, she wrote to the blind Greek scholar Hugh Stuart Boyd, chastizing him, "I don't understand your objection to the line about the *consumption of breath*. How should I, when you do not mention it? But you will, when we meet next, &, in the meantime, I kiss the *shadow* of the rod."

Sitting next to Elizabeth, Jane Austen sips her tea and smiles wryly at the words of the fragile woman next to her, her own *Pride and Prejudice* influenced Mrs Gaskell's *North and South* with its consumptive mill girls. Austen's reason to be here in this garden of the sanatorium is a complicated one. Like the shadow of the rod, the shadow of tuberculosis followed her and may have been the cause of her death. Like Mrs Barrett Browning, Ms Austen is weak and the teacup rattles in its saucer, spilling the liquid, it pools and we see that it is not tea but milk, unpasteurized, thick and creamy, a killer.

On 22 May, 1817, two months before her death — of whatever cause — Austen wrote to Anne Sharp: "An attack of my sad complaint seized me [...] the most severe I ever had — and coming upon me after weeks of indisposition, it reduced me very low. I have kept my bed since the 13 of April, with only removals to a Sopha. Now, I am getting well again, and indeed have been gradually tho' slowly recovering my strength for the last three weeks. I can sit up in my bed & employ myself. [...] My head was always clear, and I had scarcely any pain; my chief sufferings were from feverish nights, weakness and Languor. — This Discharge was on me for above a week, & as our Alton Apoth did not pretend to be able to cope with it, better advice was called in. Our nearest very good is at Winchester, where there is a Hospital and capital Surgeons, and one of them attended me, and his applications gradually removed the Evil. — The consequence is, that instead of going to Town to put myself into the hands of some Physician as I should otherwise have done, I am going to Winchester instead..." And that is where she died on 18 July, 1817, but what was it that killed her? The investigation into the cause of her death, the medical theories and subsequent diagnoses, are as complex as the plots of her novels, and as complicated as the relationships of her characters.

Despite Austen's humour in her letters and her continued work on *Sanditon* (1817), her last unfinished novel, the physician in Winchester had definitely not removed the Evil.

It is thought, variously, that the cause of her death was from Addison's disease, a suppression and destruction of the adrenal glands leading to fatigue, low blood pressure, back pain and a darkening of the skin. It is interesting to note that, at the age of fifteen, Barrett Browning also suffered from an illness with similar symptoms, and her tuberculosis may be the cause of Addison's disease through physical stress. In *Sanditon*, the character of Miss Lambe could be a description of the young Elizabeth, "Miss Lambe was beyond comparison the most important and precious, as she paid in proportion to her fortune. She was about seventeen, half mulatto, chilly and tender, had a maid of her own, was to have the best room in the lodgings, and was always of the first consequence in every plan of Mrs. Griffiths." Elizabeth believed she was descended from mulattoes, her wealthy family owned sugar plantations and mills in Jamaica; Miss Lambe is "a young West Indian of large fortune in delicate health." If Austen did suffer from Addison's disease, she would have also had a dark complexion, suffered from fatigue, vomiting and back pain, which she did.

Using her correspondence, the letters of family and friends and contemporary reports, various literary commentators and interested medical researchers and doctors have claimed to have diagnosed Austen's fatal illness. Addison's disease, the smoking gun since 1964, has been excluded in favour of a number of diseases. It is known that while writing or revising her most famous novels, Austen suffered from a number of illnesses that made it difficult for her to write. She had conjunctivitis, her constant fatigue meant she had to write with a pencil rather than a pen. Rather than the mainly healthy woman we know through biographers, Austen was probably ill throughout her life; her humour — and her sister Cassandra's editing of the letters between them — disguised the extent of her maladies. She may have had an immune deficiency caused by a postmature birth and she nearly died at the age of seven from the effects of a "putrid fever" or epidemic typhus at a boarding school in Oxford. Charlotte Brontë wrote of a similar school in *Jane Eyre* (1847), "But Helen was ill at present: for some weeks she had been removed from my sight to I knew not what room upstairs. She was not, I was told, in the hospital portion of the house with the fever patients; for her complaint was consumption, not typhus: and by consumption I, in my ignorance, understood something mild, which time and care would be sure to alleviate." Charlotte blamed the death of her sisters Marie and Elizabeth on the conditions at the boarding school and the incidents of typhus outbreaks and consumption.

In *Sense and Sensibility* (1811), an apothecary pronounces Marianne Dashwood's "disorder to have a putrid tendency, and allow(s) the word 'infection' to pass his lips." While staying with relatives near Lichfield, Staffordshire, after leaving Bath in July 1806, Austen contracted pertussis from the children. Also known as whooping cough, pertussis is an airborne bacterial disease similar to tuberculosis, the symptoms include coughing fits, discharge of mucus (cf. Addison's disease), fatigue and may lead to vomiting. By the time she had reached Southampton, the illness had become more serious. She finally recovered but suffered from a number of illnesses, several colds, an infected ear and ongoing neuralgia. It is thought that it is around the time of the writing of *Sense and Sensibility* that the disease that would eventually kill her was either contracted or manifested itself. The usual suspects are leukaemia, Hodgkin's disease, non-Hodgkin's lymphoma, systemic vasculitis and tuberculosis, all of which present similar symptoms — weight loss, fatigue, fever, night sweats, vomiting, coughing and trouble breathing.

With Addison's disease discounted, the literary/medical investigators have pointed their accusing fingers at Hodgkin's disease (also known as Hodgkin disease, Hodgkin lymphoma, and Hodgkin's lymphoma), a type of lymphoma, a blood cancer originating in the lymphatic system. The lymphatic system is part of the body's immune system and Austen's continual infections and onset neuralgia in her face were signs that her lymphocytes had grown abnormally and had metastasized. The neuralgia may have been caused by an attack of shingles Austen was unable to fight off because of the immune deficiency, the pain from the neuralgia in her face would have been intense, add that to conjunctivitis and an ear infection as well as fatigue and fevers — "It is a truth universally acknowledged, that a single woman in possession of an immunodeficient body, must be in want of a Physician."

Shingles is caused by the herpes zoster virus, which is the cause also of chickenpox and, when reactivated in the body, may cause ophthalmic zoster, a disease that affects the ophthalmic nerve causing inflammations and rashes, possibly a confusion with the signs of conjunctivitis, and also trigeminal neuralgia, a severe facial pain, sometimes known as "suicide disease." People with Hodgkin's disease show a prevalence for this virus and type of neuralgia. Other pathological prevalences include mononucleosis, anaemia, pruritis (severe itching) and back pain. The symptoms of whatever it was that was ailing her ebbed and flowed and in a moment of remission she wrote to Fanny Knight, "Many thanks for your kind care for my health; I certainly have not been well for many weeks, and about a week ago I was very poorly, I have had a good deal of fever at times and indifferent nights, but am considerably better now, and recovering my Looks a little, which have been bad enough, black and white and every wrong colour." Her mulatto-like skin may have been the result of idiopathic thrombocytopenia purpura, which causes bruise-like markings that turn red to purple to green to yellow and, in some cases, to black.

By this time, her illnesses had forced her to abandon *Sanditon*, and she was soon complaining of fevers, bilious attacks and, by early June 1817, she and her family feared for her life. After a number of seizures and extreme fatigue, she died in bed in the early morning of 18 July. In an article written in 1964 for the *British Medical Journal,* the physician and surgeon Sir Zachary Cope diagnosed her illness as Addison's disease secondary to tuberculosis, citing the episodes of fatigue, build up of mucus, skin pigmentation, back pain and apparent immune deficiency. However, fevers and night sweats were not associated symptoms, and these additional elements would indicate Hodgkin's disease — Pel-Ebstein fever is a cyclical fever associated specifically with Hodgkin's lymphoma.

After its identification in 1832 by Thomas Hodgkin, the disease was often associated with tuberculosis, one being the shadow of the other. Jane Austen's various symptoms and their relationship to one another, Addison's — Hodgkin's — Pel-Ebstein could be drawn up in a similar way to one of those Austen family trees we find in the opening pages to her novels.

But there is a further twist to the medical mystery, maybe the reason why Jane is in the sanatorium gardens rather than the cancer ward or endocrinology unit. In 2009, the social scientist Katherine White, coordinator for the Addison's Disease Self-Help Group's clinical advisory group in the United Kingdom, and who suffers from Addison's disease, suggested in a paper published in *Medical Humanities* that Austen died of disseminated bovine tuberculosis and that she was infected with the consumptive disease through drinking unpasteurized milk. Further speculation posits that Austen died from arsenic poisoning, the arsenic being in the medicines she was taking to combat all her other illnesses. For now, we will ask a nurse to replace the milk with green tea and take Ms Austen off that tuna, sprout and rice diet, just in case the arsenic theory is correct.

However interesting these retrospective literary-medical postmortems may be, we may never know what killed Austen or Barrett Browning (tuberculosis or hypokalemic periodic paralysis), but we do know what killed the man sitting on the grassy verge sketching the elongated portraits of these authors — tuberculosis and tubercular meningitis to be precise.

Fevers and headaches, nausea and vomiting, sensitivity to light, stiffness of the neck, agitation and decreased consciousness — most of us know these symptoms. The majority of them occur with a bad hangover, and the Italian-Jewish artist and sculptor Amedeo Clemente Modigliani (1884–1920) certainly had his fair share of those after moving to Paris in 1906. Modigliani was born and grew up in the port city of Livorno in Tuscany. His Sephardic Jewish family were moneylenders but went bankrupt soon after Amedeo was born. The fourth child and close to his mother, Modigliani was a sickly child, falling ill with several attacks of pleurisy and typhoid fever, and his mother took him on a tour of southern Italy seeking, like Lawrence and Stevenson, a healthy atmosphere. His visits to Rome, Capri, Naples and Amalfi stimulated his artistic sensibilities.

At the age of fourteen, while in the middle of a bout of typhoid fever, he became delirious and demanded to be taken to Florence where he could study the artworks in the Uffizi and Palazzo Pitti. At the same age, Modigliani's mother secured her son a place in the art school of Guglielmo Micheli, a painter of landscape and seascapes. At the age of sixteen, Modigliani caught the tuberculosis that would kill him twenty years later. Micheli and his students preferred painting and sketching out of doors but Modigliani, probably because of his ill health, worked mostly in his own studio, and whereas his fellow students' paintings were inspired by French Impressionism,

Modigliani's had the claustrophobic angularity of Cezanne, that stillness always on the brink of eruption.

Modigliani was an artist in perpetual convalescence, his studio a place of creativity and recovery. A disciple of Nietzsche, especially *Thus Spoke Zarathustra*, Modigliani would have agreed with Nietzsche's words from *The Gay Science*, "If we convalescents still need art, it is another kind of art — a mocking, light, fleeting, divinely untroubled, divinely artificial art that, like a bright flame, blazes into an unclouded sky! Above all: an art for artists, only for artists!"

After furthering his life-drawing studies at Florence's Accademia di Belle Arti, Modigliani, suffering from the effects of tuberculosis, moved to Venice where his bohemianism flourished under the influence of Nietzsche, Baudelaire and Comte de Lautréamont — those invalids of radicalism and style — and in 1906, he moved to a city more befitting his changing lifestyle — Paris.

Already a smoker of hashish, Modigliani fell in with the artists living in Montmartre, including Juan Gris, Pablo Picasso, Georges Braque and Henri Matisse. They used a building called Le Bateau-Lavoir, close to the banks of the Seine, as a meeting place and residency, along with writers such as Max Jacob (who gave the building its name), Guillaume Apollinaire and Alfred Jarry. A hotbed of discussion, drinking, drug-taking, creativity, poverty and disease, the Boat Wash-House was a squat, studio and school for Modigliani and others — it was also where he would begin his descent into poverty, alcoholism, violence and death.

For the first six months after arriving in Paris, Modigliani walked the streets of Montmartre dressed in the style of a bohemian artist, mixed with fellow painters, hired a studio, drank sensibly and appeared reserved and somewhat haughty. Still a mother's boy, he found it hard to shed his family's bourgeois background. When he had first rented his studio in nearby in Rue Caulaincourt, he had decorated the walls with prints from the Renaissance masters and Italian academic painters and furnished it with heavy drapes. After he had begun his descent into alcoholism and drug addiction, he ransacked the studio, tearing down the old prints and drapes and destroying his early works. Tuberculosis was affecting his work and his socializing; he camouflaged the effects of his disease by at first pretending he was an alcoholic and drug addict and then, because these substances — particularly absinthe and hashish — ameliorated the pain and gave him the confidence he needed to live a lie but also to continue his painting, drawing and sculpting, he became dependent on them in reality.

Modigliani not only destroyed his own paintings, he destroyed those of other artists, he stripped naked in public, and yet these excesses, this Saturnalia, stimulated his art and his Nietzschean ability to "create and piece together into one, what is now fragment and riddle and grisly accident." His sketching and painting became as obsessive and excessive as his drinking and drug-taking, thousands of works were destroyed by him, or lost, or given away to models and girlfriends who lost or destroyed them.

He returned home to Livorno in 1909 for a brief stay because of his worsening illness and excessive lifestyle, but he was soon back in a new studio in Montmartre and there, in 1910, he met the Russian poet Anna Akhmatova, who became his lover and muse. Even though their relationship only lasted a year, Akhmatova's long face, angular body, wan skin and deep-set eyes became the inspiration for Modigliani's future portraits and nudes.

Modigliani's poor health prevented him from joining the army at the outbreak of the First World War, but it didn't prevent him having numerous affairs and lovers, one of whom, the bohemian artist, writer and Fitzrovian alcoholic Nina Hamnett (1890–1956), died after falling forty-feet from her apartment window. In December 1917, Modigliani had his first and only one-man show at the Berthe Weill Gallery in Paris, exhibiting the nudes he had painted under the commission of his agent; however, it was closed soon after opening by the Paris police commissioner for the alleged obscenity of the artworks. Earlier that spring, he also met Jeanne Hébuterne, a Russian art student. The pair soon became lovers and moved into a studio together where Jeanne modelled for Modigliani.

Escaping the war and trying to find a healthier pace to live, Modigliani and Jeanne travelled through France and settled in Nice in November 1918. The next year, a daughter, Jeanne, was born. With the end of the war in sight, they returned to Paris in May 1919, this time to Montparnasse. There they had another child and planned to marry despite his worsening alcoholism and drug abuse. The symptoms of these two debilitating diseases are very similar to those of tubercular meningitis, a form of tuberculosis that attacks the meningitis, the membranes that connect the spinal cord and the brain. People who are more at risk of this are those who use alcohol excessively and have weakened immune systems. The symptoms of fever, light sensitivity and irritation could easily be the reasons for his using absinthe and hashish as a palliative, they may also be signs of the illness manifesting itself in his taking off his clothes, his need to work in a studio and not outside and his acts of violence and destruction. His frequent loss of consciousness due to excessive alcohol intake may have been caused by the progression of his tubercular meningitis. Alcohol and drug abuse also leads to confusion, another sign that the tubercular meningitis is moving into its last phases and, in January 1920, a neighbour found Modigliani in a delirious state clinging to the pregnant Jeanne Hébuterne.

He lapsed into a coma and, on 24 January, 1920, he died penniless in the wards of the Hôpital de la Charité. At Christie's auction rooms in New York, on 9 November, 2015, an art sale fetched $170,405,000 for Modigliani's painting *Nu couché*. The day after Modigliani's well-attended funeral, friends took the twenty-one year-old Jeanne to the home of her parents. Bereft, she climbed to the fifth floor and jumped from a window — neither she nor her baby survived. Would Zarathustra have been sympathetic? "Now it would be suffering and torture for the convalesced one to believe in such ghosts. Now it would be suffering and humiliation. Thus I speak to the hinterworldly. It was suffering and incapacity that created all hinterworlds, and that brief madness of happiness that only the most suffering person experiences."

As Modigliani sketches the faces of Austen and Barrett Browning, he asks if they would model for a new double *Nu couché*, but they demur and look across to another man standing on the ornamental bridge that crosses the little carp-filled stream. He looks back at the two women, holds his head in his hand and screams.

Edvard Munch (1863–1944) had tuberculosis as a child; his father was a doctor and army medical officer, his mother died of tuberculosis when Munch was five years old and his elder sister of the same disease when he was fourteen. The family lived in Christiania, now Oslo, and Munch spent his childhood, like Modigliani, sick and housebound, where he drew and read the tales of Edgar Allen Poe.

Baudelaire, one of Modigliani's favourite writers, translated Poe and introduced his works to France. Both Baudelaire and Poe suffered from various illnesses throughout their lives and Poe's wife, Virginia Clemm, contracted tuberculosis, coughing blood while singing at the piano at the age of twenty.

She died from the disease five years later and Poe's depression and alcoholism killed him two years after that. As in the death of Austen, there are a number of (conspiracy) theories as to the cause of Poe's death, including alcoholism, rabies, heart disease, cholera, drug-abuse, stroke, epilepsy, suicide, accidental suicide, delirium tremens, syphilis, tubercular meningitis and/or tuberculosis. Whatever it was that killed him, Poe was found delirious on 3 October, 1849 in the streets of Baltimore, wearing someone else's clothes. He spent four days semiconscious in Washington Medical College and died in the early morning of 7 October.

Charles Baudelaire (1821–1867) — who died four months before Munch's mother coughed her last — grew up and was educated in Lyon and, like Modigliani, was mother-fixated. After his father died when Baudelaire was six years old, he became traumatized by his mother's marriage to General Aupick. After he moved to Paris to study law, Baudelaire, like Modigliani later, became a dandified bohemian, visited prostitutes, experimented with drugs and alcohol and may have caught both syphilis and gonorrhoea. Illness troubled Baudelaire throughout his life, as did alcoholism, laudanum and opium abuse *and* poverty — these factors, alongside the theory of him being bipolar, may have been the cause of a stroke he had in 1866 which left him aphasic. He spent the last years of his life in a semi-catatonic state in nursing homes and eventually died on 31 August, 1867.

Both Poe and Baudelaire were, arguably, the pioneers of modernist aesthetics. Both were also drug addicts and alcoholics, both suffered from various illnesses throughout their lives and both died in sad circumstances, poor and alone in hospital rooms. In May 1861, Baudelaire wrote to his mother: "You know that when I was young I caught a venereal infection which I later thought was completely cured. After

1848, it broke out again in Dijon. Once again it was checked. Now it has returned and has assumed a new form, spots on the skin and an extraordinary fatigue in all my joints. You can believe me; I know what I am talking about. Perhaps, in the sadness in which I am plunged, my fright has aggravated the disease. But I need to follow a strict regimen and I cannot do so in the life that I am now leading."

Add to Poe and Baudelaire the *poète maudit*s Comte de Lautréamont (1846–1870 — death unknown, possibly cholera, typhoid or plague); Rimbaud (1854–1891 — thought to be tubercular synovitis but correctly diagnosed as osteosarcoma; Nietzsche (1844–1900) — the cause of his mental breakdown in 1889 is attributed to, variously, syphilis, psychosis, bipolar disorder, vascular dementia, retro-orbital meningioma, frontotemporal dementia, cerebral autosomal-dominant arteriopathy with subcortical infarcts and leukoencephalopathy syndrome and/or mercury poisoning from medication he was taking for his syphilis, and their influence on the work and life of Modigliani and Munch is clear. In the sadnesses and illnesses in which they were plunged, they struggled to create, to secure an audience, they struggled against poverty, against addictions, they all struggled against an inevitable early death and they all failed.

Baudelaire began the May 1861 letter to his mother, "I am in that horrible state of mind which I experienced in the fall of 1841. I do not intend to speak of the nervous afflictions which are slowly killing me and destroying my courage — nausea, insomnia, nightmares, fainting spells. I have spoken of them to you too often. But with you there is no need of false modesty." We will continue our tour of the sanatorium with Munch who, although not being a consumptive, became the consummate portraitist of sickness both mental and physical, a Baudelaire of paint.

Munch lowers his hand to his sides, steps off the ornamental bridge and walks towards Austen and Barrett Browning, the novelist and poet look down, cough into their handkerchiefs. The ends of Munch's neat moustache flutter in the breeze, his grey frock coat billowing out behind him. He fixes his stare on the two women, they are perfect models for one of his compositions, dark, fragile, emaciated, almost part of the bathchairs in which they sit. Modigliani has taken his sketchpad and retired to some hidden part of the garden to drink his absinthe, smoke his hashish.

Munch now stands in front of the women and says, "My fear of life is necessary to me, as is my illness. Without anxiety and illness, I am a ship without a rudder. My sufferings are part of my self and my art. They are indistinguishable from me, and their destruction would destroy my art." The two women remind him of his mother, confined to her chair by tuberculosis, gazing out at the stark Norwegian vista, as Jane and Elizabeth stare at the landscaped garden of the sanatorium. Munch bends over and whispers into Elizabeth's ear, "No longer shall I paint interiors with men reading and women knitting. I will paint living people who breathe and feel and suffer and love." Elizabeth sips her tea. Munch puts his hand on the back of Jane's chair, looks into the distance and says, "Without anxiety and illness I should have been like a ship without a rudder." Jane coughs into her handkerchief, prepares a riposte but, too late, Munch steps away and returns to the foot of the ornamental bridge, sets up an easel, canvas, palette, brushes and fixes the two women with his gaze.[2]

Unlike Modigliani, Munch never had much luck with women, he never married, became a recluse in later life and thought of his paintings as his children, he was their mother

_____

2   Subsequent quotes from Munch are also from his private
    journals.

from whom they would never be separated, unlike the four year-old Edvard, alone and sick in the dark, dark rooms in Christiania. Munch is famous for his painting *The Scream* (1893) — actually two oil paintings on the same theme, as well as pastel versions and lithograph prints. He wrote in his diary in January 1892 of the inspiration to begin the series of artworks, "One evening I was walking along a path, the city was on one side and the fjord below. I felt tired and ill. I stopped and looked out over the fjord — the sun was setting, and the clouds turning blood red. I sensed a scream passing through nature; it seemed to me that I heard the scream. I painted this picture, painted the clouds as actual blood. The colour shrieked. This became 'The Scream.'" Some medical-art commentators have suggested that the figure on the bridge could be suffering from depersonalization-derealization syndrome or, and this is where he feels an affinity with Austen, from trigeminal neuralgia.

Whatever was inflicting the twisted and tormented figure, be it mental or physical, there are obvious links to the works of Nietzsche and to Kierkegaard, those *poète maudit*s of suffering. Nietzsche understood Munch's illnesses, depression, his loneliness and failure with women, understood how nature affects the body and the mind, and Nietzsche could be writing about Munch's *The Scream* in this passage from *The Gay Science*, "Nobody equals him at the colours of late autumn, at the indescribably moving happiness of a last, very last, very briefest enjoyment; he knows a tone for those secret, uncanny midnights of the soul, where cause and effect seem to have gone awry and something can come to be 'from nothing' at any moment."

Kierkegaard's works also inspired and informed Munch's art and entries in his journal. Munch quoted from Kierkegaard's *Fear and Trembling* (1843), *The Concept of Anxiety* (1844), *Stages on Life's Way* (1845), *The Sickness Unto Death* (1849) and named a cycle of paintings *Frieze of Life — A Poem about*

Life, Love and Death, which included paintings with the titles *Death in the Sickroom*, *Anxiety*, *Ashes*, *Women in Three Stages*, *Metabolism*, *Love and Pain (Vampire)* and *The Sick Child*. Another cycle was called *The Angst of Living*.

Munch's work was directly informed by his illnesses, without which he would have struggled for subject matter; his expressionistic views of sickness, fear and anxiety were lifted directly from his own autobiography. Munch used suffering, mostly his own but that of others in his family and among his friends, to transform the realistic paintings of the nineteenth century into psychological and violently physical works of the twentieth century. His work prefigured artists such as Francis Bacon by way of Gauguin and van Gogh and he, in turn, informed the work of August Macke and Ernst Ludwig Kirchner (who spent time in the sanatorium at Davos, scene of Thomas Mann's *The Magic Mountain*). For Munch, sickness became art and art a sickness, "With every increase in the degree of consciousness, and in proportion to that increase, the intensity of despair increases: the more consciousness the more intense the despair," as Kierkegaard agrees in *The Sickness Unto Death*.

Munch's work evolved out of emotion and trauma; his many paintings, drawings and prints of *The Sick Child* were impressions and expressions of the death of his sister Sophie from tuberculosis at the age of fifteen. Munch suffered from the disease as a boy, often spitting blood the colour of the sky in his later paintings. Munch also accompanied his death-fixated father to visit patients. The variations of *The Sick Child* and *Death in the Sickroom* (1895), if put together in an exhibition, would resemble the wards in this sanatorium. Munch's colours are sombre; dark greens and reds, oranges that Bacon would use, the green of mucous, the red of expectorated blood, the orange of fever. In both paintings, the clothes worn by the mother in *The Sick Child* and the relatives in *Death in the*

Sickroom are already funereal, as if death were just the final stage of tuberculosis. Munch said of *The Sick Child* that "I opened for myself a new path — it was a breakthrough in my art. Most of what I have done since had its birth in this picture."

In *Death in the Sickroom*, the dying Sophie is surrounded by relatives, one of whom stares out at the viewer with the same expression as the people on the bridge in *Anxiety* (1895), drawing us into a collective despair, and it comes straight from Kierkegaard's *The Sickness Unto Death*: "The torment of despair is precisely this, not to be able to die. So it has much in common with the situation of the moribund when he lies and struggles with death, and cannot die. So to be sick unto death is not to be able to die — yet not as though there were hope of life; no the hopelessness in this case is that even the last hope, death, is not available. When death is the greatest danger, one hopes for death. So when the danger is so great that death becomes one's hope, despair is the disconsolateness of not being able to die."

In these paintings and their variations, Munch has locked his sister Sophie, himself and his family in an eternal zone of buffering, one in which Sophie is always dying, always about to die, always living, always dead, always sick, forever there but not there, always patient, always the patient. The anxiety of the woman who gazes out, of the people on the bridge in *Anxiety*, of the cataleptic strollers in *Evening on Karl Johan Street* (1892), is the anxiety of closure, the desire for a narrative ending, not this endless recycling of torment. Munch wrote in his journal that "I inherited two of mankind's most frightful enemies — the heritage of consumption and insanity — illness and madness and death were the black angels that stood at my cradle." A younger sister spent many years in an insane asylum and a brother died of pneumonia, while Edvard and his youngest sister Ingrid survived into old age, yet Munch feared life, he feared even more a Christian eternal life and believed, like Nietzsche in *Thus Spoke Zarathustra*, that God had been overthrown and was dead.

After his father died of a stroke in November 1889, Munch spent time in Paris, Berlin and Christiania, he also travelled through Europe, fleeing a love affair, drug and alcohol abuse. He continued producing sketches and paintings and maintaining a journal. In 1908, in Copenhagen, he collapsed Poe-like in the streets and, suffering from paralysis and auditory hallucination, was taken to a sanatorium to convalesce and kick his addictions. Despite earlier attempting suicide — he shot off part of one of his fingers — he still had thirty-six years of his life remaining.

Munch returned home to Norway in 1909 and became the newly liberated nation's state artist, garnering fame and wealth. Ever the contrarian, Munch withdrew to a country estate in order, he argued, to paint and remain sane. He turned to landscape painting but also produced more works for his *The Frieze of Life* cycle. He became more solitary in his isolated house, painting self-portraits of the ageing process and its incumbent infirmities, including one of him with Spanish influenza, caught during the pandemic of 1918–1919. Georgia O'Keeffe also survived, unfortunately Apollinaire, Schiele and Amadeo de Souza-Cardoso (a friend of Modigliani's) did not, nor did 50 to 100 million others.

Munch painted sickness, both physical and psychological. He painted his sick and dying sister, he painted self-portraits of his ravaged body, one of him with a burst blood vessel in his right eye, another, *Self-Portrait During the Eye Disease* (1930), shows him with a large purple and predatory blood clot. Clocks began to appear in some of his later works as if hurrying him along to the death he kept avoiding. In the 1930s, the Nazis had included Munch in their list of degenerative art. Munch eventually died of pneumonia brought on by cardiovascular disease on 23 January, 1944, a month after his eightieth birthday.

Now, in the eternal life of the sanatorium, he stands in front of Barrett Browning and Austen, arranges their frail limbs, their pale faces, their shawls and blankets, takes up his easel, looks at the mucous greens, the blood reds, the fevered oranges and begins to paint in order to add them to his "children."

We will leave them to it, maybe hang the finished painting with the others in reception — paintings of illness — and move into the sanatorium wards to meet some of our tubercular patients. As we do so, we will need to use the reading skill of suspending our disbelief because all of our patients will be suffering from tuberculosis as if streptomycin — the antibiotic first isolated by Albert Schatz on October 19, 1943 (three months before Munch died) and first used successfully against tuberculosis in 1946 — had not been isolated, and here the disease continues to ravage the human population. So let's strap on our cognitive-estrangement kit and proceed.

In the sanatorium, each patient has his or her own room — except the Brontës who share — the rooms are large and the distance between the rooms substantial. All doctors, nurses, orderlies and care workers must wear masks, as must all visitors. Everyone must go through a vigorous cleansing ritual and gargle with a powerful antiseptic mouthwash, they must also have their temperature taken and any anomalous readings mean they will not be admitted to the sanatorium beyond the medical anteroom. Likewise, any person exhibiting signs of a cold, influenza, asthma, bronchitis and other pulmonary infections will not be admitted beyond the medical anteroom. So let us wash our hands and forearms, gargle with the mouthwash, open wide our mouths and clamp our lips down on the thermometer, wait a while. 37°C, OK, that's fine. Put on our masks. Done. Let's enter the sanatorium proper.

The reception is a rotunda topped with an umbrella dome that allows light to flood down the walls, which are lined with paintings. Before we visit our first patient, let us examine some of these works of art. Some visitors complain, arguing that it must be distressing for the patients to witness these but, generally, they inspire recovery, instigate empathy and promote a sense of togetherness — well, maybe not for D.H. Lawrence, but more of that later.

The first painting, hung at just above head height, is *Tuberculosis in Harlem* (1940), oil on a square canvas, seventy-two centimetres by seventy-two centimetres, by Alice Neel (1900–1984). It has the sombre hues of a Munch but with a splash of outrageous pink that is at once the bedsheet the patient is lying on and the hint of an internal space infected and inflamed. The portrait shows the Puerto Rican musician Carlos Negrón in a hospital bed; his head rests atop his long neck, his emaciated chest is bare, his stomach slightly distended, a pale sheet covers his no doubt skinny legs. A square piece of gauze is taped over a wound in his chest. The man has suffered from tuberculosis since he was a child. The usual rest and recuperation, clean air and healthy food had done little to palliate his discomfort and so he underwent a thoracoplasty, a surgical procedure removing ribs to collapse and rest the infected lung. In 1945, at a sanatorium in Leysin, Switzerland, Roland Barthes underwent a similar operation, as he writes in *Roland Barthes by Roland Barthes*, "In order to perform an extrapleural pneumothorax operation, a piece of one of my ribs was removed, and subsequently given back to me, quite formally, wrapped up in a piece of medical gauze (the physicians, who were Swiss, as it happened, thereby professed that *my body belongs to me*, whatever dismembered state they restored it to me: I am the owner of my bones, in life as in death)."

In the painting, Negrón, who looks remarkably like Frida Kahlo, stares out at us, transfixing us with his gaze like the figures in Munch's paintings but, whereas in Munch the eyes are anguished or zombified, here they are dignified, evoking empathy. In this painting, we are reading the body, the not-yet corpse becoming the corpus of the man staring out at us; the artist writes the body, and what we see is "a life: studies, diseases, appointments. And the rest? Encounters, friendships, loves, travels, readings, pleasures, fears, beliefs, satisfactions, indignations, distresses: in a word — repercussions," as Barthes writes.

To the right of the Neel and slightly higher is a painting by the Cuban artist Fidelio Ponce de León (1895–1949). Modigliani-inspired, it is the very colour of sickness; pale pinks, greys, ochres, blues and blacks, it is called simply *Tuberculosis* (1934) and is oil on canvas and measures ninety-two centimetres by one-hundred-and-twenty-two centimetres. Like Modigliani, Ponce de León suffered from tuberculosis and like Munch and Modigliani he struggled with alcoholism. In the painting, five already ghostly figures, they might be nun-nurses, patients, a doctor with his hand on a skull, that are all infected, stare out at the viewer, as in Munch, as in Neel, and they look like the living dead, the now hospitalized figures of *Evening on Karl Johan Street*. It shows how pervasive tuberculosis was, tuberculosis is. This could be a family portrait of the Brontës but was painted from Ponce de León's experiences in tuberculosis hospitals. Although he lived until 1949 when streptomycin was available as a remedy, Ponce de León's excessive lifestyle and poverty meant he had to sell his paintings to buy the drug and, like Modigliani, it was a combination of alcohol, drug abuse and tuberculosis that killed him.

Of course, we have the Munch's up there, versions of *The Sick Child*, *Death in the Sick Room* and *By the Deathbed* (1896), with its five figures — prefiguring Ponce de León's

Tuberculosis — except these are standing by a deathbed not a skull, and the dead or dying figure is a mother struck down with tuberculosis. Three of the figures are as deathly pale as the corpse, the other two flame in a blood-red fever against the orange walls. The figure in the foreground, with its sunken eyes and centre-parted dark hair, resembles Franz Kafka, a skinny wrist and clenched hand reaching out to touch the still body. All of these paintings are rehearsals for death. The corpus becomes the corpse, immune against further disease, virginal and inaccessible to pain and suffering. Whereas the corpus, the body, is immured in the sanatorium, violable, awaiting failure. And the large photograph behind the reception desk, blown up to fill the whole back wall, enacts this rehearsal.

Henry Peach Robinson (1830–1901) created the combination photograph *Fading Away* in 1858, remarkably five years before the birth of Edvard Munch. It depicts a Victorian family — mother, father and sister — standing in a room attending a young woman dying from consumption. The photograph could be subtitled by a line from J.M. Coetzee's novel *Elizabeth Costello* (2003), "For that, finally, it's all it means to be alive: to be able to die."

The mother, already seemingly dressed in mourning garb, sits and looks on at the dying young girl, she looks like Queen Victoria would three years later as she mourned the death of Albert from typhoid fever. The sister stands behind the consumptive girl's bath chair, in contemplation of death, she looks like the rude in-health mirror-image of her soon-to-be-dead sister. Unlike Haworth parsonage, the building and room they are in looks immaculate with its heavy drapes and wooden furniture. The father, standing between these drapes, his back to us, staring out at the window at stormy skies, resembles Caspar David Friedrich's *Wanderer above the Sea of Fog* (1818) with its pre-Nietzschean figure staring out into an indeterminate future dwarfed by nature. *Wanderer above the Sea of Fog* was itself a composite painting, Caspar David Friedrich taking different elements of mountains, sky and geology and recomposing them in his studio. The dying girl, dressed in clothes that resemble a shroud, looks back at her mother, at a future she will not have, at an age she will not attain.

This photograph is a composite not only of five negatives but also of the sublime and the tragic, of the melodramatic and the Romantic. The consumptive young girl is not yet dead but appears already to be so, there is an incorporeal aura surrounding her; like the Lady of Shalott (Robinson would photograph the scene from Tennyson's poem in 1861), the consumptive girl appears to be already adrift towards death. In *Corpus*, Nancy writes: "And yet we won't claim that bodies are ineffable, that access to them is gained through the ineffable. The theme of the ineffable always serves the cause of a certain kind of speech — or a fable — more elevated, more refined, more secret, silent, and sublime: a pure treasure of sense, accessible to those connected to God. But 'God is dead' means: God *no longer has a body*. The world is neither the spacing of God nor the spacing in God: it becomes the world of bodies."

The father turns away, stares out onto a sublime sky, seeks refuge in denying the body of his daughter, a silence fills the room and transforms it into a Pre-Raphaelite Arthurian myth, a fable, more elevated and refined than death from tuberculosis. Yet, concurrently, the photograph is full of bodies, living, dying and already dead, already rotting. The father denies death, he has no name for it, yet the daughter in her shroud-like clothes is revealed as death, as no body.

The rubber seals on the doors through which we step into the tuberculosis ward make a sound of exhalation and suction as they open and close. The first room we come to is that of John

Keats. Let us remain quiet, open the door and step inside. The windows are closed, the curtains drawn, the light is wan. There are books on Keats' bedside table; Andrew Tooke's *Pantheon of the Heathen Gods and Illustrious Heroes*, Virgil's *Aeneid* and Percy Bysshe Shelley's *Alastor* sit in a pile next to blood-spattered handkerchiefs. While he sleeps, let us see what his medical chart tells us.

John Keats, born in Moorgate, London, 31 October, 1795, to Thomas Keats and Frances Jennings. He had three younger siblings, George, Thomas and Frances Mary. Schooled at John Clarke's School in Enfield, he was introduced to Renaissance literature, notably to the translations of Homer's *Iliad* and *Odyssey*, Virgil's *Georgics* and the satires of Juvenal by the dramatist and poet George Chapman. Keats would write a sonnet in homage to Chapman just two weeks before his twenty-first birthday, "On First Looking into Chapman's Homer."

Although outwardly healthy, Keats had already suffered from consumption-like illnesses. From an early age his breathing was never serene and like the father in *Fading Away* and the wanderer above the sea of fog, Keats places himself in Cortez's (historically erroneous) position, "Silent, upon a peak in Darien" looking out at an uncertain future. In a letter to his brother Tom, who was dying of consumption, Keats, on a walking tour of Scotland in August 1818, wrote: "After a little time the Mist cleared away but still there were large Clouds about attracted by old Ben to a certain distance so as to form as it appeared large dome curtains which kept sailing about, opening and shutting at intervals here and there and everywhere: so that although we did not see one vast wide extent of prospect all round we saw something perhaps finer — these cloud-veils opening with a dissolving motion and showing us the mountainous region beneath as through a loophole — these cloudy loopholes ever varying and discovering fresh prospect east, west, north and south."

Keats' mother had died of tuberculosis when he was fourteen, his father from a fall from a horse six years earlier. Soon after his mother's death, Keats left school and was apprenticed to a surgeon and apothecary in Edmonton named Thomas Hammond. During this apprenticeship from 1811 to 1815, Keats assisted the surgeon in his daily practice, setting broken bones, applying dressings to wounds and, in October 1815, he registered as a medical student at Guy's Hospital. Despite plans to become a surgeon and apothecary, by 1814 Keats had already resolved to become a poet, influenced more by Ovid, John Milton and Edmund Spenser than by Hippocrates, Galen and Samuel Sharp.

With Lord Byron as existential Romantic hero and Leigh Hunt as radical liberal essayist and role model, Keats continued to write poetry while studying anatomy, physiology, botany, chemistry, and general medicine. In the spring of 1815, Leigh Hunt published Keats' "O Solitude" in *The Examiner*, with its lone Romantic figure desiring to escape the pestilential city, the jumbled heap of murky buildings surrounding Guy's Hospital in Southwark, and join Caspar David Friedrich's wanderer staring out at nature's observatory. But soon this inspiration (this act of drawing in breath) would manifest itself in disease, "In solitude. — When one lives alone, one neither speaks too loud nor writes too loud, for one fears the hollow echo — the criticism of the nymph Echo. And all voices sound different in solitude!" Nietzsche claims. Having attained his apothecary's licence in 1816, Keats declared he would become a poet, but he still maintained his medical career although with doubts as to how good a surgeon he was.

Through Hunt, Keats met the Shelleys in December 1816, just after Hunt had published the two young poets plus John Hamilton Reynolds in *The Examiner*, proclaiming them a new school of youthful and naturalistic poetry. The first volume of Keats' poetry, simply titled *Poems*, was published by Charles and James Ollier on 3 March, 1817, which, although poorly promoted, reviewed and selling few copies, established Keats in the new wave of Romantic poets following the example of Wordsworth and Coleridge. The publishers Taylor and Hessey of Fleet Street saw Keats' potential, signed him to a new deal and supported him both financially and personally.

The "murky buildings" of Southwark were making Keats ill, he suffered from colds and his finances were in disarray and so, in April 1817, he escaped from inner-London to the then village of Hampstead to live with his brothers at 1 Well Walk. A few months earlier, he had written "Sleep and Poetry" and these bucolic lines must have haunted him as he and his brother George nursed their younger brother Tom who was dying of consumption. After emigrating to the USA in 1818 and living there, destitute after business failures, George and his wife would also die from tuberculosis.

Keats travelled to the Lake District, Scotland and then the Isle of Wight before returning in the summer of 1818 to continue nursing his dying brother. It is possible that it is during this period, a time when Keats was stricken with various colds and influenza-like symptoms, that he contracted *Mycobacterium tuberculosis*, "There came upon my face, in plenteous showers, / Dew-drops, and dewy buds…." — "Endymion." Tom died on 1 December, 1818 and Keats wrote to his brother George and sister-in-law Georgiana: "The last days of poor Tom were of the most distressing nature; but his last moments were not so painful, and his very last was without a pang. I will not enter into any parsonic comments on death — yet the common observations of the commonest people on death are as true as their proverbs. I have scarce a doubt of immortality of some nature or other — neither had Tom. […] During poor Tom's illness I was not able to write and since his death the task of beginning has been a hindrance to me."

Later in December 1818, he moved to Wentworth Place, not far from his Well Walk residence; the house, adjacent to Hampstead Heath, was owned by Keats' businessman friend Charles Armitage Brown. It was here in the spring of 1819, despite complaining of sore throats and colds, that he wrote "Ode on a Grecian Urn," "Ode on Indolence," "Ode on Melancholy," "Ode to a Nightingale," and "Ode to Psyche," and a few months later "To Autumn." Earlier on 17 March, he had written to George that "I look back upon that last month, I find nothing to write about; indeed, I do not recollect anything particular in it. It's all alike; we keep on breathing," and in the next paragraph stated, "I have been at different times turning it in my head whether I should go to Edinburgh and study for a physician: I am afraid I should not take kindly to it; I am sure I could not take fees — and yet I should like to do it; it's not worse than writing poems, and hanging them up to be fly-blown on the Review shambles. Everybody is in his own mess." Two months later, he was writing the six poems that enhanced his reputation, experiments in the short lyric form and representations of Keats' theory of "negative capability."

A year earlier on 3 May, 1818, he had written to John Hamilton Reynolds, "However among the effects this breathing is father of is that tremendous one of sharpening one's vision into the heart and nature of Man — of convincing ones nerves that the World is full of Misery and Heartbreak, Pain, Sickness, and oppression — whereby This Chamber of Maiden Thought becomes gradually darken'd and at the same time on all sides of it many doors are set open — but all dark — all leading to dark passages — We see not the balance of good and evil. We are in a Mist — We are now in that state — We feel the 'burden of the Mystery.'"

Keats' theory of negative capability informed not only his great odes but his life; by this time, spring 1819, he had experienced not only the death of his brother but had met and forged a relationship with Fanny Brawne, five years his junior and from a family beset with tuberculosis. She had moved into Wentworth Place with her mother in April and Keats and Brawne engaged upon an anxious, convoluted, passionate and probably unconsummated coupling. Keats' theory of negative capability became the foundation of his love for Brawne. He wrote to George on 22 December, 1817, "Negative Capability, that is, when a man is capable of being in uncertainties, mysteries, doubts, without any irritable reaching after fact and reason." Keats would martyr himself for the love of Fanny, he would embrace death for love, he would be "exquisitely miserable without the thought of soon seeing" her, he wrote on 13 October, 1819. This became not only his philosophy of love, the doubts, the uncertainties, the irritable reaching after fact but also reaching towards death. Cioran comments in *The Temptation to Exist* (2012) that, "To rejuvenate ourselves at the contact of death is a matter of investing it with all our energies, of becoming, like Keats, 'half in love with easeful death' or, like Novalis, of making of death the principle that 'romanticizes' life."

During this period, Keats wrote the darker poems "The Eve of St. Agnes," "La Belle Dame sans Merci" and "Lamia," and suffered from the first onset of serious tubercular symptoms. His possible death began to "romanticize" his relationship with Fanny, his writing and his life. "Along the chapel aisle by slow degrees: / The sculptur'd dead, on each side, seem to freeze, / Emprison'd in black, purgatorial rails," (The Eve of St. Agnes); "I saw their starved lips in the gloam, / With horrid warning gapèd wide, / And I awoke and found me here, / On the cold hill's side," (La Belle Dame sans Merci); and Lamia "breath'd death breath," but it wasn't only Lamia; in February 1820, Keats' tuberculosis ravaged his body and mind. Lines from his

"Ode to a Nightingale," "Where youth grows pale, and spectre-thin, and dies..." had come home to roost, now his doctors recommended he leave Fanny and Hampstead for a warmer and healthier location to try to escape the inevitable.

The haemorrhage had been serious. Charles Armitage Brown, who had become Keats' agent of a sort, describes how Keats "came home on the evening of Thursday, February 3rd, in a state of high fever, chilled from having ridden outside the coach on a bitterly cold day. He mildly and instantly yielded to my request that he should go to bed... On entering the cold sheets, before his head was on the pillow, he slightly coughed, and I heard him say — 'that is blood from my mouth.' I went towards him: he was examining a single drop of blood upon the sheet. 'Bring me the candle, Brown, and let me see this blood.' After regarding it steadfastly he looked up in my face with a calmness of expression that I can never forget, and said, 'I know the colour of that blood; — it is arterial blood; I cannot be deceived in that colour; that drop of blood is my death warrant; — I must die.'"

Throughout the year, Keats was beset with illness and anguish, he haemorrhaged blood, but the diagnosis of tuberculosis as a singular disease was a few years off and was not called tuberculosis until Johann Lukas Schönlein named it in 1839. The anguish was caused by doubts about his poetry, his relationship with Fanny and his accommodation — he lived variously with the Brawnes in Kentish Town and Brown and the Hunts in Hampstead. In the summer of 1820, doctors persuaded him to move south in search of cleaner and warmer air and on 13 September he left from Gravesend to join the *Maria Crowther* to sail to Italy, where he hoped to meet up with Shelley who was in Pisa. They suffered storms, doldrums and a ten-day quarantine for cholera (these could all be meteorological and medical metaphors for the past few years of Keats' life). He wrote to Brown from Naples on 1 November: "Yesterday we were let out of Quarantine, during which my health suffered more from bad air and a stifled cabin than it had done the whole voyage. The fresh air revived me a little, and I hope I am well enough this morning to write to you a short calm letter; — if that can be called one, in which I am afraid to speak of what I would the fainest dwell upon. As I have gone thus far into it, I must go on a little; — perhaps it may relieve the load of WRETCHEDNESS which presses upon me. The persuasion that I shall see her no more will kill me. I cannot q — My dear Brown, I should have had her when I was in health, and I should have remained well. I can bear to die — I cannot bear to leave her. Oh, God! God! God!"

Travelling with his friend, the painter Joseph Severn, Keats moved on to Rome and on 15 November took rooms on the Spanish Steps at 26 Piazza di Spagna. Keats' doctor, James Clarke, lived in a nearby building and diagnosed Keats' ailment as digestive in origin, prescribing walks, horse-riding, general exercise, blood letting and a starvation diet to relieve the mental exertion affecting his stomach. When Keats' health worsened and he continued to haemorrhage, Clarke changed his diagnosis to "consumption." In the 1 November letter to Brown, Keats asked, "It surprised me that the human heart is capable of containing and bearing so much misery. Was I born for this end?" It is clear that either he knew death was approaching or that he would hasten his own end by committing suicide through an overdose of opium.

On 30 November, he wrote again to Brown, "My stomach continues so bad, that I feel it worse on opening any book, — yet I am much better than I was in Quarantine. Then I am afraid to encounter the proing and conning of any thing interesting to me in England. I have an habitual feeling of my real life having past, and that I am leading a posthumous existence." This anguish and illness, this concatenation of love and death, caused Keats to become more anxious, less sure he would survive.

Keats continues to Charles Brown, "There is one thought enough to kill me — I have been well, healthy, alert &c, walking with her — and now — the knowledge of contrast, feeling for light and shade, all that information (primitive sense) necessary for a poem are great enemies to the recovery of the stomach." His writing was over, the "bright star," the "star predominant," would write no more letters, no more poems, his words eclipsed by pain.

On 9 December, he suffered a severe haemorrhage and became too ill and weak to read the letters Fanny had sent, believing the anguish her words caused him would make his illness worse. By Christmas, he had recovered enough to take short walks in the neighbourhood but had a series of major setbacks in the New Year of 1821, coughing blood and sweating profusely; he took to his bed on 10 January, nursed by the attentive Severn. In the late evening of 23 February, in the arms of Severn, Keats died. He was buried in the Non-Catholic Cemetery in Testaccio, Rome, where, one year later, Shelley's ashes were interred. Severn is also buried there.

Tuberculosis killed Keats at the age of twenty-five and there is no doubt he would have written poetry and continued to send wonderful letters to his friends and family. Yet, without the "consumption," would he have had that splendid year of 1819 where "his bright star" went supernova, producing the great odes "The Fall of Hyperion," "The Eve of St Agnes," "La Belle Dame sans Merci," "Lamia" and others? Would he have written those letters? On his deathbed, Keats was uncertain about his legacy, he doubted everything, his relationship with Fanny, what he had achieved in his life and he sought an escape from pain and anguish, he sought to "pass into nothingness."

In *The Temptation to Exist*, Cioran, writing 120 years after Keats' death, comes closest to understanding Keats' attitude to life, love and writing, when he states, "Doubt waxes by all that weakens or opposes it; it is a sickness within another sickness, an obsession within obsession."

Let us take our leave of Keats, replace his notes on the clip, take a last look at his curly locks upon the pillow, close the door behind us and let him have his "mute and uncomplaining sleep; / For he is gone, where all things wise and fair / Descend," as Percy Bysshe Shelley eulogized in *Adonaïs* (1821).

We follow the corridor to the next room or, should I say, rooms. This is where the Brontës are ensconced. The doctors have tried to separate them, give them their own accommodation where there would be less danger of cross-contamination, but they refuse to move or be separated and insist on their living and dying together in a cramped space in which our nurses and orderlies struggle to maintain sanitary standards, but they prevail against the complaints of these stubborn Yorkshire writers.

Between the time Keats was writing "An Imitation of Spenser" in 1814, his final volume of poetry *Lamia, Isabella, The Eve of St. Agnes, and Other Poems* had been published — the volume found in the drowned Shelley's pocket — all of the Brontë children were born: Maria, 23 April, 1814; Elizabeth (unknown) 1815; Charlotte, 21 April, 1816; Patrick Branwell, 26 June, 1817; Emily Jane, 30 July, 1818; and Anne, 17 January, 1820. By the time of the publication of Elizabeth Gaskell's novel *North and South* in 1855, they had all died: Maria, Elizabeth, Branwell, Emily and Anne from tuberculosis, and Charlotte from a combination — so biographers would have us believe — of phthisis (tuberculosis) with complications of dehydration and malnourishment due to *hyperemesis gravidarum* (chronic morning sickness) and possibly typhus.

Elizabeth Gaskell, in her biography of Charlotte published in 1857, wrote: "She took to her bed, too weak to sit up. From that last couch she wrote two notes — in pencil. […] I do not think she ever wrote a line again. Long days and longer nights went by; still the same relentless nausea and faintness, and still borne on in patient trust. About the third week in March there was a change; a low wandering delirium came on; and in it she begged constantly for food and even for stimulants. She swallowed eagerly now; but it was too late. Wakening for an instant from this stupor of intelligence, she saw her husband's woe-worn face, and caught the sound of some murmured words of prayer that God would spare her. 'Oh!' she whispered forth, 'I am not going to die, am I? He will not separate us, we have been so happy.'" The similarities between Charlotte Brontë's death and that of Keats are striking, striking that is if we replace "happy" with "anguished," "trust" with "doubt" and "spare" with "kill." Charlotte was just thirty-eight when she died, relatively older than her siblings at their time of death.

As we open the door, we hear a scribbling and the strained breath of the three writerly sisters and their artist brother. Both Maria and Elizabeth are already dead and buried. Their father Patrick is away at the parsonage in Haworth sermonizing and attending the sick. Their mother Maria died of uterine cancer when Anne was not quite two years old and bowel cancer killed their aunt Elizabeth in 1842. Another aunt, Tabytha Aykroyd, acted as maid and carer and regaled the children with local folklore and legend, some of which inspired *Jane Eyre*, *Wuthering Heights* (1847) and *The Tenant of Wildfell Hall* (1848).

They huddle by the fire, all sitting around a table, all scribbling into tiny books, sharing stories, creating worlds such as Glass Town, the Empire of Angria and Emily and Anne's Gondal, as fanciful and imaginary as those of Jorge Luis Borges and Italo Calvino. These books, written and made by the girls, were the size of a matchbox and contained texts, drawings and maps, they were made for Branwell's set of a dozen toy soldiers. In the unsanitary confines of Haworth, these were pockets of escape, little books filled with a need for more space, more air, more life, all fuelled by the periodicals and books brought home by their father.

It was as if the children knew that they were not long for this life, as if the literature of the house was driving them to create, to work together to construct these worlds that were to become classics of English literature. By an early age, the writerly sisters had established that, as Nietzsche writes in *Daybreak*, "under the spell of the morality of custom (*Jane Eyre*), man despises first the causes, secondly the consequences, thirdly reality (*Wuthering Heights*), and weaves all his higher feelings (of reverence, of sublimity, of pride, of gratitude, of love) into an imaginary world: the so-called higher world. And the consequences are perceptible even today: wherever a man's feelings are exalted, that imaginary world is involved in some way. It is a sad fact, but for the moment the man of science has to be suspicious of all higher feelings, so greatly are they nourished by delusion and nonsense. It is not that they are thus in themselves, or must always remain thus: but of all the gradual purifications awaiting mankind (*The Tenant of Wildfell Hall*), the purification of the higher feelings will certainly be one of the most gradual."[3]

The writerly sisters' imaginary worlds grew into gothic, romantic and social novels that influenced and inspired future generations of writers and gave birth to a literary pilgrimage second only to Shakespeare's Stratford-upon-Avon. Branwell, the painter of the most famous portrait of the sisters, became a drunk and opium addict and was unaware of his sisters' success.

---

3 Italics and brackets mine.

Originally, they sent their poems to publishers under male pen-names — Currer, Ellis, and Acton Bell — but were soon reassuming the Brontë name and meeting their literary peers.

Because of the draw of Haworth parsonage — even Cioran in *The Trouble with Being Born* proclaimed, "Emily Brontë: everything that comes from her has the capacity to overwhelm me. Haworth is my Mecca" — the writerly sisters appear to us locked in those unsanitary confines, the bleak moors at their backs, the graveyard view from the windows, winds howling, snow dusting the rooftops, crows like black dogs stalking their moods and minds. Yet the Brontë children, those of them that survived, had a happy childhood. What they saw about them, what they read in periodicals and books, they wrote about — sexual inequality, social injustice, industrial strife and mental and physical trauma. They also travelled outside of the confines of Haworth, to London to reveal themselves as women writers, to Lancashire and even to Brussels. While Branwell forsook his painting for a life of gin and laudanum, the sisters created masterpieces of literature.

Theirs was a writerly life hurtling towards a death caused by proximity and collaboration. A death by inspiration, a death by expectoration, a death expected and subsequently inspected to the point of obsession. Books on the Brontës proliferate faster than the *Mycobacterium tuberculosis*, the hospital library has a whole wing just to shelve the ever-growing Brontë juvenilia, biographies, zombie rewritings, ephemera and tribute anthologies. The question remains: would the writerly sisters be as famous and read now if they had not all died young? If consumption had not consumed them, would their village of Haworth and the parsonage have become the loci of the conspicuous consumption of bespoke merchandise?

Wuthering Heights was written by Emily Brontë when she was twenty-seven years old and was first published in 1847 under the pseudonym Ellis Bell. Emily, already suffering from tuberculosis, mirrors the cramped conditions of Haworth and her love of the open spaces of the moors within the interior and exterior locations of the novel. In the confines of Wuthering Heights and Thrushcross Grange, the cruelty of her disease is apparent in the various internments and abductions, while her wish to be able to breathe easily, to be free of illness, is expressed (literally) in the air and winds of the moors. In *A Thousand Plateaus*, Deleuze and Guattari also see this in Emily's older sister, "In Charlotte Bronte, everything is in terms of wind, things, people, faces, loves, words."

In *Literature and Evil* (1957), Georges Bataille described Emily as "the object of a privileged curse." This privileged curse, not so for Branwell, was tuberculosis. As here in the hospital room, the sisters were enclosed in a world of writing, by a proximity at once physical and hypermoral. Literature overcame the silence, the examinations of cruelty, revenge, atonement, and sexual, social and gender politics surpassed their narrow upbringing. Bataille here quotes Jacques Blondel, "Emily Brontë shows herself […] capable of emancipating herself from all prejudice of an ethical or social order. Thus several lives develop […] each of which conveys a sense of total liberation from society and morality." But this was not only an emancipation from prejudice but, as with *Jane Eyre* and *The Tenant of Wildfell Hall*, an emancipation from illness and the possibility of contagion; Catherine, Heathcliff, Jane, Mr Rochester, Helen and Arthur are means by which Emily, Charlotte and Anne liberate themselves physically from their tormented bodies, spiritual and moral severity, and their cramped and unsanitary confines. Fighting against the seriousness of their illnesses, they embrace art as life, writing as a fullness that will soon be taken away from them, a creativity that refuses the reality of their consumption. The liberation of their poems and novels is contrary to their lives, an attempted antidote to their impending deeply rooted early deaths.

As Branwell sips down a phial of laudanum, as Charlotte coughs demurely into her handkerchief, as Anne starts a new sampler and Emily stares out of the window at the glowering clouds and the vampiric dentures of the graveyard, we shall take our leave and let Georges Bataille have the last words from *Inner Experience* (1943): "At a time of confusion and anxiety when I searched frantically for something to link me to chance, I still had to kill time. I didn't want to give in to the cold then. To keep from giving in, I intended to find consolation in a book. But available books were ponderous, hostile, too stilted — except for poems of Emily Bronte."

We close the door to the sound of more scratching and scribbling, more coughing and expectorating, and walk along the corridor. Strange how the temperature around the Brontës' room is always cold; a frigid air haunts these halls, the collected breath of the siblings mists the window of the door making it look as though it is raining within, ideas percolating, contagion rife.

The temperature increases the further away we get from that room until it becomes somewhat balmy, the grey unlight brightens to a yellow blue and the view from the windows is one of sunshine and palm trees, not moon gloom and tombstones.

Buried in the same cemetery as Keats, R.M. Ballantyne's adventure novels and stories influenced the work of our next patient, the author of *Treasure Island* (1883), *Strange Case of Dr Jekyll and Mr Hyde* (1886) and *In the South Seas* (1896), Robert Louis Stevenson.

Before we knock and enter, here's what Stevenson wrote in *Essays on the Art of Writing* (1905): "A work of art is first cloudily conceived in the mind; during the period of gestation it stands more clearly forward from these swaddling mists, puts on expressive lineaments, and becomes at length that most faultless, but also, alas! that incommunicable product of the human mind, a perfected design. On the approach to execution all is changed. The artist must now step down, don his working clothes, and become the artisan. He now resolutely commits his airy conception, his delicate Ariel, to the touch of matter; he must decide, almost in a breath, the scale, the style, the spirit, and the particularity of execution of his whole design." Interesting. Now let us get a second opinion from Stevenson's specialist, Mr Gilles Deleuze, from his *Essays Critical and Clinical*: "Art also attains this celestial state that no longer retains anything of the personal or rational. In its own way, art says what children say. It is made up of trajectories and becomings, and it too makes maps, both extensive and intensive. There is always a trajectory in the work of art, and Stevenson, for example, shows the decisive importance of a colored map in his conception of *Treasure Island*. This is not to say, that a milieu necessarily determines the existence of characters, but rather that the latter are defined by the trajectories they make in reality or in spirit, without which they would not become." Stevenson only "became" when he was on a trajectory away from his illness, departing from the reality of tuberculosis, or tuberculosis with complications of bronchiectasis and/or sarcoidosis.

His novels and stories abound with doctors and characters afflicted with disease, missing limbs and molecular mutation. His trajectory towards the South Seas by way of Europe and the United States of America was made in reality, in spirit and in literature in the Caribbean setting of *Treasure Island* and the uncanny streets of Victorian London. His whole life was a coloured map that became works of art and — if X-rays had have existed at the time — the map would have shown the oceans of a diseased lung spotted with tubercular islands, as he wrote in *In The South Seas*, "The thought of death sits down with him to meat, and rises with him from his bed; he lives and breathes under the shadow of mortality awful to support; and he is so inured to the apprehension that he greets the reality with relief."

Deleuze expands this idea of flight as a *modus operandi* of literature, "To leave, to escape, is to trace a line. The highest aim of literature, according to Lawrence, is 'To leave, to leave, to escape … to cross the horizon, enter into another life … It is thus that Melville finds himself in the middle of the Pacific. He has really crossed the line of the horizon.'" That's where Melville finds himself and Stevenson also, a place where we do battle with our own Moby Dicks. For Lawrence and for Stevenson, the white whale was their own diseased bodies, their writing the *Pequod*,

"There it is again — under the hatches — don't you hear it — a cough — it sounded like a cough," Melville anticipates Lawrence and Stevenson's fear of that cough, that reminder of mortality, that flight to the South Seas.

Deleuze continues, "The line of flight is a deterritorialization," and Stevenson fled from his Edinburgh roots; his father was a lighthouse engineer and his mother came from a legal and religious background — Stevenson would graduate in law from Edinburgh University despite his poor health. He moved away from the home of his illness, the stone-grinding of his father's factories, breathing in the dust of granite blocks, his father's workers contracting silicosis of the lungs which then developed into the dangerously transmittable tuberculosis. The smog and coal-smoke darkness of Edinburgh could have been a contributing factor to the young Stevenson's weak respiratory system. Always a sickly child, he had his first attack of a tubercular nature at the age of six. As we have seen, it is uncertain whether tuberculosis was the correct diagnosis but the symptoms are similar and more than one tuberculosis specialist examined Stevenson and concluded that he had the disease.

In *Stevenson Under the Palm Trees* (2003), Alberto Manguel has Stevenson remember "the long nights of his childhood, when, gasping for breath and shaken by a hollow cough, he had sat up in his bed, with his nurse by his side, waiting for what they called the Night Hag to finish her ghastly business and go, he had told himself that if ever he had enough strength, he would use it to lead his body to the edge of any possible adventure; he would take to the road or the sea, he would set off like a new Ulysses in the hope of strange encounters but, above all, he would travel for the sake of the journey itself. He had imagined his sick bed as a boat into which his nurse would help him every night and then, when the lights went out, he would cast off into the blue darkness, breathing lightly. In this hope he had waited for morning."

His line of flight away from the cause of his illness, his father had tuberculosis, was a deterritorialization, as was Stevenson's six-thousand-mile journey to meet his future wife, to escape the solid and stolid Presbyterian family and realize his own commitments and responsibilities. On the way, by ship and then train, he almost died but managed to reach California and marry Fanny Van de Grift in May 1880. Fanny was recovering from typhoid, typhus, cholera or tuberculosis, but it is unclear which and some commentators argue that Fanny's illness was psychosomatic, owing to trauma brought on by the death of her five year-old son Hervey from scrofulous tuberculosis in 1876, the year she first met Stevenson in Paris. Stevenson was in France that year because, since 1873, when his health failed him yet again, he had spent time on the French Riviera, the Forest of Fontainebleau, Barbizon, Grez-sur-Loing, and Nemours recuperating from tubercular attacks. In 1876, he and his friend Sir Walter Simpson canoed the waterways of Belgium and France, which would lead Stevenson to write *An Inland Voyage* in 1878.

Both Lawrence and Stevenson fled Britain and sought refuge in the USA, Deleuze may have a reason for their flight. He quotes Lawrence: "'I tell you, old weapons go rotten: make some new ones and shoot accurately.' To fly is to trace a line, lines, a whole cartography. One only discovers worlds through a long, broken flight. Anglo-American literature constantly shows these ruptures, these characters who create their line of flight, who create through a line of flight. Thomas Hardy, Melville, Stevenson, Virginia Woolf, Thomas Wolfe, Lawrence, Fitzgerald, Miller, Kerouac. In them everything is departure, becoming, passage, leap, daemon, relationship with the outside. They create a new Earth; but perhaps the movement of the earth is deterritorialization itself."

Stevenson confirms this active flight in *In the South Seas*, "For nearly ten years my health had been declining; and for some while before I set forth upon my voyage, I believed I was come to the afterpiece of life, and had only the nurse and undertaker to expect. It was suggested that I should try the South Seas; and I was not unwilling to visit like a ghost, and be carried like to bale, among scenes that attracted me in youth and health." Stevenson was in flight from the sick room, an active search for deterritorialization, a constant "set[ting] forth to leeward" in search of things that were "to the European eye so foreign."

In that flight, in that foreign loci, Stevenson realized the outcome of, not only his, but the fate of every living thing; the sickness unto death is also the sickness that ends literature. He perceived his illness as a transformative, almost apocalyptic event, that not only affects him but those around him, "The tribe of Hapaa is said to have numbered some four hundred, when the smallpox came and reduced them by one-fourth. Six months later a woman developed tubercular consumption; the disease spread like a fire about the valley, and in less than a year two survivors, a man and a woman, fled from the new-created solitude." Tuberculosis is Mr Hyde, Stevenson the "phial of tincture" that changes paradise into hell, "Early in the year of my visit, for example, or late the year before, the first case of phthisic appeared in a household of seventeen persons, and by the month of August, when the tale was told me, one soul survived."

There is a sense of guilt in Stevenson's travels, a sense that his illness is operating some kind of observer effect. Manguel metaphorizes this in creating a doppelgänger for Stevenson, a Hyde-like figure who may or may not have committed rape and murder. Stevenson's cough becomes a nervous tic of guilt, "The coughing began as it so often did, without warning, first as a rasping in the back of his throat and then a hacking, dry splutter that seemed never to end," and "For a long moment, he felt that his knees were giving way and, just before losing consciousness, he saw in the handkerchief he held before his mouth a large bright stain, as crimson as the flower the girl wore in her hair."

This hint of death in a handkerchief, this almost medieval emblem of lost virginity, of murder, the loss of consciousness, of the cessation of life and so writing, inspires Stevenson, "In the morning, he woke feeling curiously better than he had in a long time, as if the wracking cough had passed like a storm, leaving him almost refreshed, without even his usual shortness of breath. Fanny wanted him to stay in bed but he wouldn't hear of it. He felt full of delicious energy, and, after breakfast, he sat down to write a new chapter of the dark Scottish romance he was composing." Time was running out, Stevenson was hurtling towards silence and he wonders that "perhaps now that life had become commonplace, that routine had set in and that the same things returned his indifferent glance day in, day out, now that there was no ardour left in his nights with Fanny who, out of concern for his health or out of mere latitude, barely brushed a goodnight kiss on his cheek before falling asleep, perhaps now he might write something worthwhile, full of true blood and real thunder. With the exception of that dark excursus that had so offended Fanny, the present book was advancing nicely and he felt that he was being ungrateful to the fates that allowed him this moment of grace."

Stevenson would die on 3 December, 1894, aged forty-four, at Villa Vailima, his home in Samoa. He was trying to open a bottle of wine and suddenly asked Fanny, "What's that? Do I look strange?" The cause of death was a cerebral haemorrhage, a murderous swirl in the brain. Stevenson wrote constantly; he was working on *Weir of Hermiston* (1896), a novel he thought of as his masterpiece, the morning before he died, the last words he wrote were, "It seemed unprovoked, a wilful convulsion of brute nature." Writing about Georges Bataille, Nick Land states that "the human animal is the one through which terrestrial excess is haemorrhaged to zero, the animal destined to obliterate itself in history, and sacrifice its nature utterly to the solar storm. Capital breaks us down and reconstructs us, with increasing frequency, as it pursues its energetic fluctuation towards annihilation, driven to the liberation of the sun, whilst the object hurtles into the vaporization of proto-schizophrenic commodification."

Stevenson actively sought the solar storm, his whole life became an "energetic fluctuation towards annihilation," a liberation from his illness in the sun of the South Seas, his proto-schizophrenic Dr Jekyll and Mr Hyde prefiguring his own haemorrhage to zero and vaporization. On second thoughts, let's not disturb him. We'll go to see our next patient whose room included a sick bed, a writing desk and a doctor's bag.

Anton Chekhov (1860–1904) ticks all the boxes for this book: a doctor, a writer and a tuberculosis sufferer. Born in Taganrog, a port city in the Rostov Oblast on the Sea of Azov in Russia, Chekhov graduated from the I.M. Sechenov First Moscow State Medical University in 1884, the year he first began to cough up blood. He had already gained a reputation as a writer for newspapers and periodicals. In 1886, the haemoptysis became serious, yet Chekhov refused to be examined and have the disease confirmed. It was as if Chekhov was living a future maxim of Nietzsche, who wrote in his notebook in the summer of 1888 that "we need art in order not to die from the truth." Chekhov would continue to create his short stories and plays, continue to treat his patients and continue to deny his illness.

On 10 December, 1884, from Moscow, he wrote to Nikolay Leikin, "For three days now for no reason at all I have been bleeding from the throat. It has stopped me working, and also from coming to Piter […] it just came out of the blue, thank you kindly! It's three days since I've been able to bring up decent white phlegm, and there's no knowing when the medicines my colleagues keep cramming into me will start to work. Apart from that I'm fine […] I imagine the causes a burst blood vessel…" That ellipsis at the end tells the true story, Chekhov must have known that the blood was from his lungs and not his throat and that it was serious enough to preclude him writing his articles and working as a locum.

Two years later, in a letter to Alexey Suvorin, Chekhov goes to great lengths to deny his tuberculosis. He replies to Suvorin's questions about his health that, "about my coughing blood. I first noticed it three years ago when I was attending the [Moscow] circuit court: it went on for about three days and caused quite a commotion in my soul and in my home. There was a lot of blood. It came from my right lung. Subsequently I've noticed some bleeding once or twice a year, and sometimes there has been a lot of blood, by which I mean what I cough up would be thick red, but sometimes not that much…" Again, that ellipsis. That omission rather than admission. That same year, 1888, the year Stevenson first set sail for the South Seas, the year Nietzsche completed *The Case of Wagner*, *Twilight of the Idols*, *The Antichrist*, *Ecce Homo* and *Nietzsche contra Wagner*, Chekhov wrote "Sleepy," a short story about Varka, a thirteen year-old infanticidal nursemaid who, tired from overwork and her abusive employees, dreams that "on the floor lies her dead father, Yélim Stépanov. She cannot see him, but she hears him rolling from side to side, and groaning. In his own words, he 'has had a rupture.' The pain is so intense that he cannot utter a single word, and only inhales air and emits through his lips a drumming sound." The ellipsis, the invisible father/author has become the deterritorialized and dying Chekhov that he refuses to see and countenance.

He continued in his letter of 14 October, "The day before yesterday, or the day before that, I don't remember exactly, I noticed some blood in the evening, but today it has stopped. I get a cough every winter, autumn and spring, and on damp days in the summer. But the only time it worries me is when I see blood: there is something sinister about blood flowing from the mouth, like the glow of a fire." For a writer so precise and demanding, so penetrating in his minute dissection of ordinary lives, this letter shows the poverty of his self-awareness. In *A Thousand Plateaus*, the tuberculosis sufferer Deleuze and the psychotherapist Guattari analyze this, "The poverty is not a lack but a void or ellipsis allowing one to sidestep a constant instead of tackling it head on, or to approach it from above or below instead of positioning oneself within it." Chekhov's short stories and his work as a doctor meant he could ignore his illness by having others suffer (in his fiction and plays) and assuage their suffering in his medical practice (Chekhov mostly treated the poor and was rarely paid for his work).

His short stories are the indirect discourse of his life with tuberculosis. Chekhov rejected his illness in favour of the differences of dynamic in writing and medicine. On 11 September, 1888, in another letter to Suvorin, "Medicine is my lawful wedded wife, and literature my mistress. When I've had enough of one, I can go and spend the night with the other. You may well call this disorderly conduct, but at least it stops me getting bored, and in any event I'm sure that neither of them is the loser from my infidelity. If it were not for medicine, I would not be devoting my leisure moments and my private thoughts to literature; I haven't the discipline to do so." Tuberculosis would have been an unwelcome suitor and Chekhov refused to acknowledge it as part of his troilistic creativity.

Aware of this, he continues his denial, his elliptic rejection of his illness in his elliptic writing style by claiming that "the point is the consumption and other serious lung diseases only manifest themselves to a particular set of symptoms, and I don't have that particular combination." The breathlessness, the coughing, the haemoptysis were classic combination symptoms of tuberculosis. Rather than informing his writing, as it had done that of Keats and the Brontës, tuberculosis deformed it, as if the tubercal bacilli had invaded the blank spaces between words or that the ellipsis was formed by a bacterial colony. Chekhov concludes, "If the bleeding I experienced in that circuit court room had been a symptom of incipient consumption, I would long ago have departed this life — that is my logic." A logical negativism against his realist positivist philosophy.

Chekhov's fictional worlds, his miniaturist portraits of everyday life and ordinary people, are world's outside of himself in the denial of what was happening inside his body; he denied his body while creating fictional others through which he metaphorized suffering. "I'm not a body," he constantly claimed, "I am a doctor" and "I am a writer." The fictional worlds he created, however realistic, co-appeared with Chekhov's denial of the reality of his disease, his world was dis-positioned through tuberculosis. 25 October, 1897, again to Alexey Suvorin: "I've had another episode of coughing blood, lasting three or four days, but now I am fine, leaping about feeling quite well. I've written two stories and sent them off," despite what he told Suvorin in a letter on 1 April of that year, "The doctors have diagnosed active pulmonary tuberculosis at the apex of my lungs and ordered me to change my way of life. The first thing I understand, but the second I don't because it is almost impossible." Chekhov was a workaholic, constantly writing, editing, attending rehearsals of his plays, yet, it was writing not the reality of everyday life that he could not change, as he explains to Suvorin, "They say I must definitely live in the country, but don't they realize that full-time country living entails constant problems with peasants, animals and the elements in all their aspects, and that you're as likely to escape getting burnt in hell as you are to protect yourself from cares and troubles in the country."

That statement sounds like a synopsis of one of Chekhov's stories. The next day, he wrote to his brother Alexander: "Here's the story. Almost every spring since 1884 I have coughed up a bit of blood. But this year, following your rebuke to me for accepting the blessings of the Most Holy Synod, I was so upset by your unbelief that in the presence of Mr. Suvorin I suffered a severe haemorrhage and was taken to the clinic. Here I was diagnosed with pulmonary apical tuberculosis and accordingly awarded the right to describe myself, should I so desire, as an invalid." Not as a writer, not as a doctor, but as an invalid, dis-positioned. There's the story. Another playwright and elliptician, Samuel Beckett, had the same problem, "What am I to do, what shall I do, what should I do, in my situation, how proceed? By aporia pure and simple? Or by affirmations and negations invalidated as uttered, or sooner or later?"

Chekhov died aged forty-four on 15 July, 1904, the same age as Stevenson. His tuberculosis was terminal. Here's the story told by Raymond Carver, who died in 1988 from lung cancer at the age of fifty: "On July 2, 1904, after midnight, Olga sent someone to get the doctor. Chekhov was delirious. When the doctor arrived, he told Olga he'd send for oxygen. Suddenly Chekhov became lucid & spoke, 'What's the use? Before it arrives I'll be a corpse.' The doctor figured out how to use the phone on the wall & called the kitchen. He ordered up champagne and 3 glasses which were delivered by a young, sloppily-dress boy. It was almost 3 in the morning. They drank; minutes later, Chekhov died. Olga asked the doctor not to tell anyone about the death until the morning; she wanted time alone with Chekhov." And we will let her have that time, as we close the door, step along the corridor to the room decorated with a strange mix of Maori designs and Mediterranean furniture.

In a letter to the translator S.S. Koteliansky on 21 August, 1919, Katherine Mansfield (1888–1923) expands Chekhov's ellipsis to enclose the world: "I have re-read *The Steppe*. What can one say? It is simply one of *the* great stories of the world — a kind of Iliad or Odyssey. I think I would learn this journey by heart. One says of things: they are immortal. One feels about this story not that it becomes immortal — it always was. It has no beginning or end. T[chehov] just touched one point with his pen (. — — .) and then another point: *enclosed* something which had, as it were, been there forever." A few days earlier, she had written to Virginia Woolf, "This is the first day I am up again and able to write letters. I have been rather badly ill, and it has left me for the moment without an idea […] except that I must go abroad into a Sanatorium until next April." Unlike Chekhov, Mansfield explored her illness, her convalescence and her impending death, she wrote within her tuberculosis not around it, sharing and comparing symptoms and places where she could get respite in letters to and meetings with D.H. Lawrence.

Mansfield reinvented herself continuously in her short stories, letters and journals; as Keats wrote, a poetic character "is not itself — it has no self — it is everything and nothing — It has no character." Mansfield's self existed in the correspondence and the journals she kept. She suffered and wrote about her suffering, she travelled in order to find a cure for her tuberculosis and wrote about those places. Often alone, she saw her suffering as a gift through which she could observe the world with an attachment and intimacy sometimes missing in the work she so admired of Chekhov. Mansfield wrote in order to stay alive, whereas Chekhov wrote in order to deny death — they are very different motives. In the short story "The-Child-Who-Was-Tired" (1910), Mansfield adapts Chekhov's plot for "Sleepy;" the child is bullied by her masters while looking after a bawling baby and she has the same thoughts of infanticide. Whereas Chekhov's Varka sought silence and hallucinated the death of her father in order to control her world, Mansfield's child seeks peace and solace in a world she cannot control, "She heaved a long sigh, then fell back on to the floor, and was walking along a little white road with tall black trees on either side, a little road that led to nowhere, and where nobody walked at all — nobody at all." Chekhov's character yearns to be part of her world, the-child-who-was-tired seeks to be alone, the solitude of the invalid. Both stories are accounts of lives interrupted by crisis, as were the lives of Chekhov and Mansfield, and of a suffering mind tortured by lack of sleep, pain and psychological stress.

In a journal entry in 1909, around the time of a miscarriage, Mansfield writes, "I think I must have caught a cold in my beautiful exultant walk yesterday, for today I am ill. After I wrote to you, I began to work but could not — *and* so cold." Mansfield's later life and work fused the forced convalescence with the desire to write and the drive to experience nature; she walks, coughs, writes. In 1917, her constant illness was discovered to be extrapulmonary tuberculosis and in a letter to her estranged husband John Middleton Murry she parrots Chekhov's letter to Suvorin twenty years earlier, "Here is the certificate which the doctor has just given me. Is it alright? He says that left lung of mine that had the *loud deafening* crack in it is 'no end better' there is a SPOT in my right lung which confirms him in his opinion that it is absolutely imperative that I go out of the country and keep out of it all through the future winters." Mansfield response is a positive one, she sees it as an opportunity not a burden. She continues, "I feel now that I've only to get into the sun and I'll simply burst into leaf and flower again."

Mansfield's vitality is similar to that of D.H. Lawrence but without the crippling disillusionment. In Mansfield's writing there is a becoming one with things, the barrier of threshold between self and other dissolves as does the difference between humans and animals, the sun and the moon, a kind of pagan spiritualism not disimilar to Acker's. Pain destabilizes the limits of the body, Mansfield described the burning in her lung as a "flat-iron" and her and Lawrence understood the materiality of the body, how the corpus affects and is affected by the would-be corpse. As Nancy explains: "A corpus of the weighings of a material, of its mass, its pulp, its grain, its gulf, its mole, its molecule, its turf, its trouble, its turgidity, its fiber, its juice, its invagination, its volume, its peak, its fall, its meat, its coagulation, its paste, its crystallinity, its tightness, its spasm, its steam, its knot, its unknotting, its tissue, its home, its disorder, its wound, its pain, its promiscuity, its odor, its pleasure, its taste, its timbre, its resolution, its high and low, right and left, its acidity, its windedness, its balancing, its dissociation, its resolution, its reason..." He finishes with an ellipsis, that fear of space, of the void.

As Mansfield writes in her journal on 19 February, 1918, "I spat — it tasted strange — it was bright red blood. Since then I've gone spitting each time I cough a little more. Oh, yes, of course I'm frightened... I don't want to find this is real consumption, perhaps it's going to gallop — who knows? — and I shan't have my work written. *That's what matters.* How unbearable it would be to die — leave 'scraps', 'bits' ... nothing real finished." She feels an interconnection with the whole world as she explains in a letter to her husband on 20 February, 1918, "...Since this little attack I have had, a queer thing has happened. I feel that my love and longing for the external world — I mean the world of *nature* — suddenly increased a million times." In June of that year, she stayed in a hotel and woke in the night to hear a man coughing in the next room, he has the same disease, she feels as though they are, "two roosters calling to each other at false dawn. From far away hidden farms."

Maybe it was the same cough Hans Castorp first heard in the Davos sanatorium, "It was coughing, obviously, a man coughing; but coughing like no other Hans Castorp had ever heard, and compared with which any other had been a magnificent and healthy manifestation of life: a coughing that had no conviction and gave no relief, that did not even come out in paroxysms, that was just a feeble, dreadful welling up of the juices of organic dissolution." Health and illness merged into one, the tuberculosis was ever-present; writing — her only desire — was changed by her disease, "even my present state of health is a great gain. It makes things so rich, so important, so longed for… changes one's focus."

Mansfield's philosophy is not some kind of holistic stew but a Nietzschean (or Lawrentian) affirmation of existence. As Mansfield writes in her journal on 21 June, 1919, "I had a sense of the *larger breath*, of the mysterious lives within lives, and the Egyptian parasite beginning its new cycle of being in a water snail affected me like a *great work of art*. No, that's not what I mean. It made me feel how *perfect* the world is, with its worms and hooks and ova, how incredibly perfect. There was the sky and sea and the shape of a lily, and there is all this other as well. The *balance* how perfect! (*Salut*, Tchehov!) I would not have the one without the other."

Mansfield's positivity sometimes led her to the point of disillusionment, as if she actually had a nondecomposable body despite the stifled breaths. On 15 October, 1919, she wrote to Murry, "A year ago I thought I was going to die, and I think I *was*. And now I know we're going to live. Don't let's forget how Sorapure (doctor) has helped. I really think I should have just died in that room upstairs if he had not taken me by the hand, like you take a little girl who is frightened of a dog, and led me up to my pain and showed it to me and proved that it wasn't going to eat me. That's what he did." Writing is a second breath — breath-words — that give her hope. But D.H. Lawrence wanted her to be realistic about her disease, she tells Murry in a letter of 9 February, 1920 that, "Lawrence sent me a letter today. He spat in my face and threw filth at me and said: 'I loathe you. You revolt me stewing in your consumption…'" These thoughts made her think she would die soon but, oddly, not because of her lungs. She felt as though something mysterious was calling her, a kind of reverse inspiration. On

18 October, 1920, she wrote to Murry, "You know, my darling, I have felt very often lately as though the silence had some meaning beyond these signs, these intimations. Isn't it possible that if one yielded there is a whole world into which one is received? It is so near and yet I am conscious that I hold back from giving myself up to it. What is this something mysterious that waits — that beckons?" Despite the pain and aftermath of pain, she continued to write, but found it increasingly difficult. On 21, November 1921, she admits to her journal, "A bad spell has been on me. I have begun two stories, but then I told them and they felt betrayed. It is absolutely fatal to give way to this temptation. Today I began to write, seriously, The Weak Heart…" And in December she wrote to S.S. Koteliansky, "Both my lungs are affected; there is a cavity in one and the other is affected through. My heart is weak, too."

Trying to see beyond the present, beyond the pain, Mansfield embraced her illness, saw it as a means by which she perceived the world; in the same letter, she claims, "And then suffering, bodily suffering such as I've known for three years. It has changed forever everything — even the *appearance* of the world is not the same — it was something added. *Everything has its shadow*. Is it really right to resist such suffering? Do you know I feel it has been an immense privilege."

By October 1922, Mansfield knew and accepted she was dying; she made a will and wanted "to get the dying over" and in her journal admonishes Chekhov for the poverty of his death: "Do the hardest thing on earth for you. Act for yourself. Face the truth. True, Tchehov didn't. Yes, but Tchehov died. And let us be honest. How much do we know of Tchehov from his letters? Was that all? Of course not. Don't you suppose he had a whole longing life of which there is hardly a word? Then read the final letters. He has given up hope. If you do you de-sentimentalize those final letters they are terrible. There is no more Tchehov. Illness has swallowed him." She wishes to be one with the world, to be a child of the sun, not to give up hope in the way Chekhov had.

That same month, Mansfield relocated to Fontainebleau, France, to stay at Georges Gurdjieff's Institute for the Harmonious Development of Man and dabbled with applying Gurdjieff's mystical teachings to "try a new life altogether," even going so far as suggesting Lawrence would benefit from a stay. From the institute, on 31 December ,1922, Mansfield wrote to her cousin, the Countess Russell, "I haven't written a word since October and I don't mean to until the spring. I want much more material; I'm tired of my stories like birds bred in cages." Ten days later, running up a flight of stairs in the institute with Murry, Mansfield had a coughing fit that resulted in a haemorrhage, and despite the administrations of two doctors, she died. The previous month, she had written to Ida Baker, "This life proves how terribly wrong and stupid all doctors are. I would've been dead 50 times in the opinion of all the medical men whom I have known." Another one who agrees with Deleuze.

Six months before her death, Mansfield wrote to S.S. Koteliansky, "Have you read Lawrence's new book? I should like to very much. He is the only writer living whom I really profoundly care for. It seems to me whatever he writes, no matter how much one may 'disagree', is important and after all even what one objects to is a *sign of life* in him. He is a living man." Better not let Virginia Woolf hear that.

In *Apocalypse*, his study of the *Book of Revelation*, D.H. Lawrence (1885–1930) concluded, "What we want is to destroy our false, inorganic connections, especially those related to money, and re-establish the living organic connections with the cosmos, the sun and earth, with mankind and nation and family. Start with the sun, and the rest will slowly, slowly happen." *Apocalypse* was his last completed book and was published posthumously in 1931. Lawrence agrees with Mansfield on many things, despite their love/hate relationship; he agrees with her that "individualism is really an illusion. I am a part of the great whole, and I can never escape. But I can deny my connections, break them, and become a fragment. Then I am wretched." His tuberculosis fragmented him and, like Stevenson, he became an exile in order to find a cure or, at least, an air that he could breathe more easily.

Lawrence wrote about the body, he expressed the body as writing. In a letter to Henry Savage on 31 October, 1913, Lawrence stated, "It is so much more difficult to live with one's body than with one's soul. One's body is so much more exacting: What it won't have it won't have, and nothing can make bitter into sweet." Lawrence explored this difficulty and the exacting state of his health in his novels, short stories and non-fiction. As Mansfield attested, Lawrence was a living man and he wrote these words only weeks before he died, "What man most passionately wants is his living wholeness and his living unison, not his own isolate salvation of his 'soul.' Man wants his physical fulfilment first and foremost, since now, once and once only, he is in the flesh and potent. For man, the vast marvel is to be alive. For man, as for flower and beast and bird, the supreme triumph is to be most vividly, most perfectly alive."

He was a sickly child who suffered from bronchitis and other chest infections. In a letter to Dr Trigant Burrow on 3 August, 1927, he writes, "As for myself, I'm in despair. I've been in bed this last month with bronchial haemorrhages — due, radically to chagrin — though I was born bronchial — born in chagrin too." He was born with breathing problems and born with rage. In 1895, he had to miss the start of his schooling because of pneumonia; the wet and polluted air of Eastwood,

Nottinghamshire could not have helped the young Lawrence's lungs. Pneumonia would be the cause of Lawrence's brother Ernest's death in 1901 and Lawrence would have another bout of the inflammatory lung disease two months after Ernest's funeral. Lawrence hero-worshipped his brother and depicted him as William Morel in *Sons and Lovers* (1913).

Writing was a way out of his illness, a way out of his circumstances, a means of controlling the cosmos, "one sheds one's sicknesses in books — repeats and presents again one's emotions, to be master of them," he wrote to Arthur McLeod on 26 October, 1913. A year before the publication of *The White Peacock* (1911), Lawrence had nursed his mother who was dying of cancer, as Paul Morel does in *Sons and Lovers*, dreading her death but wishing for it. Despite the publication of his first novel, he was depressed, began drinking alcohol and had pneumonia yet again, Lawrence called 1911 his "sick year" and claimed to be "on the brink of a complaint." Complaint is an apposite word when referring to Lawrence, "the act of complaining; an expression of grievance or a mild ailment" but also "a poem of lament, often directed at an ill-fated love" or "a satiric attack on social injustice." In November 1929, he admitted to Earl Brewster that "I do believe the root of all my sickness is a sort of rage. I realize now, Europe gets me into an awkward rage, that keeps my bronchials hellish inflamed."

In a chapter in *A Thousand Plateaus* entitled "Becoming-Intense, Becoming-Animal," Deleuze and Guattari elucidate Lawrence's complaints, "Eliminate all that is waste, death, and superfluity, complaint and grievance, unsatisfied desire, defense or pleading, everything that roots each of us (everybody) in ourselves, in our molarity. For everybody/everything is the molar aggregate, but becoming everybody/everything is another affair, one that brings into play the cosmos with its molecular components."

On Sunday 19 November, 1911, Lawrence took to his bed in Croydon with double pneumonia, he remained there close to death for a month. The doctor warned him that, if he returned to the school where he was teaching, he would become consumptive. Early the next year in a letter to his fiancée Louie Burrows he wrote, "I ask you to dismiss me. I'm afraid we are not well-suited. My illness has changed me a good deal, has broken a good many of the old bonds that held me. I can't help it. It is no good to go on." This is a clarification of how illness was the catalyst in Lawrence's philosophy to break the old bonds, the ones of marriage and sexuality, king and country, morality and immorality, this is where he becomes the escaped cock. On 3 May, 1927, he précised the story for Earl Brewster, "I wrote a story of the Resurrection, where Jesus gets up and feels very sick about everything, and can't stand the old crowd any more — so cuts out — and as he heals up, he begins to find what an astonishing place the phenomenal world is, far more marvellous than any salvation or heaven — and thanks his stars he needn't have a mission any more." The double pneumonia was Lawrence's crucifixion. In *Out of Sheer Rage* (1997), Geoff Dyer's anti-biography of Lawrence, he quotes Aldous Huxley's claim that Lawrence's "existence was one long convalescence, it was as though he were newly born from a mortal illness every day of his life."

Through illness and writing, Lawrence began to understand the molecular components of the world and he did this through a deep exploration of the body: "We can go wrong in our minds. But what our blood feels and believes and says, is always true," he wrote to Ernest Collings on 17 January, 1913. As the phoenix (sun, Christ, metempsychosis) was Lawrence's symbol, so red was his colour — Deleuze explains: "Lawrence develops a very beautiful becoming of colors. For the oldest dragon is red, golden-red, extending through the cosmos in a spiral or coiled around man's vertebral column. But when the moment of his ambiguity arrives (Is he good? Is he bad?), he still remains red for man, whereas the good cosmic dragon becomes a translucent green in the midst of the stars, like a spring breeze. Red has become dangerous for man (Lawrence, let us not forget, is writing in the midst of his fits of spitting blood)."

John Middleton Murry, Mansfield's husband, believed that Lawrence was tainted with illness and hysteria, referring to his sickly pallor and outbursts; the well-known beard was grown to cover most of his pale face but it could not hide his intensity. In 1916, while completing *Women in Love* (1920), Lawrence complained that writing was "like a malady or a madness while it lasts," and expanded on that by claiming that England was an illness, "I can't live in England any more. It depresses one's lungs, one cannot breathe," he complained on 19 January, 1917. At this point, Lawrence was not suffering from tuberculosis but his unhealthy constitution made him a very likely candidate to beomce infected.

In February 1919, Lawrence had another brush with death when he became one of the multitude afflicted by the 1918 Spanish flu pandemic that had claimed Klimt and Schiele. It was months before he fully recovered, yet there were constant reminders of tuberculosis; Mansfield had written to him that she had consumption and was dying, that she could not even employ a maid because of her disease. But Lawrence denied his illness as vehemently as Mansfield embraced it; the symptoms were those of bronchitis, pneumonia, the flu, not tuberculosis. In January 1922, he wrote to Brewster, "More and more I feel that meditation and the inner life are not my aim, but some sort of action and strenuousness and pain and frustration and struggling through… men have to fight a way for the new incarnation. And the fight and the sorrow and the loss of blood, and even the influenzas and the headaches are part of the fight and fulfilment. […] That nobody try to filch from me even my influenza." In *Ecce Homo*, Nietzsche writes, "My humaneness is a constant self-overcoming. — But I need solitude, in other words convalescence, a return to myself, the breath of free, light, playful air…" This is exactly Lawrence's philosophy and his prescription.

In *Human, All Too Human*, Nietzsche gets even closer to the radical life of Lawrence, "From this morbid isolation, from the desert of these years of temptation and experiment, it is still a long road to that tremendous overflowing certainty and health which may not dispense even with wickedness, as a means and fish-hook of knowledge, to that mature freedom of spirit which is equally self-mastery and discipline of the heart." Nietzsche goes on to adumbrate Lawrence's philosophy of contradiction, infatuation, freedom and will, obviously taken from Nietzsche's own ideas — Lawrence had, after all, read Nietzsche while convalescing in Croydon.

Lawrence had decided to leave Taormina in Sicily, where he and Frieda had been living for a number of years, and head, with stops on the way, to Taos in New Mexico's Sangre de Cristo Mountains. At the time, January 1922, Lawrence was being Lawrence: highly productive and constantly ill. He spent his time between finishing the manuscripts of *Birds, Beasts and Flowers* (1923) (poetry), his incendiary and slightly mad *Studies in Classic American Literature* (1923) and *Mr Noon* (1984) (novel) while struggling with colds, influenza and malaria. In "Pomegranate," the poem that opens *Birds, Beasts and Flowers*, Lawrence is his usual complaining self, "You tell me I am wrong / Who are you, who is anybody to tell me I am wrong? I am not wrong?" And asks in "The Evening Land," "Oh, America / The sun sets in you. / Are you the grave of our day? / Shall I come to you, the open tomb of my race." In the mad *Studies in Classic American Literature*, he complains in a pre-Sartrean voice, "But one thing we may be sure. If one wants to be free, one has to give up the illusion of doing what one likes, and seek what IT wishes done." For Lawrence, America had the potential to unmask illusion, the high desert of Taos also had the air that would make it easier for him to breathe.

As early as *The White Peacock*, Lawrence had been seeking to escape his illnesses, "I have been so glad to go away, to breathe the free air of life…" From *Sons and Lovers*, "And as soon as he was out of the wood, in the free open meadow, where he could breathe, he started to run as fast as he could. It was like delicious delirium in his veins." And from *Mr Noon*, "I never felt I could breathe among them. I never felt I could breathe — never — not till I was on board the ship coming to Germany. All the rest of the time I simply couldn't get a deep breath — I don't know why." Breathing and denial.

Lawrence and Frieda stopped off in Ceylon on their travels but Lawrence was overwhelmed by the heat, the scents, even the "nasty faces and yellow robes of the Buddhist monks," his irritability made worse by yet another influenza episode and an attack of gastroenteritis. After visiting Australia, where, as was his work ethic, he dashed off a novel, *Kangaroo* (1923), that was also a eulogy for his life in Europe, Lawrence visited the South Seas in search of some kind of paradise but also to follow in the wake of Robert Louis Stevenson.

Lawrence lived in Taos and travelled to and from Mexico until 1925, writing the novels *The Boy in the Bush* (1924), *The Plumed Serpent* (1926) and a number of essays, living constantly under the shadow of illness. In January 1925, on completion of *The Plumed Serpent* (*Quetzalcoatl* in an earlier version), Lawrence succumbed to the disease that had been haunting him for years. Close to death yet again, his body had submitted and, in addition to tuberculosis, he had influenza and problems with his bowels. He and Frieda had planned to travel back to Europe from Vera Cruz but, on the way there, Lawrence had been X-rayed by a doctor in Mexico City and had been told that his tuberculosis was active and that he should return to the high-altitude of their so-called ranch in Taos County. To everyone's surprise, Lawrence's health rallied and in *David* (1926), the play he wrote during his convalescence, Lawrence has Samuel (prophet of God) speak for him, "He needs not the fat beef nor the finer raiment, but thrashes out His anger in the firmament. Amalek has defied the living Breath, and cried mockery on the Voice of the Beyond."

Lawrence and Frieda returned to England and Nottinghamshire; Lawrence immediately caught a cold. The positivism and vitality of Taos and Mexico soon darkened and his thoughts turned to death. In an unfinished short story, "The Flying Fish," that he had started writing after discovering the extent of his tuberculosis when in Mexico City, he confesses, "He was ill, and he felt as if at the very middle of him, beneath his navel, some membrane were torn, some membrane which had connected him with the world and its day." England only made those thoughts more sombre; the weather annoyed him, some of his friends were also dying of tuberculosis, his relationship with Frieda was complicated and he needed to escape again, this time to Germany and down through Italy to Spotorno. All this time, Lawrence was aware of what he was fleeing, he had had a glimpse of it on that X-ray in Mexico City, "He had hurried perhaps a little too far, just over the edge. Now, try as he might, he was aware of a gap in his time-space *continuum*; he was, in the words of his ancestor, aware of the Greater Day showing through the cracks in the ordinary day."

Ironically, the tuberculosis affected Lawrence's sex life just as he was beginning to write *Lady Chatterley's Lover* (1928); there were rumours that he had become impotent, so there may be either humour or denial when he had Tommy Dukes claim, "'Me? Oh, intellectually I believe in having a good heart, a chirpy penis, a lively intelligence, and the courage to say 'shit!' in front of a lady.'" After the book's publication, Lawrence wrote to Dr Trigant on 25 December, 1926, "And I, who loathe sexuality so deeply, am considered a lurid sexuality specialist." However much he loathed sexuality, the erotic power of *Lady Chatterley's Lover* would make the novel a bestseller and its author a celebrity. The royalties the sales brought in enabled Lawrence to travel, to pay for doctors, medical treatment and stays in sanatoriums.

In the summer of 1927, while writing "The Escaped Cock" (also known as "The Man Who Died"), Lawrence, now in surface denial of his disease, thought his malaria had returned, but it was the tuberculosis, "he saw his thin legs that had died, and pain unknowable, pain like utter bodily disillusion, filled him so full that he stood up, with one torn hand on the ledge of the tomb." He had been in correspondence with his Sister Ada about their friend from Eastwood, Gertie Cooper, who had to have a lung and six ribs removed because of tuberculosis. Lawrence was adamant that he would not undergo such an ordeal, he preferred chloroform and the long sleep, although his denial of the word "tuberculosis" was evident in his letters, "I've been in bed three weeks with bronchial haemorrhage — brought on by sea bathing — doctor said. Am up and creeping round a bit now — and we hope to leave for the mountains in Austria," he explained to Brewster on 19 July, 1927 from Florence.

By this stage of his illness, the tuberculosis, rather than spurring him on to write out of rage and complaint, was now sapping his energy, and his output slowed to a few translations of short stories by the Italian realist author Giovanni Verga. By the autumn of 1927, the doctor's prognosis was that the tuberculosis was terminal; at most, Lawrence would live another two years. He returned to Germany and Baden-Baden but refused to enter a sanatorium, maybe he feared that he would be trapped in one, as Hans Castorp had been in *The Magic Mountain*. The Lawrences returned to Italy and Lawrence spent most of his time in Florence convalescing in bed, weak but still working on a re-write of *Lady Chatterley's Lover*, which he would finish in January 1928.

Exhausted and ill, Lawrence used his convalescent periods to edit a *Collected Poems* for the publishers Secker and supervise Pino Orioli's private publication of the unexpurgated *Lady Chatterley's Lover*. Frieda was becoming as irritable as Lawrence and had been complaining that, because of Lawrence's illness, they were unable to travel. She seemed to embody Nietzsche's maxim that, "Experience the profoundest convulsion of heart and of knowledge and emerge at last like a convalescent, with a sorrowful smile, into freedom and luminous silence — someone will still say: 'he regards his sickness as an argument, his impotence as proof that all are impotent; he is vain enough to become sick so as to feel the sense of superiority enjoyed by the sufferer.'" What Mark Leyner would call "the hedonism of suffering."

By the summer of 1928, Lawrence had managed to travel and he and Frieda spent time in Switzerland and Baden-Baden, but Lawrence's cough had become the cough that Hans Castorp and Katherine Mansfield had heard, a cough that, "isn't the human cough at all. It isn't dry and yet isn't loose either — that is very far from being the right word for it. It is just as if one could look right into him when he coughs, and see what it looks like: all slime and mucus…"

Lawrence, now gravely ill, went to Paris alone in the spring of 1929 to find a bigger publisher for *Lady Chatterley's Lover*. While there, Aldous Huxley insisted Lawrence had X-rays taken of his diseased chest. On his first visit to the doctor, Lawrence found out the extent of the tuberculosis — it had destroyed one lung and had infected the second. A second set of X-rays and examinations were arranged but Lawrence refused to attend because Frieda had turned up and wanted to take him to Majorca. Lawrence was again in denial and had, throughout his life, stubbornly refused to admit his weak constitution, had mistrusted doctors and been positive about his ongoing vitality. This obstinacy/denial is similar to Nietzsche's self-diagnosis/self-prognosis in *Ecce Homo*: "No sign at all of any kind of local degeneration; no stomach complaint for organic reasons, however much the gastric system is profoundly weakened as a result of general exhaustion. Even the eye complaint, at times verging dangerously on blindness, just a consequence, not causal: so that with every increase in vitality the eyesight has picked up again, too. — A long, all-too-long succession of years mean in my case convalescence — unfortunately they also mean lapsing, relapsing, periodically a kind of *décadence*."

Lawrence denied tuberculosis was a consequence of his life, claimed there was no pathological cause, believed that the local degeneration could be slowed by his imagination, that convalescence — in Taos, in Baden-Baden, Switzerland, in writing — was a cure, despite the lapsing and relapsing. Lawrence, like Stevenson but unlike Mansfield, deterritorialized his tuberculosis both geographically and psychologically. As Stevenson turned his illness into a murderous doppelgänger, so Lawrence created a double who, out in the world somewhere, was not ill. He even created a double of his own illness. In a letter of 29 October, 1929, he wrote to Mabel Dodge Luhan, "I feel so strongly as if my illness weren't really me — I feel perfectly well and all right, *in myself*. Yet there is this beastly torturing chest superimposed on me, and it's as if there was a demon lived there, triumphing, and extraneous to me. I do feel it extraneous to me." He goes on to say that, "Doctors frankly say — they don't know." But they did and a number of them had told him the prognosis — he was dying.

By the winter of 1929, Lawrence was still writing poetry and had had his controversial paintings exhibited in London. As if in flight from the enormity of his illness, the Lawrences kept travelling: Majorca, Florence (influenza), Baden-Baden and in September 1929 down to Bandol in the South of France where Lawrence claimed he could breathe again. Here, he spent his days in bed, writing poems and putting the final touches to *Apocalypse* in which he wrote, "We do not want to perish, either. We have to give up a false position. Let us give up our false positions as Christians, as individuals, as democrats. Let us find some conceptions of ourselves that will allow us to be peaceful and happy, instead of tormented and unhappy."

After being affected by colds, bronchitis and pneumonia in the winter of 1929–1930, Lawrence agreed to see a tuberculosis specialist who explained to him that he needed to cease work immediately and rest, preferably in a sanatorium where he could be cared for medically. Lawrence decided to remain in Bandol and edit *Nettles* (1930), his last poetry collection, "Oh, even to know the last wild wincing of despair, / aware at last that our manhood is utterly lost, / give us back our bodies for one day."

His health declining, on 3 February, 1930, he entered the sanatorium in Vence but it was too late, he contracted pleurisy and his weight had dropped to under six-and-a-half stone. On 2 March, his health deteriorated, he shed tears for the first time anyone could remember, became delirious and deterritorialized, claiming that he didn't know where he was and that he could see himself on another bed. David Herbert Lawrence died at 10:15 on 2 March, 1930. His last words were either "I am better now" or "Wind my watch." He was forty-four years old, the same age as Stevenson and Chekhov when they succumbed to tuberculosis.

Four days before he died, Jo Davidson, an American artist, arrived to sculpt a clay bust of Lawrence. Although Lawrence thought it "mediocre," it shows Lawrence's intensity and his suffering, as Geoff Dyer explains, "The closer he came to dying the more he looked like D.H. Lawrence." And, "In death Lawrence became identical with his canonic image. Death fixed the image, rendered it — and the body of work of which it was the symbolic expression — incapable of further development." Or as Nietzsche would subtitle *Ecce Homo* — *How to Become What You Are.*

Let us leave Lawrence's room, "the sizeable white bus shelter… a steeply angled roof with a Phoenix carved at the apex" and visit, slightly out of chronological order, the room of Mr Franz Kafka (1883–1924). Make sure to wash your hands. Hmmm! The door seems to be locked. I will try the access code — IB2L. Red light. Let's look through the observation window. Four familiar walls, a normal human room, if a little on the small side. Over the table on which an array of cloth samples is spread out, I can see a Post-it Note on which are written in neat German handwriting, I'll translate, "Slept, awoke, slept, awoke, miserable life." What's that on the bedspread? Is that a cockroach? I really need to get the cleaners to deal with that. Mr Kafka must have been taken down for an X-ray. Apologies for that. I'll show you to the exit.

CHAPTER 6

The Morality of Things

Immunology as Interpretation

For the next seven years, my health was sober, whereas I rarely was — and then the events of 13 February, 2003 occurred. I took notes while in hospital, some are barely legible, others make little sense but, if I add in the records from the doctors, I can get a reasonable account of what happened to me that year, despite the periods of unconsciousness and comas, being under very strong painkillers or anaesthetized.

So this is what happened, according to the discharge summary from the Hepato-Pancreato-Biliary & Endocrine Surgery Unit at the Middlesex Hospital: "This gentleman was admitted as an emergency on 13th February 2003 with an episode of vomiting. This was followed by severe epigastric pain, which radiated to the back. He was considered to have an acute abdomen. Interestingly, his amylase was not raised but his diagnosis of acute pancreatitis was upheld by the development of Grey, Turner and Cullen's sign. Subsequent CT scan of the abdomen showed that he had 95% pancreatic necrosis. It was debatable whether this was due to alcohol as an aetiology or biliary sludge was noted in the gall bladder. He was managed conservatively and steadily improved after a period in which he was in incipient respiratory failure.

The patient was placed on pancreatic rest for approximately three weeks. He had ultrasound performed, which revealed a gallbladder with sludge. He also underwent re-imaging of his pancreas, which basically showed bilateral small pleura effusions and 97% pancreatitis. On review of the splenic artery, there was the suggestion of a small pseudoaneurysm in the region of the body of the pancreas, which was not definite. We decided to proceed with pancreatic rest with peripheral T.P.N. Re-imaging of the patient on March 7 demonstrated inflammatory changes affecting the posterior wall of the stomach and again showed 95% pancreatic necrosis containing a small amount of gas. The patient was clinically doing very well and at that time we decided to proceed with a laparoscopic cholecystectomy. The patient tolerated the procedure very well and he had an uneventful postoperative course. However, he developed thrombophlebitis at the side of a vein flow and that was treated with antibiotics due to positive blood culture for *Staphyhcoccus aureus*. On 17th March, a week after the laparoscopic cholecystectomy, the patient was discharged home in a stable condition. We will follow this patient in our outpatient clinic. Yours sincerely, Mr D Zacharoulis Clinical Fellow to Mr Russell."

What follows are some of my notes on the attack and hospitalization. "Pancreatitis. Student doctors came to peer at my Grey, Turner and Cullen's signs, huge bruised, like saddlebags," and I happened to be reading Tom Wolfe's *Man In Full*, "And then Peepgass saw them... the saddlebags! The saddlebags! The saddlebags had formed! They were complete! The great stains of sweat on the tycoon's shirt had now spread from both sides, from under the arms and across the rib cage and beneath the curves of his mighty chest until they had met, come together, hooked up — two dark expanses joined at the sternum. They looked just like a pair of saddlebags on a horse." For "sweat" read "bruise." I was in and out of consciousness for the next six days, unsure of where I was and if anyone had visited. On the 19th, I wrote, "I can only swill my mouth out with water. Swill and spit into a receptacle that looks like the cardboard mould for a type of hat worn by Chilean hill tribes. Three weeks, apparently. Insulin pumped in daily for 22 hours. T.P.N. Still not sure what that stands for. Total Parenteral Nutrition. I asked the nurse. Then I asked what it tasted like and they didn't know." I wasn't allowed to eat or drink, the T.P.N. did all that through my blood.

On the 21st, I had a moment of self-reflection, "Feel more adult, more aware of my own humanity, may come out of this less arrogant, less rude, more willing to listen, more likely to ask for assistance. I think the whole experience will be a positive one for me." In *A Short History of Decay*, Cioran notes, "The man suffering from a characterized sickness is not entitled to complain: he has an occupation. The great sufferers are never bored: disease fills them, the way remorse feeds the great criminals. For any intense suffering produces a simulacrum of plenitude and proposes a terrible reality to consciousness, which it cannot elude." Doctors told me that I had nearly died the first night and that they had called K and told her to get to the hospital, as I probably would not make it to the morning. Roberto Bolaño (who died of pancreatic cancer) claims Pascal died of pancreatitis, but it may have been tuberculosis or stomach cancer, or all three.

I go on about racism, the rudeness of the patients, who has visited, who hasn't, what I'm reading, what I'm listening to on the radio, what I would like to drink and eat, "Coca-cola, grapefruit juice, tinned peaches, steak and kidney pudding." On 1 March, "16th day without food and water. Lost seven kilograms. Burning/numbing sensation in my thighs, which are wasting away. My blood sugar ranges from seven to twenty-one. Probably be a full-blown diabetic when I get out." Two days later, "I still need sleeping pills. It's too light, it's too bright; it's too night. Waking up is a slow climb out of a deep and disused well." The next day, I had a CT scan on which they found a small aneurysm in what was left of my pancreas but I hoped to be going home at the end of the following week. On the 5th, Dr Russell told me, "Oh, and we'll take your gallbladder out next Monday morning." I noted that "the aetiology of my pancreatitis was gall sludge. Keyhole surgery. One in twenty require a more invasive procedure."

I had a telephone call from a friend to inform me that another friend had died the night before. He had had an asthma attack and passed out in his garden, nobody noticed him lying there, he was found dead from hypothermia two days later. I could not attend the funeral. I was nervous about the next CT scan that would confirm my gallbladder removal, "Feel worse than I have done for a while." The procedure confirmed, I wrote, "Not that nervous before the operation. Calm. Woke up at seven, had a shower. Surgery porter came at 8:15." And further down the page, "They removed my gallbladder through my umbilicus." I was slowly becoming a body without organs. This is what they did: "A 4.5 litre pneumoperitoneum was created at 12mm pressure. Two 11mm cannulae were placed in the umbilicus and the epigastrium and two 5mm cannulae laterally. Findings: the gallbladder was markedly distended, thin-walled and contained thick sludge. The distention ceased at the cystic duct, which was 2mm in diameter and a centimetre long. There was no inflammation around gallbladder. Procedure: The Triangle of Calot was separated out. The cystic duct was then clipped with three Absolok clips. The cystic duct was divided and the gallbladder removed from the gallbladder bed. The gallbladder was then placed in a bag and extracted from the umbilicus. Spillage of thick bile was washed out with two litres of saline. Closure: 1 PDS to the umbilical fascia and 5/0 Monocryl to skin." Nice. When I came round, I remember being disappointed that the scars were very small. That disappointment would last until 2013.

The next day: "Feel like I'm back to square one. Sweating profusely, abdominal pain, exhaustion. Can just about make it to my chair, cannot concentrate to read. I can barely muster enough energy to listen to the radio. Sleep most of the day again. Do not want to see anyone. Even cotton sheets feel abrasive against my skin —hypersensitive — can feel every fold and crease and line of elastic in my D.V.T. (deep vein thrombosis) stockings. Teeth feel inches apart, nose ridiculously long, ears pendulous and scaly." But felt much better the next day and blamed the aftereffects of the anaesthetic. I was told I could sip water but also that I would have type-one diabetes and would be insulin-dependent. Over the next few days, I was allowed to eat but didn't really feel like it. I had a slight swelling in my right arm where the TPN line was and that was caused by *Staphyhcoccus aureus*. I was supposed to be discharged on the 15th but the bacterium kept me in hospital for another week.

Some of the worst moments of my stay were the increasing difficulty nurses, doctors and even anaestheticians had in getting cannulae into my ever-shrinking and disappearing veins. They probed and prodded, gouged and swore. My body wasn't having it, my hands, elbows, even my feet were purple with scabs and bruises. On the day I was supposed to go home, I noted, "Apparently they are to give me the strongest antibiotics over a 48-hour period and then reassess it on Monday. Hope to move on to oral antibiotics. And go home. Dressings off operation wounds. Three three-quarter-inch cuts at the bottom of my left-side ribcage, a second about six inches to the right an inch down and a third to the right of my umbilicus. All the scars are slightly crescent-shaped." Two days later I wrote, "Patients trail their drip trolleys behind them, they look like spectral travellers back-riding invisible bumper cars," I think I know what I meant. I had high blood-sugar readings and high ketone levels in my urine. On Tuesday, 18 March, there is a one-word entry, "Out!"

There are no entries for eleven days. I remember feeling very small sitting on my sofa. I had lost thirty kilograms and had to put a towel in the bath to stop my bones from hurting when I sat down. I was on a special diet and had regained my taste for tea. I had no energy and could just about read or stare moronically at MTV. On the night of Sunday, 30 March, I had gotten out of bed to go to the toilet but had only reached the sofa and collapsed onto it. I did not have the energy to call K but, sensing something was wrong, she came into the living room. Her face informed me that something indeed was wrong. I told her to call a taxi to take me to UCH, not wanting a local ambulance to take me to the Royal Free.

On immediate admittance to the A&E, they diagnosed another pancreatitis event and I was taken to the intensive care unit. I was anaemic, in shock and then crashed. This is what happened next: "Following a suspicious CT scan and falling haemoglobin levels, he underwent arterial angiography on 2 April 2003, where he had his gastroduodenal artery embolized. Following that, he was admitted to ITU for haemodynamic monitoring. He only required to be on ITU for approximately 24 hours. A repeat CT scan on the 7th April suggested a possible pseudoaneurysm in his splenic artery this time. He underwent a second arterial angiography on 11th April 2003 and on this occasion his splenic artery was embolized. The serial CT scans as well as clinical findings obviously suggested a recurrence of this gentleman's pancreatitis. Throughout this period, he was commenced on pancreatic rest and TPN. Despite his arterial bleeds requiring embolyzation, the patient rallied and made a gradual recovery. Upon the point of discharge, he was on a light diet. Two-week outpatient follow-up was arranged. Yours sincerely, Dr R Attaran."

My notes are sketchy over this period, just a few words, "Transferred to Middlesex. Cancer ward. Tongue cancer." I was delirious most of the time and had been temporarily placed in a cancer ward. "Gastroepiploic artery embolized. Twenty minutes to live, according to the doctor." I remember being on my back on a very uncomfortable platform, while the doctor chased around my arterial system burning off routes as I watched on the screen above my head great firework displays of what was actually my blood exploding in my body. On April the 3rd, "Steve's old bed. Feel seriously ill." And the next day, "Splenic artery embolized. 24 hours to live." There are no further entries. I was discharged on 19 May, 2003, three months after the initial attack. I convalesced for a further three months before I could return to work. During one visit to the hospital, one of my doctors feared my aorta was damaged but that wasn't the case, just an aortic echo caused by my body without that many organs. I felt relentlessly tired and my weight was still dropping, so much so that when I bumped into a friend in Primrose Hill she started to cry thinking that I had terminal cancer or AIDS or both. The weight loss was due to statorrhoea, the excretion of fat, and I was put on a course of enzymes to counter this. By December, I had started to regain weight and had returned to work full-time.

During my stays in hospital and convalescing at home, I didn't read as much as I would normally do and what I did read was mostly light, but one author helped me through those times and below is the reason why. Please excuse the repetition; the memory is layered, stratified like the London clay and writing is its erygmascope.

"My journey seemed perfect, well, at least one part of it — a dolphin swimming in a kitchen sink." I wrote these words in a diary on 3 January, 2003. I have no idea why. They may not even be my words. I would not write them now, reality television having abducted the concept of "journey" for its weight-loss and amateur talent shows, where we hear it spoken before the onset of maudlin piano or swelling strings. On 6 January, I find this, "Ask 'A' about her form of epilepsy, see if it ties in with time elision or time subduction — a mild form of narcolepsy?" For the next seven days, I visited Brussels and Amsterdam. I wrote things like, "Artaud, Peter Sellers, Tate Modern," and, "Horses drinking out of an old enamel bath, a dovecot, mole hills, a Jewish cemetery, permission to enter the tunnel." Again, I have no clue why I wrote those words. In Brussels, I noted that René Magritte and Paul Delvaux drank in La Fleur en Papier Doré and that a pregnant tabby cat rubbed herself on the brass fittings there. In Amsterdam, the prostitutes near the Oude Kirk looked like statues of saints in curving church arcades. The entries stop on 19 January, "You go away for a long time and return a different person — you never come all the way back" — *Dark Star Safari.*

On 13 January, the ambulance took me to University College Hospital, London, and then to the Middlesex Hospital (now demolished) because of acute pancreatitis and resultant complications. "It brings the unknown. A journey awakens all our old fears of danger and risk. Your life is on the line. You are living by your own resources, you have to find your own way, and solve every problem on the road. What to eat, where to sleep, what to do if you get sick." — Paul Theroux, interview, *Salon*, 2012.

Once I had regained consciousness and when I had the energy, I read novels, mostly light stuff, Jonathan Coe, Roddy Doyle, Nick Hornby, some crime fiction, nothing taxing, no Henry James, no William T. Vollmann. My diary tells me that I soon became bored with this light fare and moved on to non-fiction. I had read Paul Theroux's *The Mosquito Coast* (1981) and *Saint Jack* (1973), but had never read his travel writing. I needed to escape the drab ward, the gastrointestinal miasma, the institutional racism and bureaucratic humourlessness. "Whatever else travel is, it is also an occasion to dream and remember. You sit in an alien landscape and you are visited by all the people who have been awful to you. You have nightmares in strange beds. You recall episodes that you have not thought of for years, and but for that noise from the street or that powerful odour of jasmine you might have forgotten." — *Fresh Air Fiend* (2000).

What happened next drove me elsewhere. What happened next drove me elsewhere: *A Journey Around my Room* (1794) by Xavier de Maistre, in which de Maistre locks himself in his room and explores its walls and furniture, uses memory and digression to travel outward while journeying inward, the enclosed environment becomes the world, all worlds. De Maistre is the Magellan of the microcosm, the Drake of the domestic, the Cook of the claustrophobic. Although the ward I was in had beds for tweny patients, these people were seriously ill. We rarely spoke to each other, instead retreated into sleep or drugged unconsciousness, or we hid behind newspapers and books. The ward was sectioned off into groups of four beds, two beds facing another two. My bed was by the window, and I kept the curtains surrounding me closed whenever I could. This was my world, this bed, this pink-curtained enclosure. I was not well enough to even visit the toilet, I had a catheter and used a bedpan, not that I needed them that often, I was not allowed to eat or drink, merely wet my gums and tongue with a small sponge. I sometimes managed to shuffle and drop into the chair beside my bed. "Travel, its very motion, ought to suggest hope. Despair is the armchair; it is indifference and glazed, incurious eyes. I think travellers are essentially optimists, or else they would never go anywhere." — *Fresh Air Fiend.*

If we take de Maistre's *A Journey Around My Room* as one point of our travel compass, then the antipodal volume must be Apsley Cherry-Garrard's *The Worst Journey in the World*. Published in 1922, the memoir recounts Robert Falcon Scott and his team's harrowing and tragic expedition to the Antarctic between 1910 and 1913. He wrote, "We had been out for four weeks under conditions in which no man had existed previously for more than a few days, if that. During this time we had seldom slept except from sheer physical exhaustion, as men sleep on the rack; and every minute of it we had been fighting for the bed-rock necessaries of bare existence, and always in the dark." This is what it felt like for me to move from my bed to the armchair — a fusion of de Maistre's miniature journey and Cherry-Garrard's epic one. Somewhere between these classics of travel literature, between imagination and fact, are Bruce Chatwin, Jan Morris, W.G. Sebald and Paul Theroux. And, at that point in my life, Theroux became my Virgil (virgule), my Beatrice. "The difference between travel writing and fiction is the difference between recording what the eye sees and discovering what the imagination knows." — *The Great Railway Bazaar* (1975).

I sat in the hospital chair and noticed how my arms were welted from needles and cannulae and that "the rectangular remains of plasters and dressing gauze made my body look like an old leather suitcase from which the destination stickers had been removed." Maybe I was seeking answers and not happiness, or just searching for the truth, knowing it wasn't there. "Travel is at its most rewarding when it ceases to be about your reaching a destination and becomes indistinguishable from living your life." — *Ghost Train to the Eastern Star* (2008).

On 13 March the doctors said I could drink and eat. Because of drastic weight loss, they gave me a high-energy lemon-flavoured drink. I noted that it was the second-best drink I had ever had, the best being an ice-cold bottle of Becks I had swallowed in two gulps at the Palais Jamais in Fes, Morocco, after an eight-hour taxi journey through mountains and across desert scrub from Marrakesh. I ate some kind of soup but I didn't know what. I guessed at asparagus, as it was bland and greenish. At the bottom of that day's diary page, I had written, "Re-reading — Paul Theroux — *Mosquito Coast*." "It is hard to see clearly or to think straight in the company of other people. What is required is the lucidity of loneliness to capture that vision which, however banal, seems in your private mood to be special and worthy of interest." — *The Old Patagonian Express* (1979).

A Sunday, three days later, after a course of intravenous antibiotics — I was feeling slightly better and wrote that "*The Mosquito Coast* is better than I remember it," that I hoped to go for a walk but that "I am shaky from the insulin ingestion." Probably inspired by Lawrence and Theroux, I tried to remember the novel set in Mexico I had planned to write at university — *The Spear and the Cross*? (Does a non-existent novel warrant italics?) Theroux took me to other places, away from the medicinal/corporeal smells of the hospital and gave me the odour of jasmines, the taste of exotic fruits, the meeting of strangers, the naivety and egotism of the traveller. Like travel, here in hospital meant "living among strangers, their characteristic stinks and sour perfumes, eating their food, listening to their dramas, enduring their opinions, often with no language in common, being always on the move toward an uncertain destination, creating an itinerary that is continually shifting, sleeping alone, improvising the trip." — *Ghost Train to the Eastern Star.*

My body had become the most visited region on earth, no fold or valley left un-prodded, no arterial system un-navigated, no organ unexplored. Probes had visited my Ultima Thule, multiple hands had palpated my Hyperborea, multiform bacteria had invaded my Agartha — my very core. Charted, written about, discussed, photographed, X-rayed, CAT-scanned, my body would never be the same. If it were a geographical place, there would be maps, guides, gazetteers, GPS coordinates, topographic and bathymetric charts. Our body remains mostly exotic to us; we rarely gaze into its depths. "A true journey is much more than a vivid or vacant interval of being away. The best travel was not a simple train trip or even a whole collection of them, but something lengthier and more complex: an experience of the fourth dimension, with stops and starts and longueurs, spells of illness and recovery, hurrying then having to wait, with the sudden phenomenon of happiness as an episodic reward." — *Ghost Train to the Eastern Star.*

On 30 March I find these words, "Reading *Sunrise with Seamonsters.* Another attack of pancreatitis." Theroux had taken the title of this book from an unfinished painting by J.M.W Turner. Critics argue whether or not the painting shows sea monsters — the pinkish things in a dawn landscape could just be fish in a net. If I stare at the painting, I see my pale skin, the reddish incisions, the stitches in and across my umbilicus; these are the clouds, the monsters, the nets. From *The Happy Isles of Oceania* (1992): "Travel, which is nearly always seen as an attempt to escape from the ego, is in my opinion the opposite. Nothing induces concentration or inspires memory like an alien landscape or a foreign culture. It is simply not possible (as romantics think) to lose yourself in an exotic place. Much more likely is an experience of intense nostalgia, a harking back to an earlier stage of your life, or seeing clearly a serious mistake. But this does not happen to the exclusion of the exotic present. What makes the whole experience vivid and sometimes thrilling is the juxtaposition of the present and the past."

Joan Didion, writes, "Certain places seem to exist mainly because someone has written about them." That's how I felt, that my body existed only because of the symptoms, only because my doctors were reading me, writing my future in their notes and prescriptions, and there was "a sudden blurring, a slippage, a certain vertiginous occlusion of the imagined and the real" — Didion again. Why had I also written during these days, "Kurdish refugee. Gold bag. Cancer of the tongue"? Did I feel stateless? A refugee from my own body? Perhaps. Maybe my body was the gold bag, precious and yet empty. Frida's gold dust? I certainly did not have cancer of the tongue. Or did I imagine another organ rotting away, full of poison, the words dead, the sentences still born? "Travel is a state of mind. It has nothing to do with existence. It is almost entirely an inner experience" — *Fresh Air Fiend*.

Thirteen years later, Chitose, Hokkaido. I had moved to Japan in July 2006. "Most travel, and certainly the rewarding kind, involves depending on the kindness of strangers, putting yourself into the hands of people you don't know and trusting them with your life." — *Ghost Train to the Eastern Star*. I will allow Dr Atsushi Hasegawa and Dr Atsuhi Nobuoka of the Department of Gastroenterology, Chitose City Hospital, to explain what happened: "He has felt nauseous and thrown up since December 16th, 2006. At about 22:30, December 18th, he suddenly fainted in his room and was rushed to the emergency care unit of this hospital by ambulance. He became hospitalized with coma by diabetic ketoacidosis. He was in a coma and in a state of shock (his blood pressure 60/20), accompanied by acute renal failure by dehydration, pancreatitis and bacterial gastroenteritis. We diagnosed his illness as diabetic ketosis, coma, hypovolemic shock, acute pancreatitis, and paralytic ileus. He went into the intensive care unit. On December 24th, he recovered consciousness. His blood-sugar level was under control by insulin injection. Acute pancreatitis and ileus was also cured. He started eating food on December 25th." Once I had regained consciousness, one of the first things I asked for was a book, a collection of travel writing — Paul Theroux's *To The Ends of the Earth* (1990): "Whatever else travel writing is, it is certainly different from writing a novel: fiction requires close concentration and intense imagining, a leap of faith, magic almost. But a travel book, I discovered, was more the work of my left hand, and it was a deliberate act — like the act of travel itself. It took health and strength and confidence."

As we walk back into the gardens, we can see some of the other tuberculosis patients. With their mouths covered with white handkerchiefs, they look like a mob of displaced Japanese shoppers. Huddled together in their bath-chairs, like dormant Paralympic basketball players, we see sitting together, René Daumal (1908–1944), the para-surrealist Gurdjieff student, who wrote *Mount Analogue: A Novel of Symbolically Authentic Non-Euclidean Adventures in Mountain Climbing* (1952), an allegorical novel that claims, "Alpinism is the art of climbing mountains by confronting the greatest dangers with the greatest prudence. Art is used here to mean the accomplishment of knowledge in action," a Heideggerian allegory of transcendence, an overcoming of illness through mountaineering, a reach for breath in "the very possibility of taking action." Next to Daumal in a silk kimono is Takuboku Ishikawa (1886–1912), the Meiji Era tanka poet who wrote, "I feel so sorry for the young nurse / Dressed down by the doctor / Because her hand trembled on my pulse." And the third of the odd gang, Vivien Leigh (1913–1967), whom the director George Cukor described as a "consummate actress, hampered by beauty," more like a beautiful actress, hampered by consumption.

A colony of tuberculotic composers gather around the gates, their white handkerchiefs fluttering in the breeze as if they were surrendering to the disease: Niccolò Paganini (1782–1840), Frédéric Chopin (1810–1849) and Igor Stravinsky (1882–1971). Chopin's diagnosis was complicated, was it tuberculosis or Cystic fibrosis or alpha 1-antitrypsin deficiency or mitral stenosis or Churg-Strauss syndrome or allergic bronchopulmonary aspergillosis or hypogammaglobulinemia or idiopathic pulmonary haemosiderosis or lung abscesses or pulmonary arteriovenous malformations? Or all of those? Not counting his severe depression. We made it easy for ourselves and called it Frédéric Chopin's disease.

Talking to two other men is another patient with a complicated diagnosis, Paul Gauguin (1848–1903). Gauguin, like Stevenson, sought escape from illness in the South Seas (both men spent time on the Marquesas Islands, Stevenson travelled there in 1888, Gauguin arrived in 1901 and died there in 1903 — they never met). Gauguin's tuberculosis was made worse by his terminal syphilis, or vice versa. The other men are Aubrey Vincent Beardsley (1872–1898), dressed in a dark suit but with a swirling Art Nouveau hanky. Beardsley died of tuberculosis in Menton in the South of France, just thirty miles along the coast from Vence, the deathplace of D.H. Lawrence. Interrogating these two artists is John Ruskin (1819–1900), free of the disease now, Ruskin continues to visit the gardens and he could have been talking about *Mycobacterium tuberculosis* when he argued that "beauty of form is revealed in organisms which have developed perfectly according to their laws of growth, and so give the appearance of felicitous fulfilment of function."

Much against the advice of their physicians, a final trio stand by the bicycle sheds puffing on rolled-up cigarettes. The silver-haired Dashiell Hammett (1894–1961), swigging a Manhattan from a hip flask, once told me "I haven't any sort of plans for the future but I reckon things will work out in some manner;" eventually, the alcoholic author, who survived the Spanish flu and tuberculosis, will die of lung cancer. Cadging a light from Hammett, is another alcoholic writer, Charles Bukowski (1920–1994), whose veterinarian diagnosed his tuberculosis when Hank brought in one of his sick cats. He leans forward and in his gravelly yet velvet voice tells Hammett, "A love like that was a serious illness, an illness from which you never entirely recover." He will not recover from the leukaemia that will kill him in San Pedro, California, aged seventy-three. Hank leans towards the third man and says, "My novel *Factotum,* I got the idea, kind of, from *Down and Out in Paris and London*, I read that book and said, 'This guy thinks something has happened to him? Compared to me, he just got scratched.' Not that it wasn't a good book."

George Orwell, for that is the identity of the other man, refuses the third light from Hammett, flicks the head of a match and ignites his cigarette while rubbing the scar on his throat. He looks down at Bukowski and, in his Old Etonian monotonal drawl replies, "The blood was dribbling out of the corner of my mouth. 'The artery's gone,' I thought. I wondered how long you last when your carotid artery is cut; not many minutes, presumably. Everything was very blurry. There must have been about two minutes during which I assumed that I was killed. That wasn't a scratch old, chap. Far from it."

Despite its new resistant strains and its prevalence throughout the world to this day, tuberculosis is seen as a nineteenth-century illness, a white plague, a disease of the industrial revolution, a romantic disease written about by authors (Thomas Wolfe's *Look Homeward, Angel* (1929) — Wolfe would die of tuberculosis of the brain), depicted by artists (Cristobal Rojas' harrowing paintings of dying victims), and sung about in operas (Giuseppe Verdi's *La Traviata*).

As we step into the elevator, we press the top button, it reads "HIV/AIDS Unit" and there we will encounter two patients, Michel Foucault, the author of *The Birth of the Clinic* (1963) and Bruce Chatwin, author of *In Patagonia* (1977). We will move from the white plague (Lawrence used to wear rouge when crossing the border between the USA and Mexico because he didn't want his pale skin to be seen as a sign of TB) to what the media, in the early 1980s, scandalously, homophobically and incorrectly dubbed the "gay plague."

As a link between the two diseases, people with HIV/AIDS are more likely to be infected by active tuberculosis. The first signs of the devastation caused by the disease, and the start of the epidemic in the USA, were reported on 5 June, 1981, when the Centers for Disease Control and Prevention published their findings on cases of a rare lung infection, *Pneumocystis carinii* pneumonia, in five gay men in Los Angeles.

The door of the elevator wheezes open and we wash our hands before we enter what was previously the Jean-Paul Aron Ward (Foucault complained) and so is now the Robert Mapplethorpe Unit. Mapplethorpe famously quipped, "This AIDS stuff is pretty scary. I hope I don't get it." He also said, "You're never going to get anywhere in life if you don't live up to your obligations."

We step into the first room and close the door behind us. Michel Foucault's scalp shines under the fluorescent lights as if the great theorist were wearing a neon halo. The walls of the room are decorated with paintings by Hugh Steers (1963–1995), the Edward Hopper-like interiors showing people with AIDS in or departing from bedrooms, bathrooms and hospital rooms, all a little darker than the one we stand in.

On 6 September, 1890, Joseph Conrad piloted a small riverboat, the *Roi des Belges*, from Stanley Falls (Boyoma

Falls) down the Congo River to Léopoldville (Kinshasa) in the then Congo Free State. Conrad had been working for a Belgian trading company dealing in railways, timber and ivory and his journeys up and down the Congo, sick with malaria and dysentery, had given him the germ (so to speak) of his novel *The Heart of Darkness*, which was published in 1899. Through scientific studies, it is believed that approximately twenty years later, the first zoonotic transfer of SIV (simian immunodeficiency virus) to HIV in humans occurred in Kinshasa. The widely held concept is that this happened through butchering and/or eating chimpanzees, the genetic diversity of HIV in this area means there were many instances of the virus mutating within humans from SIV to HIV.

The chimpanzees had contracted the virus by killing and eating red-capped mangabeys and greater spot-nosed monkeys that were infected by another strain of SIV. The virus spread rapidly across the Congo River to Brazzaville and then, in part because of the railways Conrad helped the Belgians to build, throughout Western and Central Africa. In his journal of 27 July, 1890, Conrad wrote, "... Met ripe pineapple for the first time. On the road today passed a skeleton tied up to a post. Also white man's grave — no name. Heap of stones in the form of a cross. Health good now." Conrad's health was never good, what with the neuralgia, gout and depression and what horror he records here is trivial compared to the atrocities committed by Leopold II's government, armies and traders on the indigenous people of the Congo region.

In *Heart of Darkness*, Conrad writes, "No, it is impossible; it is impossible to convey the life-sensation of any given epoch of one's existence — that which makes its truth, its meaning — its subtle and penetrating essence. It is impossible. We live, as we dream — alone." This is a very pre-Foucauldian statement from Conrad. Foucault attested that the dream "is the birth of the world," "the origin of existence itself." Dreams are clues to the mysteries of being and Conrad and Foucault believed that an individual's dreams are, as Foucault's biographer James Miller puts it, a "key for solving the riddle of being." Miller goes on to write that for Foucault, "the dream is a privileged domain for thinking through what Heidegger called the unthought — a shadowy clearing where, in a moment of vision, a human being can, as it were, recognize itself and grasp its fate." And this is because the dream can "throw into bright light the secret and hidden power at work in the most manifest forms of presence."

Thirty years before HIV began to spread out from Kinshasa, Conrad had witnessed acts that questioned the ethics of existence itself, a place of the unthinkable rather than Heidegger's unthought. He witnessed humanity recognizing itself and grasping its fate — the presence of Western powers in Africa — which were the seeds of the dissemination of HIV through trade, travel and sexual economics. Conrad's solitary dream, or nightmare, may, it has been argued, be a racist and simplistic fiction about the Congo and its shadowy doubles, London and Brussels, but it does convey the secret and hidden power at work in the relationship between Europe and Africa, owner and slave, money and violence, sex and death.

Many of the workers on these colonial projects were fed on bush meat, their bodies open to the virus through cuts caused by torture and forced labour. The Irish nationalist, Roger Casement, worked with Conrad for a while in the Congo. While they were halfway between Kinshasa and Stanley Falls, Conrad's biographer Jeffrey Meyers reports that "two men were chained together and made to carry heavy loads of bricks and water and were frequently beaten by the soldiers in charge of them and that many Africans, including chiefs, died in their chains. In a grove of death," Casement "found seventeen sleeping sickness patients, male and female, lying about in the utmost dirt. Most of them were lying on the bare ground — several out in the pathway in front of the houses, and one, a woman, had fallen into the fire... All the seventeen people I saw were near their end..." The consultant David Gisselquist controversially claimed that inoculations against sleeping sickness (trypanosomiasis) were the major cause of the transmission of HIV-1 due to the mass use of dirty and infected needles between 1910 and 1940.

In 1972, Grethe Rask, a Danish doctor, opened her own hospital in Abumombazi, a village in Zaïre (the Democratic Republic of Congo). In 1975, she moved to the Danish Red Cross Hospital in Kinshasa. One year earlier, she had already presented pre-AIDS symptoms — swollen lymph nodes, diarrhoea, weight loss, and fatigue. In 1977, she returned to Copenhagen, where tests found she had what were to become classic AIDS infections — candidiasis, *Staphylococcus aureus* and a fungal infection of the lungs — *Pneumocystis jiroveci* pneumonia. She died on 12 December, 1977, her doctors puzzled by the disease. In 1987, samples of her blood and tissue were tested and found positive for HIV/AIDS.

Deleuze, writing about Foucault, explains that "an 'age' does not pre-exist the statements which express it, nor the visibilities which fill it. These are the two essential aspects: on the one hand each stratum or historical formation implies a distribution of the visible and the articulable which acts upon itself; on the other, from one strata to the next there is a variation in the distribution, because the visibility itself changes in style, while the statements themselves change their system." This is identical to Conrad's "No, it is impossible; it is impossible to convey the life-sensation of any given epoch of one's existence — that which makes its truth, its meaning — its subtle and penetrating essence." The age of HIV/AIDS was about to usher in Foucault's two essential aspects of historical formations. The easier access to sex through sexual liberation, the movement of people from continent to continent, the access to air travel, to international rail networks and the lack of cross-referencing between laboratories in the pre-computer era led to a rapid and extensive metastasis of HIV/AIDS throughout the world. Conrad's, "We live, as we dream — alone" would become a living nightmare for millions.

Born on 15 October, 1926, Paul-Michel Foucault grew up in Poitiers in an *haute bourgeoise* family; his father was a surgeon and his mother, who had wanted to be a doctor, was the daughter of a surgeon. Foucault would take up the pen rather than the scalpel, much to his parents' disappointment. He would also castrate the Paul from his birth name, the name of his father. Foucault attended the elite École Normale Supérieure in Paris to study philosophy — Bachelard and Merleau-Ponty were two of his teachers — and it was there that he first became obsessed with death, sex, suicide and the works of authors and philosophers from the wilder margins of literature, limit-experience writers such as Sade, Nietzsche, Artaud and Bataille.

Foucault was both intellectually and physically aggressive, dangerous and brilliant; he once slashed his chest with a blade, on another occasion, he chased a fellow student with a knife. As an outcast, his periods spent in the sick room with psychosomatic illnesses were counterpointed with surreptitious visits to SM clubs. Nietzsche's famous maxim from *The Gay Science*, "the secret for harvesting from existence the greatest fruitfulness and the greatest enjoyment is: to live dangerously..." fuses with his question from *Untimely Meditations*, "How did I become what I am and why do I suffer from being what I am?" These became Foucault's mottos.

He decided to follow Nietzsche's example and set out to "descend into the depths of existence with a string of curious questions on his lips." Foucault's ambition was to write something with the scope, depth and popular appeal of Sartre's *Being and Nothingness*, to write his way out of the shadow (so he saw it) that Sartre and existentialism had cast over Paris and Western culture. Foucault mistrusted Sartre's humanism, seeing the world as a place full of darker forces, *daimons*, which he would go on to analyze.

Cioran would have had advice for the young Foucault; in *The Trouble with Being Born*, he counsels, "We must beware of whatever insights we have into ourselves. Our self-knowledge annoys and paralyzes our *daimon* — this is where we should look for the reason Socrates wrote nothing." Foucault's interest in madness, prisons, illness and sexuality would become manifest in his suicide attempts, drug taking and sadomasochism; as Eugene Thacker tells us in *In the Dust of This Planet* (2011), "The demon is as much a philosophical concept as it is a religious and political one. In fact, the 'demon' is often a placeholder for some sort of non-human, malefic agency that acts against the human (that is, against the world-for-us)."

Jacques Derrida, who had a running philosophical feud with Foucault, explains the importance of the word, "it means both the soul of the dead and the revenant but also fate, the singular destiny, a kind of election, and often, in the bad sense, the unfortunate destiny, death." It is possibile, taking into consideration his obsessions with suicide, death and sex, that Foucault actively sought his own demise, that, throughout his life, he was already a revenant awaiting death in an eternal recurrence, that death was the "singular destiny" and his life was a "kind of election" towards death. Deleuze has speculated that, like his hero Raymond Roussel, Foucault chose death. The *daimon* was Foucault's motif of transcendence, while drugs and BDSM were the bad spirits that haunted him. His first major work, *History of Madness* (1961), written as a doctoral thesis, is concerned with how the insane were transformed in and by society from the sanctifiable (holy fool) to the cursed (imprisoned, tortured).

By 1966, HIV-1 subtype B had spread from Africa and had reached Haiti, probably because of Haitian professionals travelling to and from the Democratic Republic of Congo. Around 1968, HIV-1 had reached the American continent, although a few deaths from 1958 onward may be attributed to the virus. By 1968, Foucault had completed *The Birth of the Clinic: An Archaeology of Medical Perception* (1963), *Death and the Labyrinth: The World of Raymond Roussel* (1963), and *The Order of Things: An Archaeology of the Human Sciences* (1966).

It was also around this time that Bruce Chatwin (1940–1989) abandoned his studies in archaeology at the University of Edinburgh and decided that he would become a writer. His subject matter would also focus on margins, marginal people, marginal lives, marginal places, and he would continue this project throughout his life, following his particular *daimon*, in a work that has never been published — *The Nomadic Alternative*. Chatwin's obsessive restlessness was his way of asking "How did I become what I am and why do I suffer from being what I am?" His last book, published just before he died, was a collection of essays titled *What Am I Doing Here* (1988), markedly without the question mark.

By 1981, clusters of patients with Kaposi's sarcoma, crypto-coccosis (a fungal disease) and *Pneumocystis* pneumonia were being reported in hospitals in New York City and California, these were mostly gay men but also a number of drug addicts who injected intravenously. Over 120 people had died of HIV/AIDS by the end of that year. Chatwin met Donald Richards in 1977 and began an affair with the Australian stockbroker whom he described in a letter as "drawn to the idea of death." After going to Haiti with the art dealer John Kasmin in 1979,

Chatwin visited New York with Richards in February of that year. While there, he met and was photographed by Robert Mapplethorpe and had an affair with Mapplethorpe's lover and patron Sam Wagstaff. He also visited the city's bathhouses and SM clubs such as the Anvil, the Mineshaft, the Spike and the Ramrod, places where, as Chatwin's biographer Nicholas Shakespeare describes, "People were tied up and beaten; there were parts where they were pissed on. Muscular men jangled about in chains wearing nothing but leather jockstraps, caps and masks; or lay back in slings, waiting to be fist-fucked, their legs up, taking poppers, eyes rolled back, moaning." A friend of Chatwin reports "people lying in rows on their stomach waiting to be buggered and an awful lot of blood around." Chatwin had fantasies about being gang raped "by brigands, gypsies, South American cowboys," and experimented in all forms of homosexual sadomasochism while in New York. He equated promiscuity with nomadism and danger with sexuality.

In *The Viceroy of Ouidah* (1980), set in Dahomey in the early 1800s, Chatwin tells the story of Francisco da Silva, a dealer of slaves between Benin and Brazil. The novel is full of the grotesque and the violent, forced work gangs and brutal punishments. In its subject matter, if not its style, it is a successor to *Heart of Darkness*. Chatwin was working on this book while travelling to Haiti and New York City and some of his descriptions of torture, punishment and sexuality mirror the scenes he had participated in in the bathhouses and clubs, "Iron collars chafed their necks. Their backs were striped purple with welts; and when they saw the white man's ships, they knew they were going to be eaten," and "the spectators screamed with laughter as boys somersaulted on one another's backs and mimicked the motions of sodomy. When the lightning danced, the votaries of the Thundergod would axe their shoulder blades, then writhe and rear their buttocks to the sky," and he admits, "He never knew what drew him into the mysteries. The blood? The god? The smell of sweat for the wet glinting bodies?"

Among these descriptions are two paragraphs that could be portraits of Chatwin or Foucault, "His principal amusement was to follow funeral processions. One day it would be a black catafalque encrusted with golden skulls. The next, a sky-blue casket for a stillborn child, or a grey corpse wrapped in a shroud of banana leaves." Both men were obsessed with death and the dying, with the exotic eroticism and ecstasy of the Other. Both were fascinated by limit-experience and with artists at the very edges of society, Chatwin with Blaise Cendrars and Foucault with Antonin Artaud. Chatwin continues, "He lodged in a tenement in the Lower City and got a job with a man who sold the equipment of slavery — whips, flails, yolks, neck chains, branding irons and metal masks," also the equipment of sadomasochism.

In a 1971 essay "Nietzsche, Genealogy, History," Foucault contends that, "This relationship of domination is no more a 'relationship' than the place where it occurs is a place; and, precisely for this reason, it is fixed, throughout its history, in rituals, in meticulous procedures that impose rights and obligations." In *A Thousand Plateaus*, Deleuze and Guattari construct a very similar argument, "In effect, in the rich domain of personal relations, what counts is not the capriciousness or variability of the individuals but the consistency of the relations, and the adequation between a subjectivity that can reach the point of delirium and qualified acts that are sources of rights and obligations."

Power/knowledge was Foucault's overriding obsession, a continuation and re-assessment of Nietzsche's will to power. Knowledge of inmates in prison, patients in hospitals, the insane in asylums, creates power over them, creates new means, new sciences, to observe the incarcerated. For the panopticon read closed-circuit television. Foucault's archaeology stemmed from attempting to isolate a "zero-point" where madness cleaved from reason, where fools became the insane. In a 1982 epidemiology study for the US Centers for Disease Control and Prevention by William Darrow and colleagues, a gay flight attendant from Canada, Gaëtan Dugas, was labelled "Patient Zero" and, incorrectly, pinpoited as culpable of introducing and transmitting the virus throughout North America — Dugas was sexually active in California, New York and Vancouver. Darrow has since stated that the label has been misconstrued and that the original term "Patient O" meant "person from outside" of California. Foucault's archaeological "zero-point" has similarities with epidemiology, dealing with patterns and origins and to Bruce Chatwin's claim that everything has a precedent. Gaëtan Dugas had a precedent because there had been previous HIV/AIDS deaths in America. Foucault had been active on the SM scene in California since 1976, Chatwin in New York from 1979, Gaëtan Dugas in both locations throughout that period.

Foucault questions what is "normal," what is normal both physically and morally, an archaeology of "truth." His sadomasochism tests the limits of "normal" sexuality and his investigations into the prescriptions and proscriptions of "normality" as opposed to "health" exposes the power/ knowledge and political and social manipulations of the medical profession. Having worked for the auction house Sotheby's since leaving school, in 1966 Chatwin manipulated his own medical problems by blaming the close analysis of art, antiques and antiquities for causing a temporary blindness, "One morning, I woke up blind. During the course of the day, the sight returned to the left eye, but the right one stayed sluggish and clouded. The eye specialist who examined me said there was nothing wrong organically, and diagnosed the nature of the trouble. 'You've been looking too closely at pictures,' he said. 'Why don't you swap them for some long horizons?'"

Both Chatwin and Foucault used psychosomatic illnesses to change their circumstances, both were archaeologists but with very different ideas about the past. For Foucault, history elucidated the truth of the present, the past was relative and not paradigmatic. Chatwin believed that "a rigid stratification divides the years and the twain shall never meet let alone have a conversation." Whereas Foucault was a deep archaeologist of knowledge, Chatwin's excavations of the self were mostly preliminary digs, soundings for further analysis rarely conducted.

In 1954, Chatwin, aged fourteen, spent two months at the Bratt family estate on the shore of Lake Yngaren in Sweden. He was there to teach the son, Thomas, conversational English, but spent most of his time catching and categorizing butterflies, reading Chekhov, learning about Swedish furniture and design and spending more time with the aged great-uncle than with a boy of his own age. Chatwin returned to school more mature, more sophisticated with a nascent idea of where his interests would lay — travel, design and antiquities. In 1955, fleeing from a dangerous and mutually destructive affair with the serialist composer Jean Barraqué, Foucault accepted a position as a cultural diplomat and reader in French language and literature at the University of Uppsala. Here he began his research into the history of psychology and began writing *History of Madness*. After the two years he spent in Sweden, Foucault also matured, cutting down on his alcohol consumption — which may have had something to do with the hangover from the Bratt System introduced by Thomas' physician grandfather to decrease the consumption of alcohol by means of rationing.

In *The Birth of the Clinic: An Archaeology of Medical Perception*, written after Foucault had returned to Paris, he notes,

"Anatomical dispersal was the directing principle of nosological analysis: frenzy, like apoplexy, belonged to diseases of the head; asthma, pleuropneumonia, and haemoptysis formed related species in that they were all three localized in the chest. Morbid kinship rested on a principle of organic proximity: the space that defined it was local." Here we can see the similarity and the difference between Foucault and Chatwin's methodology, both using nosology, a system of classification, Foucault to understand the mechanics of power/knowledge and Chatwin to examine the "nomadic alternative," both writers unearthing alternative views of civilization's systems and histories.

Chatwin argues in an essay from 1970 that civilization "means nothing more than 'living in cities.'" And that, "this transformation depended on irrigation works, intensive agriculture, specialized skills such as pottery and metallurgy, and supervision by a literate bureaucracy, judiciary and priesthood. Civilization demands a stratified social and economic hierarchy. There is, regrettably, no indication that it is cohesive without one." For Foucault, "the more complex the social space in which it is situated becomes, the more *denatured* it becomes. Before the advent of civilization, people had only the simplest, most necessary diseases. Peasants and workers still remain close to the basic nosological table; the simplicity of their lives allows it to show through in its reasonable order: they have none of those variable, complex, intermingled nervous ills, but down-to-earth apoplexies, or uncomplicated attacks of mania." For Chatwin, "the urban civilizations of the Old World radiated outwards, excluding all who would not conform to the canons of civilized behaviour." Hence, the incarceration of the mad, the classification of diseases, the theory of normality, in a word: control.

From *The Birth of the Clinic*, "A system of coincidences then appeared that indicated a causal connexion and also suggested kinships or new links between diseases." He also wrote, "A coincidence of places, an approximate overlapping of times," in *The Order of Things: An Archaeology of the Human Sciences* (1966), and after the commercial success but negative criticism surrounding the book (most vociferously by Sartre) — and to follow his lover who had been posted there on national service — Foucault did a Chatwinesque disappearing act to take up a position at the University of Tunis where he would remain until the end of 1968. Foucault was in Tunis during the May demonstrations, strikes and occupation of buildings in France. He heard reports of it and "soundings" over the phone as his partner, Daniel Defert, happened to be in Paris at the time.

While in Tunis, Foucault was researching and writing *The Archaeology of Knowledge*, his work outlining his own methodological system of his previous books and his theories of historiography, discourse, and the episteme. Around this time, Chatwin was also working on the historiography of the unpublished *The Nomadic Alternative*, sending a book proposal to Tom Maschler of Jonathan Cape on 24 February, 1969, in which he observes, "all the civilizations are based on regimentation and rational behaviour. Nomads are uncivilized and all the words traditionally used in connection with them are charged with civilized prejudices —vagrant, vagabond, shifty, barbarian, savage, etc." In his book on Foucault, Deleuze not only explains but concurs with Chatwin's ideas about nomads, "If seventeenth-century statements wrote of madness as being the last degree of folly (a key notion), then the asylum or internment envelops it in a general concept uniting madmen, vagabonds, paupers, idlers and all sorts of depraved folk: this offers a certain 'self-evidence,' a historical perception or sensibility, as much as a discursive system."

In March 1969, Chatwin spent two weeks in Tunis securing the purchase of two door panels decorated with faces and chevrons that had been brought from New Caledonia in the mid-nineteenth century (Robert Louis Stephenson had spent a week there in July 1890). The door was a fetish to ward off bad spirits (*daimons*). The panels were sold to George Ortiz, the supposed inspiration for *Utz* (1988), Chatwin's final novel. This is not so much an overlapping of times but a coincidence of place.

From *The Birth of the Clinic*, "And it is in this sense that knowledge of life and life itself obey the same laws of genesis — whereas in classificatory thinking this coincidence could exist only once and in divine understanding, the progress of knowledge now had the same origin and found itself caught up in the same empirical process of becoming (*devenir*) as the progression of life." Chatwin's idea of precedence, Nietzsche's theory of becoming, Foucault's conception of the episteme combined in knowledge. Bruce Chatwin used to wear a dark green loden coat that resembled a swirling cape, along with his trademark white turtleneck sweaters — Chatwin was once branded one of those "polo-necked thinkers of Notting Hill" — Michel Foucault would wear a green woollen cape. Chatwin wanted "to find the other side of the coin," he was obsessed with lives "invisible to the archaeologist's spade," histories that had left "no burnt layer." In *The Use of Pleasure* (1984), Michel Foucault agrees, "There are times in life when the question of knowing if one can think differently than one thinks and perceive differently than one sees is absolutely necessary if one is to go on looking and reflecting at all." Chatwin wrote an essay "The Morality of Things," of "the journey home, the ecstasy of undressing the package, the object of the quest unveiled, the night one didn't go to bed with anyone, but kept vigil, gazing, stroking, adoring in the new fetish — the companion, the lover." Looking and reflecting. In *The Order of Things*, Michel Foucault agreed, "The skilled hand is suspended in mid-air, arrested in rapt attention on the painter's gaze; and the gaze, in return, waits upon the arrested gesture. Between the fine point of the brush and the steely gaze, the scene is about to yield up its volume."

Even though both Chatwin and Foucault "favoured looking aslant at a subject," they were both fascinated with the "gaze." In the preface to *The Birth of the Clinic*, Foucault asserts, "This book is about space, about language, and about death; it is about the act of seeing, the gaze," and continues, "We must place ourselves, and remain once and for all, at the level of the fundamental spatialization and verbalization of the pathological, where the loquacious gaze with which the doctor observes the poisonous heart of things is born and communes with itself." Foucault focuses on his medical diagnosis as part of the power/knowledge mechanisms of the medical professions and disciplinary methodologies of penal and psychiatric institutions. In the introduction to Chatwin's *Photographs and Notebooks* (1993), Francis Wyndham writes, "The extracts I have chosen only really have a direct connection with the photographs they accompany but I think they convey the general nature of his visual appetite, the *kind* of colours, forms and images which are arrested the attention of his ever curious gaze."

Gaëtan Dugas was born in Quebec City in 1952, at the age of twenty he had moved to Vancouver and started to frequent gay bars, clubs and bathhouses. He became a flight attendant for Air Canada in 1974, travelling between Halifax, Toronto, Montreal and Vancouver. He had hundreds of sexual partners in these cities and in San Francisco and New York City. In 1980, he had been diagnosed with Kaposi's sarcoma and underwent chemotherapy treatment in New York City. Dugas was cynical about the news stories and gossip in the club about a "gay cancer" and remained sexually active. In 1982, he did, however, help the Centers for Disease Control in their documentation of tracing sexual partners and therefore became a fulcrum for the 1984 cluster diagram of people with Kaposi's sarcoma, *Pneumocystis carinii* pneumonia and other symptoms in Los Angeles, San Francisco, New York City and elsewhere in the USA. Dugas would die at home on 30 March, 1984 of AIDS-related kidney failure.

From 1927 until November 1974, Chatwin worked inter-mittently for *The Sunday Times Magazine*. On a retainer of £2,000 per annum, he suggested ideas for articles, interviewed people and travelled. He assembled a thousand images for "One Million Years of Art," published in the colour magazine in the summer of 1973, which included prehistoric Tanzanian stone tools, a Chinese People's Collective painting of an operating theatre called "Acupuncture Anaesthesia" and a photograph of painted doors in Mauritania, a photograph that the *Sunday Times* had rejected for publication in 1972. The illustrations mixed and fused time periods and styles, the kind of epoch-leap that Chatwin used in his later writing and in his letters in which his "description dramatizes by leaving out links and explanations and by collapsing the time-scheme."

While having a drink at the Chelsea Hotel in New York in 1974, Chatwin announced to his editor Francis Wyndham that he was going to Patagonia. On 11 December, 1974, he ratified his position in a letter to Wyndham posted from Lima, Peru, "I have done what I threatened. I suddenly got fed up with NY and ran away to South America. I have been staying with a cousin in Lima for the past week and am going tonight to Buenos Aires. I intend to spend Christmas in the middle of Patagonia. I am doing a story there for myself, something I have always wanted to write up."

The something that he wanted to write up would be *In Patagonia*, the travel narrative, part journal, part essay, part fiction that would launch his writing career. In *Campo Santo* (2003), W.G. Sebald, comments: "Just as Chatwin himself ultimately remains an enigma, one never knows how to classify his books. All that is obvious is that their structure and intentions place them in no known genre. Inspired by a kind of avidity for the undiscovered, they move along a line where the points of demarcation are those strange manifestations and objects of which one cannot say whether they are real, or whether they are among the phantasms generated in our minds from time immemorial. Anthropological and mythological studies in the tradition of *Tristes Tropiques*, adventure stories looking back to our early childhood reading, collections of facts, dream books, regional novels, examples of lush exoticism, puritanical penance, sweeping baroque vision, self-denial and personal confession..."

Acknowledging Lévi-Strauss, the author of *Tristes Tropiques* (1955), as one of his precursors, throughout the period from 1971 to 1974, Foucault was "professor of the history of systems of thought" at the Collège de France. He used the Collège's research library in the writing of *Discipline and Punish: The Birth of the Prison* (1975), his work on the knowledge/power of prisons and how they, like their medical counterparts, developed systems to create a knowledge base in order to control inmates and then used these methodologies in society as a whole. Foucault theorized that "the workshop, the school, the army were subject to a whole micro-penalty of time (latenesses, absences, interruptions of tasks), of activity (inattention, negligence, lack of zeal), of behaviour (impoliteness, disobedience), of speech (idle chatter, insolence), of the body ('incorrect' attitudes, irregular gestures, lack of cleanliness), of sexuality (impurity, indecency). At the same time, by way of punishment, a whole series of subtle procedures was used, from light physical punishment to minor deprivations and petty humiliations. It was a question both of making the slightest departures from correct behaviour subject to punishment, and of giving a punitive function to the apparently indifferent elements of the disciplinary apparatus: so that, if necessary, everything might serve to punish the slightest thing; each subject find himself caught in a punishable, punishing universality." This not only sounds like the fantasies of a repressed sadomasochist but the philosophy of Marlborough College, the public school Chatwin attended.

After *Discipline and Punish*, Foucault began work on *The History of Sexuality*, a three-volume examination of sexuality in Western civilization. When the actor Peter Eyre used the word "sexuality" in a conversation with Chatwin, Chatwin replied in his arch Noël Coward voice, "'Sexuality' — my dear!"

The three volumes — *The Will to Knowledge* (1976), *The Use of Pleasure* (1984) and *The Care of the Self* (1984) — were published over the same period as Chatwin's *In Patagonia* (1977), *The Viceroy of Ouidah* (1980) *On the Black Hill* (1982). The Foucault titles could be subtitles for Chatwin's books as he moves from travelogue to fiction and the blurred forms between these genres. Foucault also shifts between historiography, philosophy, psychiatry, both authors using epoch shifts in experimental works. Chatwin's ninety-seven chapters span not just Patagonia in the mid-seventies but the Late Jurassic epoch, the Pleistocene, and through to the travels of Darwin. Foucault's first volume describes the changes in notions of sexuality from the seventeenth century through to the present day. Writing against the "repressive hypothesis," Foucault argues, "Those who believe that sex was more rigorously elided in the nineteenth century than ever before, through a formidable mechanism of blockage and a deficiency of discourse, can say what they please. There was no deficiency, but rather an excess, a redoubling, too much rather than not enough discourse, in any case an interference between two modes of production of truth: procedures of confession, and scientific discursivity."

Throughout *In Patagonia*, Chatwin repressed some stories, rigorously elided and blocked sexual material; there is an excess of discourse, a redoubling of knowledge, the travel narrative shot through with procedures of confession (autobiography), scientific discursivity (the search for the Mylodon, a giant ground sloth). This blockage of the discourse of sexuality, this repressive hypothesis, is evident in a letter to John Michell that Chatwin wrote from Siena in Italy on 29 October, 1977, "The pianist! Ah! The pianist! E. Hemingway, who knew a thing or two though it's fashionable to put him down, said if you take something OUT of a piece of writing it always shows. What I took it OUT of that story was the head falling backwards at the end of the mazurka, automatically with no hint of it before, and lifting him off the piano stool into the bedroom. But that is off the record and should be torn up." Chatwin had actually written, "And he played the mazurka that Chopin dictated on his deathbed. The wind whistled in the street and the music ghosted from the piano as leaves over a headstone. And you could imagine you were in the presence of genius."

The Viceroy of Ouidah was originally going to be a non-fiction narrative of the life of Francisco Félix de Sousa but Chatwin fictionalized his research, de Sousa becoming Francisco Manuel da Silva. The novel is about power and knowledge, its conception stems from a trip Chatwin made to Niger and Dahomey (Benin) in February 1972. In a letter to his wife Elizabeth, he wrote, "I have started writing a long story — may even be a short novel." A few days later, he sent a postcard to his parents, "The upper crust of Ouidah all direct descendants of a Portuguese who managed to extend the slave trade clandestinely forty years after it had in theory be abolished by the British. Fascinating material for a book." Where *In Patagonia*'s prose, despite its meanderings, had been clear and clipped, *The Viceroy of Ouidah* is over-mannered and Baroque, written in the high style of *Salammbo*, it is, like Flaubert's novella, the irregularly shaped pearl in Chatwin's oeuvre. He returned to Benin in December 1976 to do further research, while there he was arrested during a coup, strip-searched and imprisoned with hundreds of other foreigners. During this episode it is possible that his fantasy of being gang raped became an actuality. It was an episode he left out of "A Coup — A Story," his piece about the event written in 1984. After being released, Chatwin moved on to Côte d'Ivoire three days later and then flew to Brazil to continue his research. Throughout the book, there are scenes of masochism and torture, descriptions of fetishes next to whips and cicatrices, "Fixed to the wall were a pair of handcuffs and a broken guitar. There was also a stuffed civet cat, nailed, in mockery of the crucifixion, with its hind legs and tail together and its fore legs stretched apart." While a patient in the John Warin emergency ward in Churchill Hospital, Oxford, undergoing HIV tests, on 14 September, 1986, Chatwin reluctantly recounted his medical and sexual history to the doctors. He told them of his travels throughout the world, about his affair with Donald Richards (a possible source of the HIV infection) and the medical notes also record, "NB Experienced 'gang rape' in Benin (W Africa) in 1978." Doctors thought this unlikely. Chatwin also surmised that the virus could have come from Sam Wagstaff, Robert Mapplethorpe's lover.

Chatwin used the civet cat/Crucifixion scene in "A Coup — A Story," a few pages earlier, he wrote, "The next few hours I would prefer to forget." The piece is full of ellipses, those periods of elision and denial. Had Chatwin been an "object of pleasure" for the soldiers? Had he been used for pleasure? Had he contracted the HIV virus while researching his book about a slave trader? Were the episodes of masochism metaphors for gang rape? Chatwin was an unreliable narrator in both his work and his life, the gang rape could have been a fantasy or a product of his fevered mind and hypomania.

In 1984, the same year that "A Coup — A Story" was published in *Granta* magazine, Foucault, writing about sexuality in Ancient Greece, notes, "Medical and philosophical reflection describes it (the sexual act) as posing a threat, through its violence, to the control and mastery that one ought to exercise over oneself; as sapping the strength the individual should conserve and maintain, through the exhaustion it caused; and as prefiguring the death of the individual while assuring the survival of the species. If the regimen of pleasures was important, this was not simply because excess might lead to an illness; it was because in sexual activity in general man's mastery, strength, and life were at stake." Soon after leaving Brazil, Chatwin would travel to Haiti and then on to New York. In an analysis of Plato and his theories of sexuality, Foucault could be writing about the SM clubs, "The city in which those who ought to be ruled would obey, and those who were destined to rule would in fact rule: hence there would be a multitude of 'appetites and pleasures and pains.'"

In the third volume, *The Care of the Self*, Foucault focuses on Ancient Rome, and discussing the philosophy of Epictetus, writes, "The school should be thought of as a 'dispensary for the soul': 'The philosopher's school is a physician's consulting-room [*iatreion*]. You must leave it in pain, not in pleasure.'" During the early 1980s, neither Foucault nor Chatwin were mindful of their condition. Chatwin constantly complained of bronchitis, fatigue, eye problems. In December 1982, just after the publication and success of *On the Black Hill*, he had an operation on either his haemorrhoids or for a "dread stomach disorder," or, as Nicholas Shakespeare has it, "There was another reason for him to go abroad. He had just come out of St Thomas' Hospital after an operation. He convalesced with Diana Melly at her London home in St Lawrence Terrace. 'It was something genital,' she says. 'It was mysterious, painful and embarrassing and he did not want to talk about it.'" Could this have been an anal fistula? Whatever it was, Chatwin was leaving the country in December 1982, in pain, to go to Australia to do research on *The Songlines* (1987), a version of his "nomadic alternative."

Foucault was working on *The Care of the Self* around this period and analysing the writings of the Roman physician-philosopher Galen, "The increased medical involvement in the cultivation of the self appears to have been expressed through a particular and intense form of attention to the body." Both Foucault and Chatwin would experience an "increased medical involvement" and be forced to pay more attention to their bodies. From *On the Black Hill*, "'Oh, we know Benjamin,' the neighbours would say. 'The one as looks so poor.' For his shoulders had slumped, his ribs stuck out like a concertina, and there were dark rings under his eyes. He fainted twice in church. He was obsessed by death." In *The Care of the Self*, Foucault quotes Aretaeus of Cappadocia (1st century AD) — a physician who first described diabetes, bipolar disorder, asthma and uterine carcinoma, and wrote early texts on acute and chronic illnesses — on the diagnosis of gonorrhoea: "'When the semen is not possessed of its vitality, persons become shrivelled, have a sharp tone of voice, lose their hair and their beard, and become effeminate.' With gonorrhoea it is virility, the life principle, that is lost via the genitals. Hence the traits that are traditionally associated with it. It is a shameful disease — no doubt because it is often induced by a quantitative excess of sexual activity. But it is also shameful in itself because of the appearance of emasculation it produces. It is a disease that leads inevitably to death. Celsus says that in a short time it causes the patient to die of consumption." This could be a description of both Chatwin and Foucault after they were found to be HIV positive.

After returning from lecturing at University of California, Berkeley, and revisiting the SM clubs of San Francisco, Foucault was fatigued and pale. In a conversation with a student just before he returned to Paris, Foucault had summed up his thoughts on the illness: "Look at the gay community that has come into being, and look at what AIDS is doing to it. It is terrible. It is absurd. A group that has risked so much, that has won so much, is now looking to outside authorities for guidance in a time of crisis. Relying on public health officials. Listening to the doctors. It is unbelievable. The world, the play of power, the game of truth, all 'this is dangerous!' […] but that's it. That's what you've got! It should be scared of AIDS? You could be hit by a car tomorrow. Even crossing the street was dangerous! If sex with a boy gives me pleasure — why renounced such a pleasure?"

Two months after Gaëtan Dugas died, Foucault slumped to the kitchen floor in his Paris apartment. He had been suffering from fatigue, headaches and coughing fits and had had to stay in hospital on various occasions. With *The Care of the Self* unfinished, Foucault would remain in hospital. He was suffering from *Pneumocystis carinii* pneumonia, toxoplasmosis of the brain and was dying. Like Chatwin, Foucault had a "tortuous approach to telling the truth," but in his last days he "confessed" to one of his ex-lovers, the writer and artist Hervé Guibert, "invoking his childhood and its dreams" just as Chatwin evoked his summer idyll in Sweden rather than relate the story of gang rape. Hervé Guibert would be diagnosed with AIDS in 1988 and write a trilogy — *To the Friend Who Did Not Save My Life* (1990), *The Compassionate Protocol* (1991) and *The Man In The Red Hat*

(1992) — his own history of sexuality and living with HIV/ AIDS. He also made a film *La Pudeur ou l'impudeur* (*Modesty or Immodesty*) about the last year of his life. After attempting suicide, he died on 27 December, 1991 aged thirty-five.

The performance artist Bob Flanagan featured in the film *Sick: The Life and Death of Bob Flanagan, Supermasochist* directed by Kirby Dick and first released in 1997. Flanagan died the year before, aged forty-three, from cystic fibrosis, and the movie portrays his stark and honest views on his illness, impending death and his use of masochism as a sexual stimulant and as therapy to help him cope with his disease. The film is a graphic and humorous portrait of a dying man who enjoys severe torture under the direction of his partner Sheree Rose. In the 1992 video for Nine Inch Nails' "Happiness in Slavery," Flanagan undergoes an extreme version of Kafka's the Condemned in "In the Penal Colony," the difference being Flanagan is enjoying the pain, his blood feeding the plants of the garden beneath the torturing machine. This from his *The Pain Journal* (1996), 25 April, 1995: "Getting hard to breathe again. Thought I was doing much better, but it never lasts. My mood has been improving, though. And I've got a renewed interest in sex, mostly fantasizing about this alligator clip thing, and trying it out a little bit with a couple of clips here and there, those jagged little teeth biting into my tender spots as I grab hold of something like the bed rail and squeeze until the pain floats off a little, turns sweet almost, until it's time for another clip. It's almost like eating hot chili peppers, except that the taste buds for this delicacy are in my balls, not my mouth." Flanagan wanted his death filmed, his last dying breaths, and he planned for a camera to be placed in his coffin to record his putrefaction.

In 1983, Foucault told an interviewer, "I believe that [...] someone who is a writer is not simply doing his work in his books, but that his major work is, in the end, himself in the process of writing his books. The private life of an individual, his sexual preference, and his work are interrelated, not because his work translates his sexual life, because the work includes the whole life as well as the text." This was a statement contra to his agreement with Barthes concerning the death of the author and on 25 June, 1984, Foucault would die from what *Le Monde* claimed to be complications from septicaemia and "cerebral suppurations." This diagnosis, like Foucault's work, twisted the truth, his family wanted the cause of his death suppressed — power/knowledge. Truth and denial, Foucault used both with extreme elasticity. In reality he had died of AIDS-related complications just as the first reviews of *The Use of Pleasure* and *The Care of the Self* were published.

On 25 May, 1984, Chatwin wrote to Elizabeth, "not doing so badly in complete seclusion: Paris — nightmare." On 2 July, he wrote to Penelope Tree, "A disaster with the Australian book — in that another, by accident, had cannibalized it — temporarily." The Australian book was *The Songlines*, Chatwin's fictional non-fictional account of Aboriginal culture and the nomadic life. In it, the narrator quotes from Rimbaud, "My health was menaced. Terror came. For days on end I fell asleep and, when I woke, the dark dreams continued. I was ripe for death. My debility led me along a route of dangers, to the world's edge, to Cimmeria, the country of black fog and whirlpools." Cimmeria was a mythical land that bordered the kingdom of the dead. There are these border zones, these bufferings, between illness and health, living and dying in liminal hospital beds.

On 23 April, 1984, the US Department of Health and Human Services announced that Dr Robert Gallo and other researchers at the National Cancer Institute had discovered the cause of AIDS — it is the retrovirus HTLV-III, now known as HIV, which, over a period of time caused acquired immunodeficiency syndrome (AIDS). The National Cancer Institute had originated a diagnostic blood test to screen for and identify HTLV-III and hoped to develop a vaccine against the virus. In June, the National Cancer Institute, in a joint conference with Dr Gallo and Professor Luc Montagnier, from the Pasteur Institute on Rue de Vaugirard, Paris (the street Foucault lived on from 1979 to 1984 and where he was run over by a car and hospitalized in 1982), announced that Dr Montagnier's discovery of Lymphadenopathy Associated Virus (LAV) and Dr Gallo's HTLV-III virus were identical and the likely cause of AIDS. In October, bathhouses and private sex clubs were closed by San Francisco health officials because of high-risk sexual activity. New York City and Los Angeles enforced the same laws in 1985.

Chatwin had become seriously ill in Java "with amoebas and all that" that the doctors thought was cholera. During the writing of *The Songlines*, Chatwin's health declined and he seemed unconsciously aware that time was pressing, "I'm writing something very odd, which although set under a gum tree somewhere in the MacDonnells has nothing much to do with Central Australia. No, that is wrong, it has everything and nothing to do with Central Australia and I need desperately to know certain things." In November 1984, he had a "nasty virus on his face" which looked like chicken pox and also bronchitis. On 21 May, 1985, Chatwin visited Mount Athos for a spell of contemplation and recuperation but was unhappy with his work on the book and was "tempted to tear the whole thing up." On 29 July, he complained of "soggy fish and chips on the boat; catarrh on the by-pass" as he drove through Europe on his return to Homer End. On 14 September, he confesses, "God knows when the book'll be finished." On 7 November, 1985, Chatwin and Elizabeth flew to Kathmandu for a three-month stay and also visited Hong Kong and China. In Yunnan

Province, during a feast, Chatwin ate a one-thousand year-old black egg and became immediately ill. The first reported AIDS case in China was of a tourist in Yunnan who had become infected through sharing needles while injecting heroin.

By the end of 1985, AIDS cases had been reported in every region of the world, a vaccine had still not been created. On 25 July, Rock Hudson died of AIDS, he had been diagnosed a year before and was the first American celebrity to admit that he had the disease. Throughout the world 20,303 cases of AIDS had been reported.

In January 1986, Chatwin wrote to Wyndham, "Have fled from disease-ridden Kathmandu: the world's No 1 capital for complaints of the upper respiratory tract." From Jodhpur, India, where he had escaped to, he complained to John Kasmin that, "The cold and cough has been hard to shake off. A dry cough always is." And goes on later in the letter, "I have at last been cutting some fresh furrows with the book, and I don't think I have quite the same sinking feeling that all the rest of it was in chaos." On 9 February, he wrote to Murray and Margaret Bell, "As for my own 'Awful Mess' I've now got to the critical stage in which there is a sudden shift from Australia, in order to answer Pascal's assertion about the man sitting quietly in a room. If it comes off, then I'm on the downward stretch. If not, dinner is a real crisis." And at the end of the letter, "I wasn't really on best form on our little jaunt a. because of my cold b. the uncertainty of what I was doing."

Chatwin returned to Homer End in May, his health perilous and *The Songlines* proving problematic. His asthma worsened, he was troubled by night sweats and lumps had developed under his skin. He was even unable to go walking because of fatigue and this affected his work on the "Awful Mess." In *Songlines*, Chatwin quoted a letter from Kierkegaard, "Above all, do not lose your desire to walk: every day I walk myself into state of well-being and walk away from every illness; I have walked myself into my best thoughts, and I know of no thought so burdensome that one cannot walk away from it… but by sitting still, and the more one sits still, the closer one comes to feeling ill. Thus if one just keeps on walking, everything will be all right." By August 17, he had finished a first draft and immediately flew to Zurich to work with his editor Elisabeth Sifton, he was too exhausted to go to New York as they had originally planned. On August 18, coughing, anaemic and with diarrhoea, he was admitted to a Swiss clinic. His weight had dropped to 66 kilos. The doctors ran a number of tests for malaria and other diseases plus one for toxoplasmosis. He recovered enough to return to his hotel where from his bed, for the next five days, he and Sifton worked on the manuscript, but Chatwin couldn't concentrate and left most of the editing to Sifton, assuring her that the illness wasn't AIDS.

Elizabeth arrived in Zurich on 1 September and went straight to the hotel. Chatwin was in bed shivering, sweating, his immune system breaking down. Elizabeth thought he was dying and persuaded him to go back to the clinic. They ran another set of blood tests, the results showed "HTLV-III-Virus-Antikörper / HIV positive." On 12 September, the Chatwins flew back to London, an ambulance was waiting to take the gravely ill writer to hospital where the doctor recorded in his notes that Chatwin had pre-AIDS. As Foucault's illness had been withheld from the press, so Chatwin's parents and brother were told that the diagnosis was pneumonia. During their investigations the doctors also discovered *Penicillium marneffei*, a rare human-pathogenic fungus and that the right side of Chatwin's brain had been damaged, affecting his reason.

On 13 October, Chatwin explained "the collapse" in a letter from hospital to Gertrude Chanler, "Trust me to pick up a disease never recorded among Europeans. The fungus that has attacked my bone marrow has been recorded among 10 Chinese peasants (China is presumably where I got it), a few Thais and a killer-whale cast up on the shores of Arabia. The great test comes when we find out whether I can go on producing red blood cells on my own." Chatwin's denial of the diagnosis was immediate, his grasping of an exotic source for his illness was as fanciful and unreasonable as a killer whale being washed up on the shores of Arabia. On 3 November, 1964, he reiterates the fantasy to Murray Bail and claims he is "an A1 medical curiosity;" he wasn't, he was HIV positive with pre-AIDS symptoms and a poor prognosis. He tells Bail, "I finished the book — title The Songlines — which, to all the publishers distaste, I insist on calling a novel." In the book, Chatwin had quoted from Sun Tzu's *Art of War*, "Wild beasts, when at bay, fight desperately. How much more is this true of men! If they know there is no alternative, they will fight to the death." Chatwin would not believe that there was no alternative; in a letter to Cary and Edith Welch on 12 December, 1986, he wrote, "my illness was a dramatic episode. I have always known — from a fortune-teller or from my own instinctive promptings? — that I would be terribly ill in middle-age, and would recover. All summer, while I was putting the final touches to the book, I was obviously sickening, but preferred to put it out of my mind…"

In May 1986, the International Committee on the Taxonomy of Viruses changed the official name of the virus that caused AIDS from HTLV-III to HIV. The World Health Organization reported eight-five countries, now officially including the Soviet Union and India, with 38,401 cases of AIDS. In *The Order of Things*, Foucault states that literature "breaks with the whole definition of genres as forms adapted to an order of representations, and becomes merely a manifestation of a language which has no other law than that of affirming — in opposition to all other forms of discourse — its own precipitous existence." Chatwin was in ludic denial of his illness and was about to embark on writing another book that broke with the whole definition of genres as a means of affirming his own precipitous existence.

In the same letter to Cary and Edith Welch, Chatwin had admitted, "I'm at present at work on a tale — a Hoffmann-like tale set in Prague — in which a collector of Meissen porcelain (a man I met there in 1967) systematically destroys his collection on his deathbed…" For the first quarter of 1987, Chatwin's red blood cell count had stabilized and he was well enough to travel to the south of France, Milan and to Accra, Ghana, where Werner Herzog was directing *Cobra Verde*, his film version of *The Viceroy Ouidah*. Denial and travel, denial and creativity. During this period, Chatwin's peregrinations and writing of *Utz* were attempts to recapture his youth and his health. In *The Order of Things*, Foucault explains: "But in setting itself the task of restoring the domain of the original, modern thought immediately encounters the recession of the origin; and, paradoxically, it proposes the solution of advancing in the direction of this ever-deepening recession; it tries to make it appear on the far side of experience, as that which sustains it by its very retreat, as that which is nearest to its most visible possibility, as that which is, within thought, imminent; and if the recession of the origin is thus posited in its greatest clarity, is it not the origin itself that is set free and travels backwards until it reaches itself again, in the dynasty of its archaism?"

Chatwin's continuing denial included the impossible "task of restoring the domain of the original," his body and mind were in an "ever-deepening recession," he was encountering the limit-experience of his life even in remission and his death was imminent. In writing *Utz*, Chatwin was travelling backwards and reimagining the archaic dynasty of Meissen (eighteenth century) and further back to Rabbi Judah Loew ben Bezalel and the legend of the golem of Prague (late sixteenth century).

Back at Homer End in May 1987, after receiving a copy of the about-to-be-published *The Songlines*, Chatwin confessed to the classicist and historian Robin Lane Fox, "This is a failed attempt to write the book that you above all people believed in. But time is short. Of course, it's fragmentary and probably baffling and you never expected it would have anything to do with Australia." Published on 25 June, a month later, *The Songlines* became the number-one bestseller on *The Sunday Times* list. That was the good news, but by then his doctors were sure the pre-AIDS had become full-blown. On March 19, the US Food and Drug Administration, the FDA, had approved zidovudine (AZT), the first anti-retroviral drug, as treatment for HIV. In April, Chatwin's doctor, Bent Juel-Jensen, placed him on an AZT treatment programme, which, at first, had optimistic results. Over the next few months, Chatwin travelled to Vienna, Prague, Steiermark, home to Oxford and then to the Chateau de Seillans in the south of France to convalesce, walk when he was able to and to finish the writing of *Utz*.

On 15 September, as part of the publicity for *The Songlines*, Chatwin flew from New York for the Toronto Harbourfront Reading Series, but had to cancel all scheduled interviews because of sickness and vomiting. Back in the UK, his doctors were worried that his P24 antigen (viral protein) had again become positive. But Chatwin continued to work and travel, to the West Indies, back to France, home to Oxford. On 11 December, in a letter to Murray Bail, he exclaims, "I, for what it's worth, yesterday, finished a novel. Quite a carry on! The title — *Utz* simple as that! The most that can be said for it is that it was designed as an entertainment to carry me through those rather beleaguered months."

71,751 cases of AIDS had been reported to the World Health Organization by December 1987, with an estimated five to ten million people living with HIV. Randy Shilts' piece of investigative journalism, *And the Band Played On: Politics, People and the AIDS Epidemic*, which includes an analysis of Gaëtan Dugas and the "Patient Zero" theory, was published earlier that year. The book reports on the early years of HIV/AIDS in America and how, through the indifference and ineptitude of government health officials, was nosologized as a gay disease (a cancer) before being recognized as a viral epidemic.

After having changed agent and signing with Wylie, Aitken and Stone in January 1988, Chatwin finished writing *Utz*. He and Elizabeth then left Homer End for a holiday (that's if Chatwin ever went "on holiday") to Guadaloupe. On 8 February, his publisher Tom Maschler issued a statement on Chatwin's behalf, "I am most honoured to be nominated for the Thomas Cook Travel Award; but *The Songlines* has been published as fiction on both sides of the Atlantic... the journey it describes is an invented journey, it is not a travel book in the generally accepted sense. To avoid any possible confusion, I must ask to withdraw from the shortlist." Published that year, Deleuze's monograph on Foucault, *Foucault*, announces, "In a certain way Foucault can declare that he has never written anything but fiction for, as we have seen, statements resemble dreams and are transformed as in a kaleidoscope, depending on the corpus in question and the diagonal line being followed. But in another sense he can also claim that he has written only what is real, and used what is real, for everything is real in this statement, and all reality in it is openly on display."

Both Foucault and Chatwin worked within a multiplicity of genres: travel, fiction, history, law, psychiatry, philosophy, archaeology, palaeontology, epistemology and, at the same time, none of these. Deleuze's analysis of Foucault's corpus is as applicable to Chatwin's works and methodology: "He will not concern himself with what previous archivists have treated in a thousand different ways: propositions and phrases. He will ignore both the vertical hierarchy of propositions which are stacked on top of one another, and the horizontal relationship established between phrases in which each seems to respond to another. Instead he will remain mobile, skimming along in a kind of diagonal line that allows him to read what could not be apprehended before, namely statements. Is this perhaps an atonal logic? It is natural for us to have misgivings. For the archivist deliberately refuses to give examples. He believes that he never stopped giving them in the past, even if at the time he was unaware that they were examples." Genres elide, the truth is malleable, partners multiply, denial is both imminent and immanent. Chatwin and Foucault shunned categorization in their work and life, were evasive about the details of their life and their dying.

Chatwin, now dependent on Elizabeth for care, planned to write a "Russian" novel tentatively titled *Lydia Livingstone*, another located in a South African village and a one-act ballet; he also planned to travel to Sudan, write a libretto for a musical of *The Songlines*, but was "hardly able to hold a pen," yet in February, he told Murray Bail, "We're off on a world tour — I hope!" Always contradictory in letters, he twice quoted Cyril Connolly's aphorism, "inside every traveller an anchorite is longing to stay put." But by 5 May he was back in hospital and back in denial, "It's no good," he apologized to Harriet Harvey-Wood, "I've been in hospital on and off for 3 months a. with an ordinary stomach disorder of the tropics b. with undiagnosed malaria (temperature of 106°) caught on the famous trip to Ghana. I simply can't face any engagements and have work to do." Chatwin's refusal to accept the truth was, in a sense, the equivalent of his non-acceptance of categorization. Deleuze on

Foucault again, "Above all, what we have done is to discover and survey that foreign land where a literary form, a scientific proposition, a common phrase, a schizophrenic piece of non-sense and so on are also statements, but lack a common denominator and cannot be reduced or made equivalent in any discursive way. This is what had never before been attained by logicians, formalists or interpreters. Science and poetry are equal forms of knowledge." For Chatwin, "the truth" was a foreign land, his denial a "schizophrenic piece of non-sense," he turned the science of diagnosis into the poetry of dissembling.

Chatwin's stays in the Churchill Hospital were becoming more frequent and lengthy, he had chronic diarrhoea, wasn't eating and in constant abdominal pain. The fungus had spread to his brain (maybe a scientific reason for the schizophrenic nonsense) causing toxic brain syndrome resulting in hypomania, and his facial spots were diagnosed as Kaposi's sarcoma. Still in denial, Chatwin hoped to convert to the Greek Orthodox faith, he told Gertrude Chanler, "I am entirely concerned with the matter of healing. There is no point in setting out to write a book about healing. If a book has to be born, it will be born." He continues, "I hope to divide my life into four parts: a. religious instruction b. learning about disease c. learning to heal d. the rest of the time free to give my undivided attention to Elizabeth and the house." The book he planned to write was to be called *Sons of Thunder*, telling the story of the AIDS virus, and was to include scientific studies by virologists at the Radcliffe Medical Foundation and his own archaeological theories of culture and healing in an attempt to find the "primordial" virus somewhere in Africa.

On 7 July, 1988, the *London Review of Books* published a letter by Chatwin which was signed, "Bruce Chatwin Oxford Team for Research into Infectious Tropical Diseases, Oxford University." The letter criticizes a review of Randy Shilts' *And the Band Played On* by John Ryle, *The Forbidden Zone* (1987) by Michael Lesy and *Crisis: Heterosexual Behaviour in the Age of Aids* (1988) by William Masters, Virginia Johnson and Robert Kilodny. Chatwin opens with a quote from the review: "'There is no good news about Aids. With a total of 85,000 cases reported at the beginning of this year the World Health Organization estimate of the true figure is nearer 150,000. Their global estimate for HIV infection is between five and ten million. Most HIV-positive individuals have no symptoms and don't know they are infected: but the majority of them — possibly all of them — will eventually develop Aids and die; in the meantime, of course, they may infect anyone they have sex with and any children they bear.'" And he counters, "This is hogwash. The word 'Aids' is one of the cruellest and silliest neologisms of our time. 'Aid' means help, succour, comfort — yet with a hissing sibilant tacked onto the end it becomes a nightmare." Without getting semiological, Chatwin is attacking the "name" not the disease, the signifier not the signified, the categorization and not the thing. Chatwin denies the diagnosis, the taxonomy, the nosology, he denies language, yet, as Foucault writes in *The Order of Things*, "though language no longer bears an immediate resemblance to the things it names, this does not mean that it is separate from the world; it still continues, in another form, to be the locus of revelations and to be included in the area where truth is both manifested and expressed." Chatwin does not accept this manifestation of the truth and its expression, refuses the locus of revelations that is both diagnosis and prognosis, preferring agnosis. He is going to die. He continues, "In one case in the US an infected person suddenly became HIV negative. We should, in fact, take Mr. Ryle's own figures. There have been 800,000 infected persons in the United States, of whom 80,000 have died. That means nine survivors to one death. This can mean only one thing: that some mechanism, pharmaceutical or otherwise, is keeping them alive." In a letter from two weeks previous to the *LRB* fantasy diatribe, Chatwin told Gertrude Chanler, "I get better by the day — although the neuropathy in my legs makes me very tottery. Yesterday, I went to the neurologist who said he could treat it right away, but with steroids — which is obviously out! The nerves should heal entirely within five years."

Doctors had told him that his belief that he would survive, recuperate and convalesce was a fantasy, his planning of novels and travels were means to deny the future. He concludes the letter to the *LRB*, "What is most horrifying about Mr. Ryle's article is the callous cruelty with which he condemns hundreds of thousands of people to death. If a young man who has just been told that he is HIV positive got hold of the article, the chances are he might commit suicide. There have been many such cases." On 25 July, he wrote to Henry Marshall, "I've had malaria anaemia semi paralysis of the hands and feet — all now better but I'm still a wheelchair case." In that wheelchair another symptom of the hypomania manifested itself — Chatwin began a frenzy of buying, spending thousands of pounds on artworks, antiques, Russian icons, rolling through Mayfair with plastic bags crammed with *objets d'art*, only for the purchases to be cancelled or returned by Elizabeth. If Foucault was the "new archivist," Chatwin was becoming the "new Utz."

Chatwin was so weak that on 16 August he dictated a letter to Elizabeth for Gertrude Chanler, "The pills are working a bit but it's slow. Am now trying to prevent wild travel schemes." But Chatwin was planning another trip to Mount Athos and possibly back to Australia, dictating again, "I haven't really been sick except that I had undiagnosed malaria for 13½ months and the fungus came back, necessitating a blood transfusion... I hope to be much better by the winter and we're both looking forward to coming to Australia." On 1 September, he combined his travels, research and writing in a trite explanation to Emma Bunker, "You can study nomads in the Inner Mongolia milieu. You can also catch outrageous diseases in the same area." And lapses into wishful thinking, "As to HIV, the situation is much less of a problem here than in America because people have learned not be hysterical… I shall be in San Francisco shortly after Christmas on our way to Australia." *Utz* was published three weeks later and was shortlisted for the Booker Prize. It didn't win.

Chatwin travelled to the Chateau Seillans on 20 November, planning to start work on *Lydia Livingstone.* Between trips to Paris for treatment and blood transfusions, Chatwin spent his days on the sun-filled terrace barely able to hold a pen. 1 December, 1988 was declared the first World AIDS Day by The World Health Organization — by this date, Chatwin was obviously dying yet still refusing to utter the name of his disease.

After more blood transfusions in early January 1989, Chatwin finally seemed to be coming to an understanding of his fate, telling Werner Herzog, "I am dying. You must carry my rucksack, you are the one who must carry it." By the middle of January, Elizabeth had arranged for a doctor to fly out and accompany Chatwin back to the London Lighthouse, a centre for people with HIV/AIDS. On 15 January, he was carried from the terrace back to his bedroom. During the night, he lapsed into a coma. An ambulance took him to a hospital in Nice and he was put on a ventilator. On 17 January his brother Hugh arrived. Elizabeth, not wanting Chatwin to be kept alive artificially, requested the oxygen and medication to cease. He died at 1:30pm on 18 January aged forty-eight. On the morning of 9 March, Robert Mapplethorpe died of complications from an AIDS-related illness, he was forty-two.

As we leave the HIV/AIDS unit, I would like to make two notes in my case study. First, "The journey thus pre-empts the need for hierarchies and shows a dominance. The 'dictators' of the animal kingdom are those who live in an ambulance of plenty. The anarchists, as always, are the 'gentlemen of the road.'" And second, "Prefer what is positive and multiple: difference over uniformity, flows over unities, mobile arrangements over systems. Believe that what is productive is not sedentary but nomadic." Foucault or Chatwin? Foucault sums up both men's attitudes to life in his preface to the English translation of *Anti-Oedipus*, "Develop action, thought, and desires by proliferation, juxtaposition, and disjunction, and not by subdivision and pyramidal hierarchization." I will leave the final words to one of Chatwin's biographers, "When the writer Richard Sennett arranged a meeting between Chatwin and Michel Foucault, the French philosopher who wrote a several-volumed *History of Sexuality*, the encounter wasn't a success: the two men 'took one look at each and decided no.'"

From Mount Athos on 5 June, 1985, Chatwin had sent a postcard by means of an apology to Susan Sontag, "Sorry to have missed you in London: but as you see, I've been out of the world a bit. Not too seriously! I'll be coming to NY in the Fall. As always, Bruce." And it is to Dr Sontag's office we will go to get a second opinion on AIDS and its metaphors. Although Chatwin and Foucault only met once, Edmund White, friend of Foucault and Sontag, remembers Chatwin coming to Paris, "suffering from a mysterious 'wasting' syndrome, though he never named it. He said it was a rare disease you got either from eating whale meat or from being around Chinese peasants in Fukion. Bruce couldn't bear to be afflicted with an ordinary disease that was killing everyone around him. He always wanted to be rare, exotic, unique." And White remembers: "Robert Mapplethorpe had first sent him to me in New York and we'd had sex immediately, standing by the

front door, half undressed. That was what people did in the late
seventies in New York. I'd been impressed by Bruce's odorless
body, constant laughter, and jewel-bright eyes, but we never
slept together again. Every time I saw Bruce after that, usually
while we were dining in an expensive Paris restaurant, I'd recall
us that first time sniffing each other's genitals like dogs — and
he'd be regaling the table with his latest anecdote, sounding out
and working up a version of the novel he was working on."

Of Foucault, White writes: "Toward the end of his life Foucault thought the basis of morality after the death of God might
be the ancient Greek aspiration to leave your life as a beautiful,
burnished artefact. Certainly in his case his gift for friendship,
his quick sympathy, his gift for paradox, his ability to admire,
left his image a man, as an exemplary life, highly burnished.
The people who said his promiscuity or his death from AIDS
diminished him were just fools." And he goes on to ponder:
"David Rieff, Susan Sontag's son, said to me, 'I guess you have
to start all over again. You're too famous to live in New York,
now right?' Was that true — was I famous? I didn't feel famous,
though Susan (Sontag) had told me, 'You'll never be really poor
again.' She had already arranged for me to receive a cash award
from the American Academy of Arts and Letters and to win a
Guggenheim. She was famous; people nudged each other when
she walked past." So let us knock and enter and discuss the cases
of Michel Foucault and Bruce Chatwin with the eminent doctor.

"Metaphor," she explains, by way of Aristotle's *Poetics*,
"consists in giving the thing a name that belongs to something
else," so Foucault's pneumonia and Chatwin's fungus were
metaphors for HIV/AIDS, Foucault's archaeologies and
Chatwin's songlines were metaphors for their own lives. And
she quotes John Donne whom, thinking he was close to death,
meditated, "and so our *Health* is a long and regular work; But
in a minute a Canon batters all, overthrowes all, demolishes all;

a *Sicknes* unprevented for all our diligence, unsuspected for all our curiositie," and I will extend that quote, "nay, undeserved, if we consider only disorder, summons us, seizes us, possesses us, destroyes us in an instant." As White mentions above, Foucault's enemies believed he deserved the illness, but both he and Chatwin were not aware of the disease when they were most sexually active. As Sontag explains when she, like Hitchens, challenges the war metaphor, "The metaphor implements the way particularly dreaded diseases are envisaged as an alien 'other,' as enemies are in modern war; and the move from the demonization of the illness to the attribution of fault to the patient is an inevitable one, no matter if patients are thought of as victims. Victims suggest innocence. And innocence, by the inexorable logic that governs all relational terms, suggests guilt."

Foucault agrees and sees in this an expression of knowledge/power, "In order to punish, one needs to know the nature of the guilty person, his obduracy, the degree of his evilness, what his interests or his leanings are." Chatwin observes the same knowledge/power/guilt dynamics in the Australian Aboriginals, "There was an awesome power in these apparently passive people who would sit, watch, wait and manipulate the white man's guilt." Was Foucault and Chatwin's denial an expression of guilt? Was their naming of HIV/AIDS as something else a metaphor for the alien "other," an invading enemy? HIV/AIDS proliferates paranoia, intensifies hysteria, invites apocalyptical fantasies, whereas, and she quotes Nietzsche, Sontag wants to "alleviate unnecessary suffering," and would like "to calm the imagination of the invalid, so that at least he should not, as hitherto, have to suffer more from thinking about his illness than from the illness itself — that, I think, would be something! It would be a great deal!" She explains, "The purpose of my book was to calm the imagination, not to incite it." Could a philosopher who attempted to build archaeologies of medical perception, of the human sciences, of knowledge, who wrote histories of insanity and sexuality, admit a "generic rebuke to life and to hope" and not be able to deal with a personal apocalypse? Could a writer who attempted to connect and correspond different spaces, different ages and different genres, live for two years or more knowing he had the spectrum of illnesses that would eventually kill him?

However much Sontag is against interpretation, it is integral to human reasoning that we interpret in order to know. In *The Order of Things*, Foucault explains, "Divination is not a rival form of knowledge; it is part of the main body of knowledge itself. Moreover, these signs that must be interpreted indicate what is hidden only in so far as they resemble it; and it is not possible to act upon those marks without at the same time operating upon that which is secretly indicated by them." Foucault ignored the "signs and outward correspondences" of his illnesses, the great archaeologist of knowledge was incapable of discovering the cause of his headaches, his fatigue, his inward gaze became blurred, he failed to interpret the signs, to fully understand the metaphor, the resemblance, of what was hidden.

Foucault's correspondences and Chatwin's associative histories work as metaphors for interpretation, yet they both failed to self-diagnose. This may be because HIV/AIDS "is a clinical construction, and in furtherance. It takes its identity from the presence of *some* among a long, and lengthening, roster of symptoms (no one has everything that AIDS could be), symptoms which 'mean' that what the patient has is this illness." It is, like syphilis before it, "the great masquerader," as were both Foucault and Chatwin. We can see this in *The Order of Things*, "Where one mode of thought predicts the end of history, the other proclaims the infinity of life; where one recognizes the real production of things by labour, the other dissipates the chimeras of consciousness; where one affirms, with the limits of the individual, the exigencies of his life, the other masks them beneath the murmuring of death." The presenting symptoms mask the real cause, where the other is a chimera, an opportunistic disease noisily drowning out the real murmuring of death. Chatwin's work is evasive, novels masquerading as travel narratives, fictionalized non-fiction, his letters are a series of masks donned just as pen hits paper. Nicholas Shakespeare explains Chatwin's creative methodology when writing *The Viceroy of Ouidah*, "Bruce used the 'patchiness' of his material as his excuse for recasting de Souza as a bi-sexual wanderer. He attributes to his fictional creation his own impulses, desires and abhorrence of domesticity. De Souza's Bahia phase is the time in which he puts away his masks and becomes fully himself." But only in fiction and only when the fiction is accompanied by the presenting symptoms of non-fiction and mutates back to the opportunistic narrative of the novel.

Dr Sontag sits back in her chair, her fingers pyramided above the desk, the silver streak (poliosis) in her hair illuminated by the overhead fluorescent strip-lights. She gets up and replaces the book *AIDS and Its Metaphors* (1989) on the shelf, she looks through the other books, *Against Interpretation* (1966), *Under the Sign of Saturn* (1980), *Regarding the Pain of Others* (2002), finally, using her right index finger to tip the top of another volume towards her, she pulls it out and places it cover upwards on the desk. The drawing on the cover is of a wind-swept Asclepius, naked apart from his billowing robe, a snake curled around his left arm, the title above reads *Illness as Metaphor* (1978). She opens the book, thumbs to its first pages, looks me in the eye and reads without looking down at the words, begins to read and then stops abruptly. She closes the book, gets up, takes me by the crook of the arm and says authoritatively, "Let's go to your office. I think we need to have a little chat."

CHAPTER 7

Death Kit

Consultation as Conclusion

"Your art is most alive and dangerous when you use it against yourself. That's why I pick at my scabs." As we walk through the hospital, me trailing in Dr Sontag's wake, her streaked hair forming a black and white contrail behind her as she strides through the corridors, I have to admit to her that I did not read *Illness as Metaphor* before I wrote this book. Well, let me qualify that; I did not re-read *Illness as Metaphor*. I didn't want it to affect my ideas on the subject, infect my thoughts, I didn't want its virus of influence making me anxious that I was misdiagnosing or replicating, cancer-like, her theories. I did read other books that informed and inflamed me — Elaine Scarry's *The Body in Pain* (1985), Philip Sandblom's *Creativity and Disease* (1982), Nietzsche's *The Gay Science* — but I knew these books would lead me elsewhere, direct me to hitherto unknown departments in the hospital, whereas I was nervous that *Illness as Metaphor* would have trapped me in the X-ray lab constantly examining the very bones of my material. However, I did read *AIDS and Its Metaphors* because of Sontag's connections with Chatwin and Foucault, and am now prepared to consult with the good doctor on her examination of disease and art. So we're going to my office for a consultation from which I hope to develop a conclusion and not a concussion.

But before we reach my office — and I'm hoping she is in a good mood — a few extra thoughts on illness and art, some advice and sage words from other doctors and patients, artists and writers, some theories of the bleeding human edge between health and sickness, creativity and death. A liminal commonplace.

Ben Marcus: "Language turns out to be the most unruly of medicines, the most unknowable, and yet, provided we collaborate with it, still among the most powerful."

Lauren Slater: "The fact is, or my fact is, disease is everywhere. How anyone could ever write about themselves or their fictional characters as not diseased is a bit beyond me. We live in a world and are creatures of a culture that is spinning out more and more medicines that correspond to more and more diseases at an alarming pace. Even beyond that, though, I believe we exist in our God-given natures as diseased beings. We do not fall into illness. We fall from illness into temporary states of health. We are briefly blessed, but always, always those small cells are dividing and will become cancer, if they haven't already."

Julian Barnes on Daudet's *In the Land of Pain*: "How is it best to write about illness, and dying, and death? Despite Turgenev's impeccable example, pain is normally the enemy of the descriptive powers. When it became his turn to suffer, Daudet discovered that pain, like passion, drives out language. Words come only when everything is over, when things have calmed down. They refer only to memory, and are either powerless or untruthful." And, "The prospect of dying may, or may not, concentrate the mind and encourage a final truthfulness; may or may not include the useful *aide-memoire* of your life passing before your eyes; but it is unlikely to make you a better writer. Modest or jaunty, wise or vainglorious, literary or journalistic, you will write no better, no worse. And your literary temperament may, or may not, prove suited to this new thematic challenge."

Albert Camus: "Illness is a monastery with its own rules, asceticism, silence, and inspiration."

John Berger: "In illness many connexions are severed. Illness separates and encourages a distorted, fragmentated form of self-consciousness. The doctor, through his relationship with the invalid and by means of the special intimacy he is allowed, has to compensate for these broken connections and reaffirm the social content of the invalid's aggravated self-consciousness."

Alphonse Daudet: "Since learning that I've got it for ever — and my God, what a short 'for ever' that is going to be — I've readjusted myself and started taking these notes. I'm making them by dipping the point of a nail in my own blood and scratching on the walls of my *carcere duro*. All I ask is not to have to change cell, not to have to descend into an *in pace*, down there where everything's black and thought no longer exists." And, "Sterility. That's the only word that gets close to describing the horrible stagnation into which the mind can fall. It's the condition believers call accidie. This note, made quickly, is wooden, inexpressive, solipsistic; but it was written during cruel illness."

E.M. Cioran: "Whatever his merits, a man in good health is always disappointing. Impossible to grant any credence to what he says, to regard his phrases as anything but excuses, acrobatics. The experience of the terrible which alone confers a certain destiny upon our words — is what he lacks, as he lacks, too, the imagination of disaster, without which no one can communicate with those *separate* beings, the sick. Having nothing to transmit, neutral to the point of abdication, he collapses into well-being, an insignificant state of perfection, an impermeability to death as well as of attention to oneself and to the world. As long as he remains there, he is like the objects around him; once torn from it, he opens himself to everything, knows everything: the omniscience of terror."

I can barely keep up, not just with those writers but the pace Dr Sontag is setting along the hospital corridors. I think she's got it in for me. On the way, we've passed some wards that we never got to visit. The neurology department, whose patients include Siri Hustvedt and her convulsive-conversion disorder; Jean-Dominique Bauby and his locked-in syndrome; John Scalzi and his Haden's syndrome — a locked-in viral epidemic (maybe we should move him to isolation); Malcolm Lowry and his delirium tremens (maybe he should be in the alcohol dependency unit); Lewis Carroll and his migraines; Stendhal with his Stendhal syndrome (Lou Gehrig and all that); and, of course, Alice with her Alice in Wonderland syndrome, otherwise known as "lilliputian hallucinations," which I remember suffering from during my migraine attacks, that problem with the size of people's heads.

Next door is the dermatology department. Yes, I know you were itching to visit and the fact that we have to skip it is a little rash but Vladimir Nabokov, Dennis Potter, John Updike and Nicholson Baker are a little sensitive when undergoing treatment and I promised them we wouldn't intrude. However, I persusaded them to provide short statements about their condition. Nabokov: "I continue with the radiation treatments every day and am pretty much cured. You know — now I can tell you frankly — the indescribable torments I endured in February, before these treatments, drove me to the border of suicide, a border I was not authorized to cross because I had you in my luggage."

Dennis Potter, Doctor: "How do you feel about trying one of the new retinoids? Hmm?... Do you understand the question?"
Philip E. Marlow: "Er, no, I don't think so."
Doctor: "I'm asking you if you'd like to try one of the new..."
Philip E. Marlow: "I don't understand the question because I seem to have regressed into a helpless, pathetic condition of total dependency, of a kind normally associated with infancy.

The last time I experienced anything remotely like this was in my bloody pram, being poked and drooled over by slobbering cretins, who turned out to be escapees from the local loony bin. They thought they were doctors and nurses!"

John Updike, "She glances at me and does not know I am a leper. If I bared my arms and chest she would run screaming. A few integuments of wool and synthetic fibre save me from her horror: my enrolment in humanity is so perilous." Finally, and in his own peculiarly arch yet honest manner, Nicholson Baker: "I'm a psoriatic myself, and though Updike has said lots of what can be said about the disability, there is more, and there might come a time when I would want to have a scaly-rinded character imagine himself or herself as smooth as a golf course. So no — I couldn't talk about psoriasis with Updike: I'd be too scared of hearing something from him that I would itch to use before he'd used it, or of tempting him with a flake or two of my own experience that I would want to keep for myself — or of hearing him say something similar to something I'd already noted down and was planning to use, and having my note killed by his passing mention." Maybe on your next visit to the hospital, we can examine these wards more closely.

Yes, you've got me, I've been prevaricating and procrastinating, putting off the inevitable, but we've reached my office and the doorplate screams my name. I open the door and usher the good doctor in. She walks around my desk covered in anatomical atlases — Mansur ibn Ilyas (c.1390), Hieronymus Brunschwig (c.1450-c.1512), Andreas Vesalius (1514–1564), Shinnin Kawaguchi (1736–1811), Julien Bouglé (1868–1903) — and she sits in my chair, rocks back a little and steeples her fingers, more pointed than the pyramid of earlier. She looks around the room, taking in the books on the shelves and the artworks on the wall — Ken Currie's *Three Oncologists*,

Chiharu Shiota's *During Sleep*, Sir Edward Poynter's *A Visit to Aesculapius*, Francis Picabia's *Portrait of a Doctor*, etchings by Käthe Kollwitz, while Damien Hirst's *Pain Killers* illuminates the whole of one wall and a Robert Mapplethorpe self-portrait (the one with his disembodied head and hand holding a black beskulled cane taken a year before he died) stares self-confidently down and back at her from above the door.

She gestures to the seat in front of my desk, the patient's seat. I sit down, my forehead and palms beginning to sweat. Nietzsche's words flash into my mind: "Thus some thinkers confess to views which are plainly not calculated to increase or improve their reputation; some downright call down the disrespect of others upon themselves when by keeping silent they could easily have remained respected men; others retract earlier opinions and are not afraid of henceforth being called inconsistent: on the contrary, they strive to be called so, and behave like high-spirited riders who like their steed best only when it has grown savage, is covered with sweat, and is tamed." I look up, gulp. "Shall we begin. The good doctor says, not asks.

Illness as Metaphor, first published in 1978, examines the language used to describe disease and the diseased. Mainly focusing on cancer and tuberculosis, Sontag analyzes the wider context of semiotic and cultural reactions to illness. She does so through the personal experience of being treated for uterine and breast cancer at the time she was writing the essays that make up the book. It opens, "Illness is the night-side of life, a more onerous citizenship. Everyone who is born holds dual citizenship, in the kingdom of the well and in the kingdom of the sick. Although we all prefer to use only the good passport, sooner or later each of us is obliged, at least for a spell, to identify ourselves as citizens of that other place." I have a problem with that. Illness, rather than being the "night-side of life," throws into sharp relief, in fact, emblazons our lives with spotlights. Rather than groping around in the dark for reason and meaning, illness makes us focus on the minuscule and the profound. "Onerous"? In what sense? Only if we feel guilt about our illnesses, about the burden placed on others, on family and friends, doctors and nurses. Illness as citizenship, I quite like the metaphor but it doesn't work, my passport is stamped with immunizations, with prescriptions, with blood glucose counts, asthma peak expiratory flow test results. "That other place" is the locus of my being. Seeing illness as negative already skews the theory, the prognosis may be incorrect.

I need to consult someone who lived with illness all of his life and who has examined the nature of disease and interpretation. Nietzsche argues: "All the visions, terrors, states of exhaustion and rapture experienced by the saint are familiar pathological conditions which, on the basis of rooted religious and psychological errors, he only *interprets* quite differently, that is to say not as illnesses. Thus the daemon of Socrates too was perhaps an ear-infection which, in accordance with the moralizing manner of thinking that dominated him, he only *interpreted* differently from how it would be interpreted now." Interpretation is a matter of quantum decoherence, observing metaphors in their relationship with/to illness creates a Socratic ear infection resulting in misnomers and the proliferation (or metastasization) of metaphor — illness as metaphor as metaphor.

Dr Sontag raises her eyebrows and retorts, "My point is that illness is not a metaphor, and that the most truthful way of regarding illness — and the healthiest way of being ill — is one most purified of, most resistant to, metaphoric thinking." Why the denial of metaphor? In a world of the simulacrum, everything is a metaphor for itself. So illness is a metaphor for illness, the naming of it is a metaphor for a future well-being, a diagnosis is a metaphor for an approaching death, everything to do with illness is indirect discourse. Deleuze and Guattari, "The 'first' language, or rather the first determination of language, is not the trope or metaphor but *indirect discourse*. The importance some have accorded metaphor and metonymy proves disastrous for the study of language. Metaphors and metonymies are merely effects; they are a part of language only when they presuppose indirect discourse." So metaphor is an effect of language, not a cause, they presuppose meaning, cloaking and revealing simultaneously. There are many illnesses in illness (see HIV/AIDS).

Sontag establishes that she wishes to "de-mythicize" cancer, that the very naming of it causes suffering, yet it is not the disease itself that is wrapped in myth but the fear of death; cancer is a metaphor for death's rapid approach, for the shrinking of time, for the elision of space between the hospital bed and the grave. Is it "cancer" that is unutterable?

My father died on 27 May, 2016. I am writing this conclusion on 25 June, 2016. He had been ill for a few months. As far as I know, the cancer went undetected until the New Year when, undergoing his usual tests, they discovered that the prostate cancer had returned. Within a few months, it had metastasized and, as I wrote above, my mother called me to tell me he had developed bowel cancer. Mark Leyner argues, "In traditional folktales, the revenge of the father for his son's Oedipal ideation is, of course, to pass along to that son a genetic predisposition for prostate cancer, which is precisely what my father, in fact, did." I think I need to have my prostate checked and I wince as I imagine Dr Sontag snapping on those latex gloves.

On the morning of 27 May, the phone rang at 6am and I knew he had died. Until a few days before this, I had never seen my father in a hospital bed, I had never seen him look ill, even when he was undergoing chemotherapy twenty-odd years ago. But he looked small under the white sheets, old (he was seventy-six), frail, his hair had almost gone because of the latest bout of chemotherapy, his skin was pocked with what looked like acne, there were bruises on his neck and his bottom lip hung down. He had always been a well-dressed man and one of the only things he said that day, I mentioned earlier that he had been all but incoherent, that I could understand was "the green and the orange — wrong." I asked what he meant, then realized he was wearing a green top and orange bottoms and wanted them to match.

Dr Sontag looks at me with what might be compassion and says: "Treatment also has a military flavor. Radiotherapy uses the metaphors of aerial warfare; patients are 'bombarded' with toxic rays. And chemotherapy is chemical warfare, using poisons. Treatment aims to 'kill' cancer cells (without, it is hoped, killing the patient). Unpleasant side effects of treatment are advertised, indeed overadvertised. ('The agony of chemotherapy' is a standard phrase.) It is impossible to avoid damaging or destroying healthy cells (indeed, some methods used to treat cancer can cause cancer), but it is thought that nearly any damage to the body is justified if it saves the patient's life. Often, of course, it doesn't work. (As in: 'We had to destroy Ben Suc in order to save it.') There is everything but the body count." I agree, I say. My mother thinks it was the chemotherapy that killed him.

The doctors had told my mother and brother that the cancer had metastasized and was terminal, they could give him medication to keep him alive for a few weeks otherwise he would be dead within three or four days. They decided that they didn't want to keep him alive artificially, that he was suffering and, in his more lucid moments, he had told them that he just wanted to die. He was at peace. He knew what was wrong with him, how serious it was and that he just wanted to go home. There was no use for, no use of metaphor, there was no disguising what was going to happen or what was happening. In the saying of it, "death" not "cancer," "it is not a matter of rediscovering some primary word that has been buried in it, but of disturbing the words we speak, of denouncing the grammatical habits of our thinking, of dissipating the myths that animate our words, of rendering once more noisy and audible the element of silence that all discourse carries with it as it is spoken," as Foucault would have it. It is not the de-mythicization but the de-silencing. The truth was not intolerable, there were no lies, no equivocation, the sentence was one of death and there was no use for metaphor, metaphor was moribund.

Derrida argues, "This notion of an imagination that produces metaphor — that is, everything in language except the verb *to be* — remains for critics what certain philosophers today call a naively utilized *operative concept*." I found that my mother and brother's decision to allow my father to die — the doctor had signed a do-not-resuscitate order under advice — was both reasonable and compassionate. Metaphor collapsed in the speed of the verb *not to be*. To de-mythicize illness was a naively utilized operative concept. My father was dying and not from "a long illness" but rapidly, before our eyes. I had seen him about a month before for one of my parents' Sunday lunches, he looked ill but not death-bound, he laughed and joked and drank the red wine he so enjoyed. His cancer was not a slow death and had nothing to do with the metaphors of "idleness" and "sloth."

Sontag claims, "Cancer is a rare and still scandalous subject for poetry; and it seems unimaginable to aestheticize the disease." So cancer is then some kind of bodily Auschwitz and can be aligned with Theodor W. Adorno's statement that "to write poetry after Auschwitz is barbaric"? What nonsense. The writer and critic Clive James was diagnosed with B-cell chronic lymphocytic leukaemia in April 2011, his response was an outpouring of writings on poetry — *Poetry Notebook 2006–2014,* books of poetry — *Sentenced to Life* (2015) and even a verse translation of *The Divine Comedy* (2013). In June 2014, David Bowie discovered that he had liver cancer, he kept it a secret from all but his closest friends, family and people with whom he was collaborating. He underwent chemotherapy treatment while continuing to work on a number of projects. A three-CD compilation album, optimistically titled *Nothing Has Changed*, was released in November 2014, the cover showing Bowie staring back at his reflection. Tracks on it include, "Where Are We Now?," "New Killer Star," "Slow Burn," "Let Me Sleep Beside You," "Shadow Man," "Survive," "Loving the Alien," "Time Will Crawl" and "Ashes to Ashes." The cancer had metastasized by November 2015 and Bowie knew he was dying. On 7 December, he attended the Manhattan premiere of his musical *Lazarus*, a follow up to *The Man Who Fell To Earth*; it was his last public appearance, the cancer was terminal. On 8 January, 2015, Bowie's ISO Records released his 25th album *Blackstar*, which Bowie had conceived, written and produced while suffering from liver cancer. He had also started recording songs for a follow-up album but died on 10 January; he had been working and writing, aestheticizing his illness right up to the day he died. Writing *Illness as Metaphor* while being treated for uterine and breast cancer IS aestheticizing it.

I concur with Dr Sontag on her diagnosis of the romanticization and glamorization of tuberculosis in the eighteenth and nineteenth centuries, the spectral figures of Chopin, Keats and Stevenson, the artistic denial of Lawrence, the illness as editor of Mansfield and Orwell. Kafka denied his tuberculosis and believed it to be a symbol, a sign of his "general bankruptcy," a manifestation of character, similar to Gregor Samsa's transformation into a beetle. I also concur with Dr Sontag's notes on passions and their supposed link to disease but, when illness strikes, desire is the first thing to wither, it is not a lack of desire that causes cancer but cancer that causes a lack of desire. As I noted in my 2003 hospital diary, "the fetishization of nurses is absurd."

Following my family's wishes, my father returned home on the Tuesday. I visited and he seemed much better. He could eat and drink a little, his skin was much improved and his mind sharper. My brother had washed and shaved him, dressed him in matching pyjamas. I climbed the stairs to his bedroom and we chatted. Apart from a few occasions when he drifted off, he was lucid and my brother and I asked him questions, "Where was the favourite place he had visited?" Answer: Sri Lanka, possibly the site of the first ever hospital (c.380 BC) and a place D.H. Lawrence disliked with a vengeance. What was his favourite drink, "Red wine. No, port. No, brandy. No, Cognac." We talked some more but he was tired and so I kissed him on the forehead and said I'd return the day after tomorrow. He gestured towards the dressing table, on it was a watch. It was the last thing he gave me; a stainless-steel watch I had coveted since I was a teenager. You might not think that odd, a father giving his son a watch, but the strange thing is, he had already given me that watch some years before. I thought it was in a box with my other watches. But, no, my father had found it among my books stored in his loft and he had had it mended and had been wearing it all those years without me knowing. He would take it off when I came over for lunch, hide it, ask me if I still had it. There was no shame in my father's eyes, no bitterness, they shone with the blue intensity they had always had, with humour and intelligence. The cancer was not a "hidden assassin," it was him, his body. He wasn't "depressed or unsatisfied" with his life as Sontag claims two-thirds or three-fifths of cancer patients are, he said repeatedly that he had

had a good life and loved his wonderful family. His "human condition" was one of acceptance not despair.

My father was an amateur artist; in the 1970s, off work for months with a bad back, he painted copies of classical paintings, Giovani Bellini's *The Virgin and Child* (1480–1490), Frans Hals' *The Laughing Cavalier* (1624), Théodore Géricault's *The Charging Chasseur* (1812), Eugene Delacroix's *Arab Horseman Attacked by a Lion* (1849–1850) and a number of landscapes. The paintings are still on the walls of our living room, the landscapes lost. What made my father choose these paintings to copy I'll never know. They are all difficult to execute.

I look at my father's hands above the sheets, they are skinny, each finger distinct in its crookedness, and I think of John Berger on Bellini's Madonna, each finger is separate and outlined, so that together the fingers are almost like the keys of the piano. Then there is the cavalier's lace cuff, of which John Berger writes, "Every cuff he painted in his portraits informs on the habitual movements of the wrist it hides." The sheets hid my father's emaciated body and I watched it twitch, his knees rising and falling as if he were rowing, as if he could not wait to get to the other side. As Berger writes of Hals' portrait of Captain Michiel de Wael, "It is like watching a departure for a journey we haven't the means to make." The laughing cavalier's eyes follow you around the room so, even if my father were absent, the glare of Tieleman Roosterman, a rich Dutch cloth merchant, would track my movements, spy on my sips from the brandy bottles, gulps from the port, swallowings of cherry brandy. I can feel the gaze on me now as I type these words, as I stare back at the intricate embroidery on the man's sleeve. The eyes are humorous, wry but also protective, caring. The painting is calming, humorous, showing generosity.

The next painting, Théodore Géricault's *The Charging Chasseur* or *Officer of the Chasseurs Commanding a Charge*, is anything but calm, but because my father's version is about a quarter of the size of the original (349cm x 266cm) that hangs in the Louvre (I remember being shocked at its measurements when I saw it), the horror of Géricault's action portrait is diminished in my father's version. But if I study the original (well, a larger colour reproduction on Wikipedia) I can see that my father had included all of the detail and the events of and in the painting but miniaturized them, as if making war personal, violence domestic, fear of death intrinsic to the house in which he lived and died. The craquelure of the grey-blue crowds resembles my father's dry and cyanotic lips. The officer is looking back at what he has done with that curved sword, he appears indifferent to the carnage, his black and scarlet plumed hat, the gold braiding of his velvet tunic, the fur cape, the white jodhpurs, the black leather riding boots resolute and skilful in the brass stirrups, all are clean and pristine, not a drop of the blood that must have recently been spilled. But the grey horse he is riding, its skin dappled just like my father's, the magnificent rearing stallion with its blond mane, its black leather and brass studded bridle, its leopard-skin covered saddle, sees what is in the very near future, men and other horses in a fire-and-brimstone, red in tooth and hoof battle, destroyed cannons, dying men, dying horses. If you look very closely, on the horse's right hindfoot, there is a smear of blood to indicate what the horse has gone through. To the left of the downturned sword (defeat, acceptance of death) is a second horse's head replicating the bulging eyes of the terrified stallion as if to say, here is another and another follows, and standing next to the second scared horse is a bugler sending a call for others and yet more others to join the in the violence. The officer and the soldier look back on their past indifferent, steely gazed, tight-lipped, while the horses *forcené* — literally "going mad" — see their death in the unfolding events.

I always thought I knew what the stern yet nonchalant officer was staring back at, it was Eugene Delacroix's *Arab Horseman Attacked by a Lion* (1850). If the look back is memory and the horse's petrified gaze the future, then Delacroix's lion, horse and horseman seem locked in an eternal recurrence of violence, survival and death. Which figure represents life, which death? The horseman's sword, about to plunge between the lion's shoulders, is equally matched by the lion's outstretched left front paw about to strike the horseman's face with its extended claws while, simultaneously, it bites into the rearing horse's chest. The horseman's leg and the lion's tale describe a corresponding ballet of balance between life and death, past and future, locked together in a trilogy of existence, endurance and obliteration.

Of course, when I studied these paintings, they became metaphors for my father's disease and death; paintings illuminate as they cloak, reveal as they obscure. The Géricault/Delacroix horsemen could be my father looking back at the past, indifferent to the future while locked in a fight against death, or the cavalier smiling at a private something while his gaze penetrates those who examine him. If I didn't know why he chose these paintings to copy, that goes doubly so for Bellini's *The Virgin and Child* (1480–1490), my father was not religious, he would have found no succour in the church or its iconography, maybe he painted it for my mother.

Retrospective metaphors are as abhorrent as present ones yet I wanted to show that the paintings created while my father was ill are works of convalescence and all works of art can be metaphorized for the purposes of criticism and biography; illness does not need another level of metaphor, which all criticism, whether it denies it or not, becomes. Sontag glosses the supposed psychosomatic causes of cancer — female sanguinity and melancholy (Galen) or grief and anxiety (Sir Astley Cooper, surgeon and anatomist 1768–1841) were the cause of breast cancer. Sontag contrasts the Ancient and nineteenth-century manic-depressive diagnosis with late-twentieth century theories of what she terms "that forlorn, self-hating, emotionally inert creature, the contemporary cancer personality." My father was not forlorn, self-hating or emotionally inert. While physically inert and being carried up the stairs to his bedroom, he was cracking jokes with the ambulance staff, warning them about scratching the wallpaper, or knocking over the ornaments. If my father's emotions had anything to do with his illness, in the last few days before he died, he would have gone into remission, however oxymoronic that sounds. Here, I concur with the good doctor as she insists: "Moreover, there is a peculiarly modern predilection for psychological explanations of disease, as of everything else. Psychologizing seems to provide control over the experiences and events (like grave illnesses) over which people have in fact little or no control. Psychological understanding undermines the 'reality' of a disease. That reality has to be explained. (It really means; or is a symbol of; or must be interpreted so.) For those who live neither with religious consolations about death nor with a sense of death (or of anything else) as natural, death is the obscene mystery, the ultimate affront, the thing that cannot be controlled. It can only be denied. A large part of the popularity and persuasiveness of psychology comes from its being a sublimated spiritualism: a secular, ostensibly scientific way of affirming the primacy of 'spirit' over matter. That ineluctably material reality, disease, can be given a psychological explanation. Death itself can be considered, ultimately, a psychological phenomenon." My father had no belief in the "spirit," had no time for spiritualism however sublimated; he understood the "reality" of his disease, its materiality, as if he had replaced the Madonna and child's haloes with the cavalier's wide-brimmed hat and the Arab horseman's turban.

As we are at a point of agreement, I will allow her to carry on: "Cancer remains the most radical of disease metaphors. And just because it is so radical, it is particularly tendentious — a good metaphor for paranoids, for those who need to turn campaigns into crusades, for the fatalistic (cancer = death), and for those under the spell of ahistorical revolutionary optimism (the idea that only the most radical changes are desirable). As long as so much militaristic hyperbole attaches to the description and treatment of cancer, it is a particularly unapt metaphor for the peaceloving." When I was sitting by what would be my father's deathbed, I was thinking through what I had read about cancer, and Sontag, Mukherjee and Hitchens (to varying lengths) all agree on the triteness and inappropriateness of the military metaphors surrounding it. I saw nothing in my father's eyes that was combatant. He wasn't paranoid, surely you can only be paranoid about what you are unsure of and he knew he had bowel cancer. My mother and brother were not on a crusade to keep him alive, they were not on a campaign to resuscitate him, they WERE fatalistic, they understood that my father's cancer did equal death. He could have had a further course of chemotherapy but they had no revolutionary optimism that the most radical cancer treatment was desirable. Dr Sontag agrees and interrupts, "The understanding of cancer supports quite different, avowedly brutal notions of treatment. (A common cancer hospital witticism, heard as often from doctors as from patients: 'The treatment is worse than the disease.') There can be no question of pampering the patient. With the patient's body considered to be under attack ('invasion'), the only treatment is counterattack." I nod. My father just wanted to die in peace.

Dr Sontag begins the final paragraph of the book with, "But at that time, perhaps nobody will want any longer to compare anything awful to cancer." Sitting there in the bedroom where my first books on history and the art books from where he copied the paintings still sat on the shelves, I did not want to compare anything with cancer, with terminal illness, it was and it will be unmetaphorical.

My father had already been taken to the funeral home by the time I got to my parents' house. I did not want to see the body. My brother was exhausted having slept very little while caring for my father. I comforted my mother and agreed to do all the administration, declare the death at the registry office, inform the solicitors, but first I had to collect the death certificate. I asked my mother where the doctor's surgery was located. "You know, she said, the one on Hanworth Road just passed the pond." This was the same surgery I had gone to as a boy to see Dr Griffin and then Dr Aswani. I hadn't visited the place in thirty-six years. At 1pm, I walked along the High Street, past the disfigured church, past the pond pocked with algae, across the gravel drive and into Clifford House Medical Centre. When I used to visit, I walked across the gravel and then followed a path around the back to the garden where double doors allowed you access. This time, I walked into the reception and told the receptionist that I had come to collect my father's death certificate. They all expressed their commiserations and asked me to sit in the waiting room, Dr Sen would be down shortly. The reception room was in the same space as the old one but the walls were a royal blue and the posters were about malaria, the Zika virus, HIV/AIDS. I sat at the back as I always had done and memories returned slowly like the drops of saline in an intravenous drip. The cold stethoscope on my back, the comedy of the reflex hammer, the faint yet overriding smell of disinfectant and antiseptic. I heard footsteps coming down the stairs, stairs that I had climbed on many occasions. I stood and a dapper Indian gentleman introduced himself as Dr Sen. He had been called out during the previous night and had declared my father dead. He too offered his commiserations and handed me an envelope. I thanked him and left, crossing the road to the pond. I sat on a bench and stared at the surface of the pond covered in algae or blanket weed, a few ducks gliding through the green, a pair of moorhens squabbling over something or other.

I opened the envelope and unfolded the certificate. I read it. It was brief and to the point. I will let Dr Sontag rewind to a point she makes in the early pages of *Illness as Metaphor*, "While TB takes on qualities assigned to the lungs, which are part of the upper, spiritualized body, cancer is notorious for attacking parts of the body (colon, bladder, rectum, breast, cervix, prostate, testicles) that are embarrassing to acknowledge. Having a tumor generally arouses some feelings of shame, but in the hierarchy of the body's organs, lung cancer is felt to be less shameful than rectal cancer." My mother, remember, had told me my father had bowel cancer. I read it again, "Cause of Death." And in Dr Sen's handwriting, "prostate cancer and rectal cancer." Rectal cancer. Bowel cancer was a polite metaphor.

Deleuze and Guattari, on the trail and case of Frank Kafka, note that he jotted down in his diary in 1920, "Metaphors are one of the things that makes me despair of literature," and they continue, "Kafka deliberately kills all metaphor, all symbolism, all signification, no less than all designation. Metamorphosis is the contrary of metaphor," and they conclude, "Instead, it is now a question of a becoming that includes the maximum of difference as a difference of intensity, the crossing of a barrier, a rising or a falling, a bending or an erecting, an accent on the word." My father had crossed the barrier, the buffering had stopped and left a blank screen.

While Dr Sontag takes her leave, flouncing out the door ignoring my entreaties to say and my expressions of gratitude, let me see if I can track down Mr Kafka. I'll call the sanatorium reception. "Hello. Yes, has Herr Kafka returned to his room

yet? Yes, of course. Oh, I forgot about that. I'll turn it on now."
I access my computer and sign into the CCTV monitoring
system. I wait for the blank screen to connect and watch the
digital buffering. The patients can turn the channel off at any
time, but Herr Kafka's is broadcasting and I can see him sitting
in the room. We'll watch as we look through his case notes.
Diagnosed with tuberculosis in 1917, although he had signs
of the disease before this, Kafka came to believe that writing
was helpless when confronted with life. His illness was not a
metaphor for anything, it killed metaphor, annihilated the
symbolic, erased signification, annulled designation. In a diary
entry on 20 December, 1921, he admits, "Undeniably, there is
a certain joy in being able calmly to write down: 'Suffocation is
inconceivably horrible.' Of course it is inconceivable — that is
why I have written nothing down." The range of the word is not
sufficient for the illness, "suffocation" is the distribution of states
of his tuberculosis. On 24 May, 1922, he explains, "The constant
variety of the form it takes, and once, in the midst of it all, the
affecting sight of a momentary abatement in its variations."
Writing is the line of escape from the deterritorialized body,
but an escape that is the eternal recurrence of the same —
what Tom McCarthy calls "buffering." On 12 June, 1923, "The
horrible spells lately, innumerable, almost without interruption.
Walks, nights, days, incapable of anything but pain." His
illness had become him, pain had taken over from thought,
like the lion, Arab and horse in the Delacroix painting, Kafka,
tuberculosis and pain are "no longer man or animal, since
each deterritorializes the other, in a conjunction of flux, in a
continuum of reversible intensities." Kafka continues: "More
and more fearful as I write. It is understandable. Every word,
twisted in the hands of the spirits — this twist of the hand is
their characteristic gesture — becomes a spear turned against
the speaker. Most especially a remark like this. *And so ad*

infinitum. The only consolation would be: it happens whether you like or no. And what you like is of infinitesimally little help. More than consolation is: You too have weapons." "Every word, twisted in the hands of the spirit" equals "it is even less a question of a simple wordplay." Words have failed him, this diary entry was not supposed to have been read by anybody, words are empty, they are absence, whereas pain and illness are replete and present in their communication. Life never arrives, the waiting room is always full, the castle is never breached ("the crossing of a barrier"), the trial never goes to court, the inscription is never finished.

The diary entry of 12 June, 1923 was the last Kafka wrote that still survives. On 10 April, 1924, unable to eat because of the severity of his layryngeal tuberculosis, he was taken to a sanatorium in Kierling (Klosterneuburg, north of Vienna) where he was put under the care of a Dr Hoffmann (uncanny). While there he worked on his short story "The Hunger Artist," he could not take nourishment, even drinking water was difficult: "Scorning the use of the chair he sat at the scattered straw pale, in a black vest, with startlingly protruding ribs, now nodding politely, answering questions with a strained smile, or poking his arm through the bars so that its thinness might be felt, but repeatedly collapsing into himself, not caring about anything or anyone, not even for the — for him — so important striking of the clock that was the only item of furniture in the cage, but just looking straight in front of him through almost closed eyes, every so often sipping water from the tiny glass, to moisten his lips."

Kafka's hunger artist exists in a world (a cage) of self-dissimulation, of a deterritorialization of the body; the hunger artist is all patients, Frida Kahlo, Denton Welch, Christopher Hitchens, Kathy Acker, John Keats, Katherine Mansfield, D.H. Lawrence, you — dear reader — and he is I. He enacts what Heidegger, writing about Nietzsche, calls "the raging discordance between truth and art," and Kafka, the dying Kafka, alone in his room (his cage), presents "the raging discordance between health and illness."

We watch him and he watches back, he says "he much preferred those invigilators who sat right in front of his bars, who were not content with the dim night-light in the hall, but aimed at him the beams of electric torches that the manager had left at their disposal." So we'll carry on invigilating and observing in the hope that Herr Kafka can assist with the discharge. At one point, the hunger artist feels that "his body was hollowed out; his legs for dear life pressed against one another at the knee, but continued to scrape against the ground as if it were not the real thing, as if the real thing was still being sought." This is how illness feels and the expression of it, how writers and artists create within illness or are unable to, the body is empty of anything except pain, life is not the real thing and that "real thing" is still being sought, the eternal recurrence of the same, the buffering, the endless repetition of the creative spark.

John Berger observes of Kahlo: "It is necessary to return to pain and the perspective in which Frida placed it, whenever it allowed her a little respite. The capacity to feel pain is, her art laments, the first condition of being sentient. The sensitivity of her own mutilated body made her aware of the skin of everything alive — trees, fruit, water, birds, and, naturally, other women and men. And so, in painting her own image, as if on her skin, she speaks of the whole sentient world." As does the hunger artist, as do we all when lying in bed staring at the ceiling, our body the real thing still being sought, the deterritorialized unhealthy body. Berger continues, "There is no screen; she is close up, proceeding with her delicate fingers, stitch by stitch, making not a dress, but closing a wound. Her art talks to pain, mouth pressed to the skin of pain, and it talks about sentience and its desire and its cruelty and its intimate nicknames." In 2013, the Japanese artist Ishiuchi Miyako photographed Kahlo's sunglasses, dresses, prosthetic leg and other artefacts for a catalogue of Kahlo's belongings from The Blue House museum.

So the hunger artist has no screen between his body and his audience, like a patient has no screen between their unhealthy body and their doctor. Illness and creativity are intimate nicknames that seek the real thing, as the hunger artist says, "Try and explain the art of starving! It needs to be felt, it's not something that can be explained." Illness and creativity cannibalize themselves, auto-cannibalize, consume themselves as they perpetuate; the body decays, the pages are turned, the paint dries and cracks, the music fades, the hunger artist dies and is replaced by a panther that "seems not even to miss freedom; the noble body furnished almost to bursting-point with all it required seemed even to have brought its own freedom with it; it appeared to be located somewhere in its jaws; and his love of life became so powerfully out of its throat that it is no easy matter for spectators to withstand it. But they steeled themselves, clustered round the cage, and would not budge." Here Kafka replaces illness with life, the feeling of being trapped in a diseased and malfunctioning body with a being that carries its own freedom with it.

In editing "A Hunger Artist" during the last few days of his life, Kafka created out of decay — this is not a metaphor, it is a metamorphosis. Kafka died of starvation, just as the hunger artist did, just as Gregor Samsa did, illness metamorphoses into art in Kahlo, Welch, Hitchens, Acker, et al. Art metamorphoses into silence (the starvation of the sign). In both "A Hunger Artist" and "Metamorphosis," the starved men give narrative way to things that are retrievably alive, the hunger artist by the panther and Gregor Samsa by his younger sister Greta, "And it felt like confirmation of their new dreams and their fond intentions when, as they reached their destination, the daughter was the first to get up, and stretched her nubile young body." As illness triumphs, life begins again, an eternal recurrence of the same. Cancer is life that has lost all control. Pain is the reminder of what life is. Creativity within and about illness is a recollection of the focusing aspect of pain.

Thomas Bernhard, who suffered from tuberculosis and was a patient at the Grafenhof sanatorium in Sankt Veit im Pongau, Austria, from 1949 to 1951, claims that "the sick don't like allying themselves with the sick, or the old with the old. They run away from one another. To their destruction. Everyone wants to be alive, nobody wants to be dead. Everything else is a lie. In the end they sit in an armchair or in some wing-chair and dream dreams of the past which bear not the slightest relation to reality. There ought to be only happy people — all the necessary conditions are present — but there are only unhappy people. We understand this only late in life. While we are young and without pain we not only believe in eternal life, but have it. Then comes the break, then the breakdown, then the lamentation over it, and the end. It's always the same." It's always the same. Kafka wanted life, if he couldn't have it, he wanted his writings to be destroyed just as he would be destroyed by laryngeal tuberculosis, just as living with pain at an early age and believing he was going to die caused Bernhard to start writing.

Creativity is a means of understanding illness, whether it be Kahlo's immersion in her pain or D.H. Lawrence's denial of his tuberculosis. It is a way of writing through your affliction as with Hitchens or writing around your disease in the manner of Foucault. Illness redirects the focus of creativity, see Welch, Bernhard and Bowie. Creativity can also modify the illness, deflect the mind from the body to the page or canvas, see Karinthy, Zorn and Modigliani.

I look up at the computer screen. Herr Kafka is writing in a notebook. I use the mouse to zoom in and read: "He did have pains all over his body, but he felt they were gradually abating, and would finally cease altogether. The rotten apple in his back and the inflammation all round it, which was entirely coated with a soft dust, he barely felt any more. He thought back on his family with devotion and love. His conviction that he needed to disappear was, if anything, still firmer than his sister's. He remained in this condition of empty and peaceful reflection until the church clock struck three a.m. The last thing he saw was the sky gradually lightening outside his window. Then his head involuntarily dropped, and his final breath passed feebly from his nostrils."

I turn off the camera, pick up a copy of Nietzsche's *Writings from the Late Notebooks* (2003) and read, "Brave and creative men never see pleasure and suffering as ultimate questions of value — they are accompanying states, one must want both if one wants to achieve anything. Something weary and sick in the metaphysicians and religious men is expressed in their foregrounding problems of pleasure and suffering. Morality, too, only has such importance for them because it's considered an essential condition for the abolition of suffering." Both Kafka and Nietzsche understood the importance of suffering, of working within that suffering and using it as source material. Pain and artistic production were accompanying states. They did not want to abolish suffering, they wanted to understand it, use it. If I can bring Dr Sontag back into the consultation as conclusion, she agrees: "The melancholy character — or the tubercular — was a superior one: sensitive, creative, a being apart. Keats and Shelley may have suffered atrociously from the disease. But Shelley consoled Keats that 'this consumption is a disease particularly fond of people who write such good verses as you have done...' So well established was the cliché which connected TB and creativity that at the end of the century one critic suggested that it was the progressive disappearance of TB which accounted for the current decline of literature and the arts." Well, I wouldn't go that far.

Both creativity and illness speak of transformation, metamorphosis, of the page and the canvas and of the body and so the mind. "A third thing is the absurd sensitivity of the skin to little stings, a kind of helplessness in the face of every little thing. This seems to me to result from the immense squandering of all one's defensive energies which every *creative* deed, every deed that derives from one's ownmost, innermost depths has as its precondition," Nietzsche claims. The body weakens as it creates, becomes vulnerable to infection, helpless in the face of the world but then immunizes itself against this through an understanding of the font of creativity. Or, as Nietzsche states, "And how could I bear to be human if the human being were not also a composer-poet and riddle-guesser and the redeemer of coincidence? / *To redeem that which has passed away* and to re-create all 'It was' into a 'Thus I willed it!' — that alone should I call redemption." "*To redeem that which has passed away* and to re-create all" is Kahlo's paintings, Welch's journals, Barthes' *Roland Barthes on Roland Barthes*, Hitchens' *Mortality*, Keats' letters, Lawrence's letters, Chatwin's *Utz* and Foucault's unfinished *History of Sexuality*.

If we look at the final prognosis of most of the artists in this study, we have to ask, "Would the works they created have been as powerful without the experience of illness?" In the cases of Kahlo, Welch, Keats, the Brontës, Stevenson, even Lawrence, the answer must be no, they would not have been. Tuberculosis informed the writings of Barthes, Bernhard and Orwell; cancer inspired the late polemics of Hitchens and the politics of Acker; HIV/AIDS, however obscurely, infected the theories of Foucault and the archaeological obsessiveness of Chatwin. Deleuze concurs: "We mean that they are themselves astonishing diagnosticians or symptomatologists. There is always a great deal of art involved in the grouping of symptoms, in the organization of a table [tableau] where a particular symptom is dissociated from another, juxtaposed to a third, and forms the new figure of a disorder or illness. Clinicians who are able to renew a symptomatological picture produce a work of art; conversely, artists are clinicians, not with respect to their own case, nor even with respect to a case in general; rather, they are clinicians of civilization." Artists are doctors and patients, they manifest symptoms, diagnose them, and look for a cure through creativity.

Deleuze and I differ here, in that I see the artist as a self-curing patient with a Borgesian library of anatomical maps and medical dictionaries, as Ballard argues, "Doctors are always complaining about the fact that their patients read more medical journals and know more about medicine than they do themselves." But Deleuze and I come to some agreement with his second opinion when he notes: "Illness is not a process but a stopping of the process, as in 'the Nietzsche case.' Moreover, the writer as such is not a patient but rather a physician, the physician of himself and of the world. The world is the set of symptoms whose illness merges with man. Literature then appears as an enterprise of health: not that the writer would necessarily be in good health (there would be the same ambiguity here as with athleticism), but he possesses an irresistible and delicate health that stems from what he has seen and heard of things too big for him, too strong for him, suffocating things whose passage exhausts him, while nonetheless giving him the becomings that a dominant and substantial health would render impossible. The writer returns from what he has seen and heard with bloodshot eyes and pierced eardrums. What health would be sufficient to liberate life wherever it is imprisoned by and within man, by and within organisms and genera? It is like Spinoza's delicate health, while it lasted, bearing witness until the end to a new vision whose passage it remained open to." Let us hope we are all nascent Spinozas, biding our time in the waiting room.

Well, that is it. Martin Bax notices in *The Hospital Ship* that "the patients they picked up this way were unable to give a coherent account of the way things were in the world. They were concerned to tell you the details of their own particular misfortunes but it was impossible to obtain any idea of what was happening in general." I hope that isn't the case and you enjoyed this journey around the hospital and that the case notes have stimulated your interest. We could have spent more time with the individuals here but before you leave I'd like to prescribe other books yet to be written: Frida Kahlo and body deterritorialization, Denton Welch's metamorphosis from artist to writer, the Brontës and insanitary incest, Kathy Acker's diagrams of dis-ease and even Michel Foucault's AIDS and its metonyms.

I'd like to leave you with a *memento mori* to read on your journey home. A hemisphere of pain stretches to the horizon. According to legend, the hospital's foundations are at Epidaurus in Greece, others insist that it was first built in the jungles of Ceylon. Buried in its confines, you might find dream theatres where, wielding spectral scalpels, fugue-state surgeons remove organs, splint limbs and suture skin. You have visited here before, millennia ago, when a sculpture of Asclepius stood above the entrance. You came as someone else and left as another, your body, a Theseus' ship of replaced parts — even your eyes have changed colour, from the deepest blue to a stormy grey with golden forays of cumulonimbus — is near collapse, the bones brittle, the muscles rebellious, the blood murderous. Coincidentally, you are here on a Thesean matter, to penetrate the labyrinthine hospital with its endless wards and countless departments to find the one person who can help you with your ailments, with your illnesses, with your dis-ease. The most serious ailment you have — whether or not it is psychosomatic or hypochondrial — is that you are shrinking, your skin is tighter, your hair is falling out. Although you have lived for thousands of years, the aging process retarded itself when you were in your mid-fifties, give or take, and since that point in time, apart from the brain shunts, the heart bypasses, the liver and lung and kidney transplants, the removal of gall bladder and spleen and appendix, the replacement hips and knees and shoulders and elbows, the plastic surgery on face and chest and buttocks, the hair weaves, the Botox, the iris implants, the prosthetics, you always thought that something was not quite right, something was indeed seriously wrong. And you have come here today, walked across the earth on your shrivelling feet, because you feel the process accelerating, you are less than half the size you were two months ago, the height of a four year-old, and your skin is pink and healthy, your hair — what's left of it — pale and fine, your teeth white and tiny and your memory is fading, your language with it. And so you head on in, push open the heavy rubber doors with their cloudy plastic windows and stride up to the reception desk, pulling your trousers up as you go, and you stand and stare at a young woman who is, in turn, staring at a screen until she turns and smiles and you see gold fillings and white ones also and she asks if she can help you and in a voice you no longer recognize you ask if you could see the doctor and you can no longer remember the word "urgent," so you say that you want to see the doctor very much and the woman types something and continues to smile. You look at the other patients waiting in the reception area and there are millions of them, billions, a mess of humanity, hunters with predator-raked chests, gladiators with severed limbs, Somali tribesman with spectacular and alien bubals, Nez Perce with gunshot wounds, powdered geishas with third-degree burns, and you look at them and although you feel sympathy for these people, you also feel yourself shrinking further, faster. There's a reduction in your body mass and your cerebral heft and a tooth falls out and then another and you feel as though you are swimming in your own clothes and you look up at the young woman receptionist who is still typing away, still smiling and you gulp and feel tears coming to your eyes and a throbbing, insistent need to scream. Without looking at you, possibly noticing your diminishing form, or disgusted by the snot that is gathering around your nostrils, she pushes a concertinaed piece of paper towards you. You take it and unpleat the pages, it is a map of the hospital and its myriad spaces. She then places a plastic ring on the table and you pick it up and notice that the glass it confines magnifies things and you hold it to the map and see the tiny blue lines that delineate the wards and the departments and the theatres and the intensive care units and the nurses' stations and the waiting rooms and the cafeterias and the chapels and musallahs and the pujas and the zendos and the toilets and the bathrooms. The drawing is minuscule and you notice that the rooms radiate out of a centre, an omphalos, and the lines could be the fine thread of a capture spiral or an auxiliary spiral, the omphalos the hub of a giant web, the corridors the radii. You unravel the map further and you have to spread it on the floor because it is too large and unwieldy to hold and you clear chairs to the side and the pages open and open and still there's not enough room, yet there appears to be thousands of pages and you notice that the blue lines are growing more definite, becoming thicker, you can see the wards and departments becoming larger and sub-dividing. You stop unfurling the pages because a large red arrow has appeared and you put your finger on it, all stubby and pink, the nails tiny, and you step out of the puddling clothes and crawl naked along the length of the red arrow, your knees fat, your chubby thighs trembling, the returning blue of your eyes sparkling, a line of drool from your toothless mouth forming a trail behind you. The floor is cool and smells of bleach, each tile in the floor is a captured universe of spots and dashes, galaxies and nebulae, the odd supernova. The map now unfolds itself and there are walls appearing and doors within them and on the doors there are signs that mean nothing to you, just squiggles and pins and the arrow stretches on and turns corners and turns corners and turns corners. All the walls and doors and ceilings look the same and all the people look different and although you do not know this, cannot know this, do not care, there are Polish miners coughing, Zulu warriors without limbs, New York office workers wearing face masks, Armenian peasants so thin they look as though they might snap. There are Napoleonic cavalrymen walking, English archers shuffling, Indian sappers trailing IV stands, Patagonian-Welsh farmers in wheelchairs, Chinese court bureaucrats on gurneys. You are barely able to crawl now, you can no longer reason the arrow's direction and something or someone, the person for whom you were searching, raises you from the floor and carries you to the very tip of the arrow into a room with bright lights and green walls and your vision blurs and your fingers furl and you are covered in a waxy fat streaked with blood. And hands thrust you cowl first toward a warm dark space, the cage of her wetness, a place you know and do not know, and then there is nothing but subtraction and then nothing more than a remote and isolate dot.

Thank you so much for coming. I am afraid visiting hours are over.

Selected Bibliography

Acker, Kathy *Bodies of Work* (London, 1997)

——, *Great Expectations* (New York, 1982)

——, *Hannibal Lecter, My Father*, (New York, 1991)

Acker, Kathy and Wark, Mckenzie, *I'm Very Into You — Correspondence 1995–1996* (South Pasadena, 2015)

Amis, Martin, *Money* (London, 2000)

——, *The Information* (London, 2008)

Aristotle, *Problems: v. I, Bk. 1–19: 15* (Harvard, 2011)

Austen, Jane, *Jane Austen's Letters* (Oxford, 1995)

Ballard, J.G., *Crash* (London, 2014)

——, *Extreme Metaphors — Collected Interviews* (London, 2012)

——, *Miracles of Life*, (London, 2008)

Baker, Nicholson, *U and I* (New York, 1992)

Banks, Iain, *The Quarry* (London, 2013)

Barrett Browning, Elizabeth, *Complete Works* (Hastings, 2013)

Barthes, Roland, *Camera Lucida* (New York, 1981)

——, *Roland Barthes by Roland Barthes* (New York, 2010)

Bataille, Georges, *Literature and Evil* (London, 2012)

——, *On Nietzsche* (London, 2004)

——, *The Bataille Reader* (Oxford, 1977)

Baudelaire, Charles, *Baudelaire: A Self-Portrait—Selected Letters* (Oxford, 1957)

——, *Selected Poems* (London, 1986)

Bax, Martin, *The Hospital Ship* (London, 2013)

Berger, John, *A Fortunate Man* (Edinburgh, 2015)

——, *The White Bird* (London, 1985)

Bernhard, Thomas, *Correction* (London, 2003)

——, *Wittgenstein's Nephew* (London, 2013)

Blanchot, Maurice, *The Space of Literature* (Lincoln NE, 1989)

Bolaño, Roberto, *The Unknown University* (London, 2015)

Bukowski, Charles, *The Most Beautiful Woman in Town* (San Francisco, 2013)

Burroughs, William S., *Blade Runner* (Berkeley, 2010)

——, *Naked Lunch* (London, 2005)

——, *Queer* (London, 1985)

——, *The Place of Dead Roads* (London, 1984)

——, *The Soft Machine* (London, 2014)

Butler, Judith, *Gender Trouble* (New York, 2006)

Camus, Albert, *The Plague* (London, 2010)

Carver, Raymond, *Elephant and Other Stories* (London, 2003)

Céline, Louis-Ferdinand, *Guignol's Band* (New York, 1969)

——, *Journey to the End of the Night* (New York, 2006)

Chekhov, Anton, *A Life in Letters* (London, 2004)

Chatwin, Bruce, *Anatomy of Restlessness* (London, 1997)

——, *In Patagonia* (New York, 2003)

——, *Photographs and Notebooks* (London, 1993)

——, *The Songlines* (London, 1987)

——, *The Viceroy of Ouidah* (London, 1982)

——, *Under the Sun, the Letters of Bruce Chatwin* (London, 2011)

——, *Utz* (London, 1989)

Cioran, E. M., *A Short History of Decay* (London, 2010)

——, *The Temptation to Exist* (New York, 2012)

——, *The Trouble with Being Born* (New York, 2012)

Clapp, Susannah, *With Chatwin: Portrait of a Writer* (London, 1998)

Coetzee, J. M., *Elizabeth Costello* (London, 2004)

Conrad, Joseph, *Heart of Darkness* (London, 2007)

Daudet, Alphonse, *In the Land of Pain* (London, 2002)

Deleuze, Gilles, *Cinema 1* (Minneapolis, 1997)

——, *Desert Islands and Other Texts 1953–1974* (New York, 2004)

——, *Essays Critical and Clinical* (Minneapolis, 1997)

——, *Foucault* (London, 2006)

Deleuze, Gilles and Guattari, Félix, *A Thousand Plateaus* (Minneapolis, 2005)

——, *Anti-Oedipus* (London, 2009)

——, *Kafka: Toward a Minor Literature* (Minneapolis, 1986)

Deleuze, Gilles and Parnet, Claire, *Dialogues II* (New York, 2007)

——, *Gilles Deleuze from A to Z* (Minneapolis, 2011)

Derrida, Jacques, *The Death Penalty* (Ithaca, 1977)

Didion, Joan, *The White Album* (New York, 2009)

Dillon, Brian, *Tormented Hope, Nine Hypochondriac Lives* (London, 2010)

Donne, John, *Selected Prose* (London, 2015)

Dyer, Geoff, *Anglo-English Attitudes* (London, 2013)

Dylan, Bob, *Chronicles: Volume One* (New York, 2005)

Empedocles, *The Fragments of Empedocles* (Chicago, 1908)

Flanagan, Bob, *The Pain Journal* (Los Angeles, 2001)

Foucault, Michel, *History of Madness* (London, 2006)

——, *Language, Counter-memory, Practice: Selected Essays and Interviews* (Ithaca, 1980)

——, *Madness and Civilization: A History of Insanity in the Age of Reason* (New York, 1988)

——, *The Birth of the Clinic* (London, 2003)

——, *The History of Sexuality: An Introduction, Vol. 1* (New York, 1990)

——, *The History of Sexuality: The Use of Pleasure, Vol. 2* (London, 1992)

——, *The History of Sexuality: The Care of the Self, Vol. 3* (London, 1986)

——, *The Order of Things* (London, 2002)

Freud, Sigmund, *The Uncanny* (London, 2003)

Gaskell, Elizabeth, *The Life of Charlotte Brontë* (London, 1998)

Ginsberg, Allen, *Collected Poems, 1947–1997* (New York, 2006)

Heidegger, Martin, *Being and Time* (New York, 2008)

——, *Nietzsche: Volumes One and Two* (New York, 1991)

Herrera, Hayden, *Frida* (New York, 1983)

Higgs, John, *I Have America Surrounded—The Life of Timothy Leary* (London, 2006)

Hippocrates, *Hippocratic Writings* (London, 1983)

Hitchens, Christopher, *Mortality* (New York, 2012)

Hölderlin, Friedrich, *The Death of Empedocles: A Mourning-Play* (Albany NY, 2008)

Hustvedt, Siri, *The Shaking Woman or A History of My Nerves* (London, 2011)

Huysmans, Joris-Karl, *Against Nature (A Rebours)* (London, 2003)

Kafka, Franz, *Diaries* (New York, 1988)

——, *Metamorphosis and Other Stories* (London, 2007)

Kahlo, Frida, *The Diary of Frida Kahlo: An Intimate Self-Portrait* (New York, 2006)

Karinthy, Frigyes, *A Journey Round My Skull* (New York, 2008)

Keats, John, *Selected Letters* (London, 2014)

——, *The Complete Poems* (London, 1977)

Kierkegaard, Søren, *The Sickness Unto Death* (London, 1989)

Land, Nick, *Fanged Noumena, Collected Writings 1987–2007* (Falmouth, 2011)

——, *The Thirst for Annihilation* (London, 1992)

Lawrence, D.H., *The Complete Plays* (Pickering, 2009)

——, *The Complete Poems* (London, 1994)

——, *The Letters of D. H. Lawrence* (Cambridge, 2002)

——, *The Selected Letters of D. H. Lawrence* (Cambridge, 2000)

Leyner, Mark, *Gone with the Mind* (New York, 2016)

Malcolm, Janet, *Reading Chekhov: A Critical Journey* (London, 2012)

Manguel, Alberto, *Stevenson Under the Palm Trees* (Edinburgh, 2005)

Marcus, Greil, *The Old, Weird America* (New York, 1997)

Mann, Thomas, *The Magic Mountain* (London, 1999)

Mansfield, Katherine, *The Collected Stories of Katherine Mansfield* (London, 2007)

——, *The Letters and Journals: A Selection* (London, 1991)

Martineau, Harriet, *Life in the Sick-Room: Essays by an Invalid* (Boston, 1844)

McCarthy, Tom, *Recessional—or, the Time of the Hammer* (London 2016)

——, *Satin Island* (London, 2016)

McCormick, E.H., *The Friend of Keats: A Life of Charles Armitage Brown* (Melbourne, 1989)

Melville, Herman, *Moby Dick: or the Whale* (New York, 1992)

Meyers, Jeffrey, *Joseph Conrad: A Biography* (New York, 2001)

Miller, James, *The Passion of Michel Foucault* (New York, 1993)

Mukherjee, Siddhartha, *The Emperor of Maladies: A Biography of Cancer* (London, 2011)

Munch, Edvard, *The Private Journals of Edvard Munch* (London, 2006)

Nancy, Jean-Luc, *Corpus* (New York, 2008)

Nietzsche, Friedrich, *Daybreak* (Cambridge, 1997)

——, *Ecce Homo*, (Oxford, 2007)

——, *Human, All Too Human* (Cambridge, 1996)

——, *Selected Letters* (Chicago, 1996)

——, *The Birth of Tragedy* (London, 2003)

——, *The Gay Science* (Cambridge, 2001)

——, *Thus Spoke Zarathustra* (London, 2003)

——, *Untimely Meditations* (Cambridge, 1997)

——, *Writings from the Late Notebooks* (Cambridge, 2003)

Orwell, George, *Homage to Catalonia* (London, 2000)

Peace, David, *1977* (London, 2000)

Poe, Edgar Allen, *The Complete Poetry Of Edgar Allen Poe* (New York, 2008)

Rimbaud, Arthur, *Complete Works, Selected Letters* (Chicago, 1975)

Roth, Philip, *Nemesis* (London, 2010)

Sacks, Oliver, *Awakenings* (London, 2012)

——, *Migraine* (London, 1995)

Scarry, Elaine, *The Body In Pain* (Oxford, 1987)

Sebald, W.G., *After Nature* (London, 2003)

——, *Campo Santo* (New York, 2005)

Shakespeare, Nicholas, *Bruce Chatwin* (London, 2000)

Solanas, Valerie, *SCUM Manifesto* (London, 2004)

Sontag, Susan, *Illness as Metaphor & AIDS and Its Metaphors* (London, 2002)

Stephen, Julia Princep, *Notes from Sick Rooms* (London, 1883)

Stevenson, Robert Louis, *Essays on the Art of Writing* (London, 2006)

——, *In the South Seas* (London, 1998)

Stiegler, Bernard, *Acting Out* (Stanford, 2009)

Thacker, Eugene, *In the Dust of This Planet* (London, 2011)

Theroux, Paul, *Dark Star Safari* (London, 2002)

——, *Fresh Air Fiend* (London, 2000)

——, *Ghost Train to the Eastern Star* (London, 2008)

——, *The Great Railway Bazaar* (London, 1975)

——, *The Happy Isles of Oceania* (London, 1992)

——, *The Old Patagonian Express* (London, 1979)

——, *To The Ends of the Earth* (London, 1990)

Thomas, Dylan, *The Collected Poems* (New York, 2010)

Updike, John, *Self-Consciousness* (London, 1990)

——, *Trust Me* (New York, 1987)

Vollmann, William T., *An Afghanistan Picture Show* (New York, 2013)

Warhol, Andy, *The Philosophy of Andy Warhol* (London, 2007)

Warhol, Andy and Hackett, Pat, *POPism: The Warhol Sixties* (New York, 1980)

Welch, Denton, *A Voice Through a Cloud* (Cambridge MA, 1996)

——, *In Youth Is Pleasure* (Cambridge MA, 1994)

——, *Journals* (London, 2011)

White, Edmund, *Inside a Pearl: My Years in Paris* (London, 2014)

Whitman, Walt, *The Complete Poems* (London 2004)

Winnicott, D.W., *Home Is Where We Start from: Essays by a Psychoanalyst* (New York, 1986)

Woolf, Virginia, *A Writer's Diary: Being Extracts from the Diary of Virginia Woolf* (Orlando, 2003)

——, *On Being Ill* (London, 1930)

Worthen, John, *D. H. Lawrence: The Life of an Outsider* (London, 2006)

Zorn, Fritz, *Mars* (London, 1982)

Zweig, Stefan, *Nietzsche* (London, 2013)

Acknowledgments

I'd like to thank:

For encouragement, anecdotes and beers: Fiona Barham, Lisa Cradduck, Paul Ewen, Gary Hughes, Melissa Mann, Mathilde Menusier, John Murphy and Vince Wade.

For advice, ideas and time: Anthony Auerbach, Stephen Barber, Simon Crump, Marlene Haring, Stewart Home, Tom McCarthy, Susana Medina and Sarah Stodola.

Repeater Books

is dedicated to the creation of a new reality. The landscape of twenty-first-century arts and letters is faded and inert, riven by fashionable cynicism, egotistical self-reference and a nostalgia for the recent past. Repeater intends to add its voice to those movements that wish to enter history and assert control over its currents, gathering together scattered and isolated voices with those who have already called for an escape from Capitalist Realism. Our desire is to publish in every sphere and genre, combining vigorous dissent and a pragmatic willingness to succeed where messianic abstraction and quiescent co-option have stalled: abstention is not an option: we are alive and we don't agree.